MW00778514

Joy and Pain

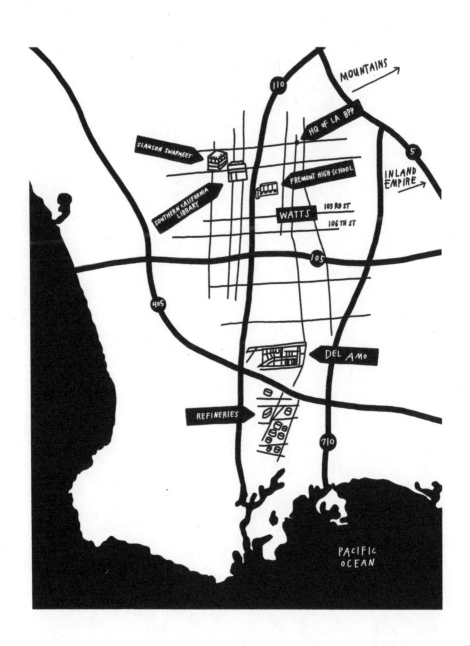

Joy and Pain

A Story of Black Life and Liberation in
Five Albums

Damien M. Sojoyner

UNIVERSITY OF CALIFORNIA PRESS

The publisher and the University of California
Press Foundation gratefully acknowledge the
generous support of the George Gund Foundation
Imprint in African American Studies.

University of California Press
Oakland, California

Library of Congress Cataloging-in-Publication Data

Names: Sojoyner, Damien M., author.
Title: Joy and pain : a story of black life and liberation /
    Damien M. Sojoyner.
Description: Oakland, California : University of
    California Press, [2022] | Includes bibliographical
    references and index.
Identifiers: LCCN 2022005548 (print) | LCCN 2022005549
    (ebook) | ISBN 9780520390416 (cloth) | ISBN
    9780520390423 (paperback) | ISBN 9780520390430
    (ebook)
Subjects: LCSH: African Americans—California—Los
    Angeles—Social conditions. | Discrimination in
    criminal justice administration—California—Los
    Angeles.
Classification: LCC E185.86 .S6555 2022 (print) | LCC E185.86
    (ebook) | DDC 305.896/073079494—dc23/eng/20220323
LC record available at https://lccn.loc.gov/2022005548
LC ebook record available at https://lccn.loc
    .gov/2022005549

Manufactured in the United States of America

31 30 29 28 27 26 25 24 23 22
10 9 8 7 6 5 4 3 2 1

To Elaine and Godfrey, whose love has always been unconditional.

To Shana, whose love has enabled me to reach levels I never thought possible.

To Naima and Nesanet, whose love gives my life true meaning.

CONTENTS

Acknowledgments ix

Introduction: Look at California
I

ALBUM I: HIDDEN IN PLAIN SIGHT

A Side: A Place Called Home
18

B Side: Manufacturing a Problem
47

ALBUM 2: THE HEART OF REBELLION

A Side: A True Education
60

B Side: Watts to the Future
78

ALBUM 3: ALL THAT GLITTERS

A Side: Nonprofit Management
98

B Side: All Power to the People
119

ALBUM 4: CRUEL AND BEAUTIFUL

A Side: Shelter from Paradise
132

B Side: Socialist Visions
160

ALBUM 5: LIBERATORY VIBES

A Side: Freedom Ain't Free
174

B Side: The Price of Freedom
189

Closing Note: Freedom on the Mind
204

Grounding Materials 209
Works Cited 217
Illustration Credits 222
Index 223

ACKNOWLEDGMENTS

Writing a book is never an individual endeavor, and to that end there are many, many people who have contributed to the crafting of this project. I am forever grateful to the stewards of the Southern California Library—Michele Welsing, Yusef Omowale, and Raquel Chavez. They have been constant sources of intellectual, communal, and political support and inspiration throughout the course of this project. There are also so many people with whom I had the opportunity to engage at SCL whose insight has been beyond valuable. While I run the risk of leaving some people out of the list, this book could have not been completed without the wisdom of Linda, Shanae, and the late Annette McKinley.

My colleagues in the Anthropology Department at the University of California, Irvine have been tremendous in their unwavering support throughout the duration of the project. I would like to extend a huge note of thanks to Kristen Peterson and Valerie Olson, who read over chapter drafts and were tremendous in their thoughtful, critical feedback. Many thanks to Bill Mauer and Doug Haynes, who, via their administrative capacity, provided invaluable resources to ensure the completion of the book. I am thankful for the many brilliant people whom I have been able to work with at UCI including Stephanie Jones, Janelle Levy, Guilberly Louissaint, Diana Gamez, Ian Baran, Isabel

Gonzales, Miguel Abad, LaShonda Carter, Sofia Pedroza, Chaz Briscoe, Camille Samuels, Monique Azzara, Rojelio Munoz, Isabel Soifer, Darren Turner, and Josh Johnson.

This project could not have been completed without the support of the UC Consortium for Black Studies in California facilitated by Robin D. G. Kelley, Aisha Finch, Stephanie Batiste, Nahum Chandley, Dayo Gore, Imani Kai Johnson, Cheryl Harris, Frances Saunders, and Van Do-Nguyen. Many thanks to Dayo Gore for hosting a fantastic symposium at the University of California, San Diego, that was instrumental in the development of key tenets and ideas that informed the basis of the book.

I am especially indebted to the editorial staff at the University of California Press. Kate Marshall has been a staunch advocate of the book and provided so much encouragement and thoughtful feedback. Thank you so much to Enrique Ochoa-Kaup, who has been extremely patient with me as I pushed the concept of a deadline to its most extreme definition. My most sincere thanks to the readers who took extreme care with the manuscript and opened up numerous possibilities for the book to develop and become a much more thoughtful, nuanced project.

I have had the opportunity to present various facets of *Joy and Pain* to a range of audiences and I am grateful for the feedback and support that I have received. Many thanks to Ezekiel Joubert, Miguel Zavala, Jose Paolo Magcalas and the Ethnic Studies Collective at California State University, Los Angeles; Jonathan Rosa and the Department of Education at Stanford University; Sabina Vaught and the Carceral Studies Consortium at the University of Oklahoma; Jheanelle Brown and the Broad Art Museum; Coco Massengale, Danielle Greene, and the Critical Studies of Blackness in Education community at Stanford University; Dylan Rodriguez and the Department of Media and Cultural Studies at the University of California, Riverside; Raja Swamy and the Department of Anthropology at the University of Tennessee.

Over the years there have been so many friends and colleagues who have read over chapter drafts, patiently discussed the frameworks and ideas, and pointed me in needed directions. I am especially thankful to Orisanmi Burton, Ryan Jobson, Savannah Shange, Fred Moten, Juli Grigsby, Sarah Haley, Connie Wun, Anthony Johnson, Tiffany Willoughby Herard, Craig Gilmore, Sabina Vaught, Emily Thuma, Erica Meiners, Bianca Williams, Ashanté Reese, Ashon Crawley, Shana Redmond, Robin D.G. Kelley, Sandra Harvey, Rachel Herzing, Dylan Rodriguez, João Costa Vargas, Stefano Harney, SA Smythe, Melissa Burch, Avery Gordon, Gaye Theresa Johnson, Ruth Wilson Gilmore, Pem Buck, Karen Williams, Andrea Del Carmen Vasquez, Chrissy Hernandez, Sónia Vaz Borges, Priscilla Ocen, Keisha-Khan Perry, Ujju Aggarwal, Andrea Morrell, James Doucet-Battle, Setsu Shigematsu, and Anthony Jerry. I thank you so much for your brilliance and kindness.

Throughout this process I have been supported by a tremendous collective of friends who have been bedrocks throughout the process. Milton and Erica Little, Maggie and Steve Pulley, John Norwood and Tula Orum, Mark and Tish Arana, Senta and Felton Newell, Amy and Damon Ross, Ke'Yuanda and Jonté Robertson, Adrian Guillemet and Kim Baker Guillemet, Pernell and Keila Cox, John and Nadia Ward, Reggie Fears, Brian and Amika Rikuda, Jerrin West, Chane Morrow, Jamila Webb, Asmahan Thompson, Alex and Melinda Nickelberry, Chris Harris, Rocio Silverio, Nesanet Abegaze, Alix Chapman, George and Lauren Turner, Anneeth Kuar Hundle, Byron Davis, LaKisha Moore, Banch Abegaze and family, Jerome McAlpin and family, Angel Martin and Ron Thompson, Jodi Skipper, Sylvia Nam, Mohan Ambikaipaker, Steven Osuna, Courtney Morris, Angelica Camacho, Samar Al-Bulushi, Erica Williams, Hyman Scott, Brittany Matt, Reggie and Paula Gautt, Che Rodriguez, Yousef Al-Bulushi, Jonathan Gomez, Sandra Hearst and family, Steve and Deyna Hearn, Aaron Gautt, Kris McCain, Raja Swamy, Claudia Peña, Ernest, Andreas Beasley, Troy, Anthony Johnson and Johanna Almiron, and the Sage Garden Community and family network.

Thank you so much to Leslie Poston, who in addition to possessing many talents and skills is one of the most thoughtful and patient thinkers and editors whom I have had the chance to work with. Leslie took so much time to meticulously go through every single word of this book, and I am thankful for her time and expertise.

A special note of thanks to Elizabeth Robinson and her late husband and longtime partner, Cedric Robinson. The inspiration for this book came many years ago during a meeting that I had with Cedric in his office at the University of California, Santa Barbara. During the interim, I had many conversations with Cedric and Elizabeth about the direction and flow of the project. Over the years, Elizabeth has graciously invited me to speak about various aspects on the radio program *No Alibis*, hosted on KCSB. Our discussions both on and off the air were foundational to the production of the book, and I am forever grateful for our continued friendship.

The perseverance of a strong family network including Alicia, Laura, Esther, Earl, Lela, Cheryl, Ann, Tony, Jasmine, Carolyn, Sheldon, Austen, Curtis, Diana, Carter, Christian, Aunt Imani, Jamila, Kamila, Mekyle, Aunt Jesse, Denise, David, Hope, Rashida, Ron, Uncle Ron, Kelsey, Jodia, Richard, Callee, Kim, Sam, Sheila, Alison, Derezet and Jimmy Moore, Selina Morris, Richard James and Janie, Brenda, Constance Lynn, Lolita, Anthony, Tracy, Ron Prince, Mr. and Mrs. Addison, Jo-Carolyn, Tina, Jacqui, Cheryl Merchant, Nick, Gina, and Dana have inspired me to continue to want to do better and place the needs of the Black community in all of my actions. Shelia and Wilson Crawford and their children Nikia and Wilson provided me with constant support and laughter. Michael Johnson's funny wit and understanding demeanor provided me with relief during the most stressful of times. Herbertean and Keith Morris and their wonderful family, Keiana, Rodney, Whitneigh, and Taran, have always been warm and inviting. Friends and family are very important to me and luckily, I have a very large family. For anyone who I forgot to mention, please charge it to my head and not my heart.

My sister, Leslie Schnyder, has been a wonderful, supportive sibling whose passion for life is only matched by her energy. Godfrey and Elaine Schnyder have been kind, caring, and most of all, loving parents who have had the patience to support me through all of my good and bad decisions. Their ability to make life fun and enjoyable enabled me to get through some of the most difficult times of completing the book.

Finally, this book could not have been written without the love and commitment from Shana, Naima, and Nesanet Sojoyner. Shana has been tremendous in her support through the highs and lows that have occurred throughout the process. I am forever in her debt and thank her a million times over for her kindness and generosity. Naima and Nesanet have been blessings manifested over and over again. They have brought nothing but joy, laughter, and love to my life. Everything I do is for them and my love for them is unwavering.

Look at California

WELCOME TO LOS ANGELES

Los Angeles is the type of place where you can ride by buildings every day for years and have no idea what happens within those walls. It is the kind of city where something is not missed until it is torn down and replaced. This is not for a lack of curiosity, rather it is simply that in a place so vast, it is difficult to ever know the inner beauty of all the nooks and crannies. Having grown up in the region, I must have driven past the Southern California Library more than five hundred times without ever knowing its name, not knowing that one day, it would come to have one of the most profound impacts on how I think about and engage with the world.

Despite living in close proximity to the SCL as a child and adolescent, my first introduction to its work happened when I was far away from Los Angeles, living in Austin, Texas, and read a collection of essays titled *Without Fear ... Claiming Safe Communities without Sacrificing Ourselves: A Reader.* Published by SCL, the volume addressed the development and fight against the carceral state and its relationship to issues including education, housing, and the political economy. The framing of the carceral state as less a material site (such as prison) of physical violence or brutal extraction and more as a set of constant micro and macro engagements against Black people and with state structures that animate the carceral state helped to reorient my understanding of carcerality and, specifically, the struggle against the carceral state. The archival records and contemporary strategies of anticarceral organizers reveal that the long struggle against the carceral state situates the vast nexus of prisons, courts, police officers, universities, prosecutors, social workers, financers, probation officers, jails, public defenders, academics, detention centers, legislators, real estate developers, and the litany of other bureaucratic administrators and officials into a set of fraught relationships that are neither static nor omniscient. Similarly, the details of these relational engagements with Black communities are the lifeblood of the multifaceted violence that permeates throughout the carceral state. The liberation struggle against the carceral state has been situated in this relational manner in part because this is how Black people experience the carceral state—but also, it is an organizing strategy that has been tried and tested as effective against something that is seemingly everywhere and nowhere at the same time. Rather than set up an impossible task of shutting down every single prison "tomorrow," organizing strategies have developed to locate critical nodes within the relational structure and expose the absurdity and fragility of these connections. Similar to *Without Fear,* this book frames the carceral state and liberation efforts against the carceral state as based upon a set of relationships that extend beyond the physical walls of a prison and into the daily lived experiences that affect nearly every aspect of Black life.

Little did I know that two years after I read *Without Fear* I would connect with key members of SCL and begin a project that would help me reconceptualize carcerality and forever change how I engage with just about everything in the world.

SOUTHERN CALIFORNIA LIBRARY AND MARLEY

The Southern California Library is not a library in the typical sense. It is an archive that houses the collections of radical-left organizations from the International Oil Workers Union to the Los Angeles chapter of the Black Panther Party. It is also a community hub. Founded in 1963 by Emil Freed, a labor organizer and communist agitator, SCL moved to its current location in South Central Los Angeles in the early 1970's. Under the care of Yusef Omowale and Michele Welsing, SCL continued to serve as a key meeting site for community organizations and developed a very specific and intentional relationship with the surrounding neighborhood. It is through this relationship that I came to understand SCL as a central part of the intellectual infrastructure throughout the many neighborhoods of Black Los Angeles. Attuned to the discrepancy between "what is thought to be" and "what is," SCL documents the lived experience of Black Los Angeles and the wide-ranging impact of the expansion of the carceral state for Black communities in the region. As the host of workshops, classes, seminars, and organizing sessions, SCL emerged as an intimate part of the regional communal struggle against the carceral state. Most importantly, SCL has developed into a space that has allowed people to just be. In a neighborhood where residents are constantly asked to fill out surveys and give the most detailed and highly confidential information for the most basic of services and/or as part of surveillance schemes, SCL has intentionally crafted a culture where people are allowed to be, even if it is for a fleeting moment, free. The creation of such an environment has engendered accountability for the space and the investment in a particular set of expectations that are based in mutual respect and honesty.

It was through this struggle, and at the library, that I met Marley, who along with SCL is the primary driver of the book. I had heard a great deal about Marley and his comrades from Yusef and Michele in the weeks leading up to our meeting. Marley, who was born in 1992 and was 16 years old when we first met, had come into SCL looking to learn, but importantly, he was looking to organize within his community. Nineteen ninety-two is a critical year in Black Los Angeles as it marks the Los Angeles Rebellion and the coalescence of a unified radical politics that made strident structural demands upon the city through mass mobilization. Raised within such a political awakening, Marley and his peers were well attuned to the viciousness of the carceral apparatus as well as the power of organizing and political education. Yusef and Michele instantly realized the charismatic leadership style that effortlessly poured out of Marley. On a consistent basis he was bringing more and more of his peers into conversations with Yusef, Michele, and Raquel. We first met at a political education course that I facilitated at SCL. The course was structured on the explosion of prisons that happened in California during the 1970s and through the late 1990s. Marley was a participant in the course, and it is fair to say that we did not get off to the best start. While Marley is naturally gregarious and has boundless amounts of energy, that was not the case during our first set of engagements. Marley often recalls his first impression of me as a mix of disdain and dismissiveness. As he has stated to me on several occasions, his first thought was, "Who is this tall, light-skin dude, walking in here, going to tell me about my neighborhood?" The course was six weeks long. During that time we engaged in difficult conversations, and I quickly realized that if I did not have Marley's respect, then I was going to lose the class. What I also learned was that Marley and his peers valued radical honesty and mutual accountability. They would push the conversation in a manner that would cut through the "niceties" and conventions of polite conversation. Having grown up in a context where every aspect of the state (such as school, health care, social work, housing) had overpromised and underdelivered, they knew honesty to be in short supply. Thus, they demanded radical honesty of each other, and likewise, it was demanded of me. It was after this threshold was passed that my relationship with Marley began to change. Marley and his comrades utilized SCL as an intellectual and social space that coalesced into a symbiotic bond that was built upon respect, love, and care.

Born and raised in the neighborhood surrounding SCL, Marley embodies both the spirit of Black freedom and the angst of Black vulnerability within the carceral state. A young organizer of extreme talent, he represents the tensions, contradictions, and desires of Black men who are raised within a regime defined by particular forms of gendered, racialized, and sexualized violence. Yet, what Marley and many of his peers possessed was a boundless capacity to care and nurture each other, regardless of the complete absence of any state support aside from that which defined their lives as illegible and criminal and at odds with the social mores of a proper, respectable citizen and thus in need of constant surveillance and reform. There was an unwavering capacity to love in the midst of a truly repugnant carceral apparatus that was built and maintained upon repression, violence, and general containment. This means Marley and his peers had a capacity to love despite being subjected to forms of state violence where children were forcibly removed from their families under the guise of parental negligence, where families undertook herculean efforts to secure modest forms of housing, where going hungry was commonplace within much of the neighborhood. For Marley and his peers, the policies and edicts of the carceral regime made the struggle to obtain the basics of life not an exceptional reality, but the norm.

It was within this particular social milieu that Marley and his friends and family organized, laughed, and supported each other. It was also here that they mourned, fought, and dealt with the seemingly impossible odds of being Black. Being Black in a place that was predicated upon an intense disdain and hatred for expressions of Blackness that expanded beyond particular forms of servility and docility that were prescribed by the carceral state. Such a limited framework of Blackness did not square with the traditions that Marley and his comrades adhered to. Rather than accept this framework, they resisted and articulated ways of being that flew in the face of a set of pitiful options.

It is within this space that I present just a portion of what is the life of Marley. Situated as various snapshots of Marley, to explore Marley's life is to explore the life of Blackness in Southern California. The focus on Marley in this manner provides an opportunity to understand the multifaceted nature of Black life in Southern California through a specific instance. My hope is that the nuanced and complicated facets of his life and the importance of the Southern California Library to Black people in South Central Los Angeles register to a community living in the midst of an ongoing struggle.

FRAMING AND STRUCTURE OF THE BOOK

At the risk of sounding old, the structure of the book forms a record collection. Each chapter is an album, and each album details one aspect of the carceral state apparatus across an A side and B side. Located within a genealogical practice where Black music is the embodiment of political struggle, joy, love, hurt, and creativity, music is the thematic undercurrent that animates the multifaceted nuance of the Black lived experience across time and space. As articulated by Shana Redmond and Clyde Woods, Black music is a key interlocuter that informs intellectual traditions across generations and is central to processes of memory and cultural assertions that affirm Black political thought (Redmond 2013; Woods 2017). Within such a framework, Black music serves as the cultural analog that gives breadth to the dynamisms that are at the vortex between the daily lived experiences and historical knowledge production of Black life. Mapped along such terrain, the book utilizes music as a conduit to frame and situate the complexity of Black intellectual thought.

The template of an album provides an archetype that positions the ethnographic narrative in conversation and dialogue with the historical renderings derived from the archival collections housed at the Southern California Library. The beauty of an album is the interplay between the A side and the B side. The A side is very often constructed with songs that speak to emotive sentiments that tap into visceral capacities such as love, hurt, and exhilaration. B sides are very often constructed with a more mediative sensibility and are intended to be sat with as a means to digest the complexity of arrangements and the risks that artists take on a project. With this template in mind, the album format functions as the ideal model to situate the articulation of Black thought and cultural making.

Following this structure, each album focuses on an institutional site that maps the jagged terrain of the fight against the carceral state and details how carcerality has become imbricated within several key structures of state governance. Marley's lived experiences on the A side of the album animate the connections between carcerality and housing, non-profits, health care, and education, while on the B side, a multifaceted engagement with the Southern California Library documents the many layers of the carceral state and the long fight against carcerality in the state of California. The A side of each album is ethnographic in that it details a particular set of lived experiences that coalesce around the struggle within and against the carceral state. The core of the ethnography is informed by a series of recorded conversations, field notes, interviewer-written narratives, and multiplatform social media engagement. The B sides of the albums offer a deeper dive into the history and context that informs the lived experience of Marley and also animates the intellectual life and organizing work taking place at the Southern California Library. Importantly, the archival documents utilized in the B sides were curated through the steadfast work of the Southern California Library as critical texts in the formal and informal political education process that was central to organizing efforts against the carceral state.

Music is the background to this story, a constant presence during my engagement with Marley and the Southern California Library. During our many journeys throughout Southern California, Marley and I were always listening to or talking about music. As an informal policy, SCL always had music playing and holds a fairly extensive music archival collection. The "throwback" to the days of records is an intentional effort to build a cohesive set of chapters that are in dialogue with each other. From the opportunities I've had to form solid friendships with musicians, I've found that a common thread amongst them all is an immense fondness for the album construction process. Each selection on a record needed to be placed in a very specific location in order to achieve the desired goal of building a cohesive project that followed a particular theme or vision. In that same vein, *Joy and Pain: A Story of Black Life and*

Liberation in Five Albums is built as a set of albums—or chapters—that collectively demonstrate the relational organizational structure of the carceral state and, importantly, organizing efforts against the carceral state.

While music is the overlay to the framing of the book, the true inspiration for the structure comes from two sources that have been foundational to my understanding of Black life in the United States: *We Charge Genocide* by the Civil Rights Congress and the *Parable* series by Octavia Butler.

Akin to the cohesive building of a record on a set of albums, *We Charge Genocide* is a collection of chapters such that, while each is damning on its own, the collective weight of the petition brings to bear the overwhelming nature of genocidal violence. In 1951 the Civil Rights Congress (CRC) published *We Charge Genocide* as a petition to the United Nations. Edited by William L. Patterson, the CRC asserted "that the oppressed Negro citizens of the United States, segregated, discriminated against and long the target of violence, suffer from genocide as the result of the consistent, conscious, unified policies of every branch of government" (Patterson, 1951, xi). *We Charge Genocide* painstakingly documented the multifaceted nature of genocidal violence levied against Black people in the United States. Attending to matters of economic, social, political, educational, and legal oppression, the petition presented voluminous evidence of genocidal acts that the United States condoned and perpetuated against Black people. The petition exposed the United States as not a bastion of freedom and democracy. In an international arena, it presented a country whose core values were indebted to traditions of racial exploitation and violence.

Over seventy years later, many of the founding tenets of the *We Charge Genocide* petition hold true. So much so that several community organizations around the country have recently adopted the framework of the petition as a centerpiece to their organizing platforms and campaigns. In the wake of the expansion of the carceral state as the most ubiquitous formation of state terror, the framework of *We Charge Genocide* is a most appropriate model to understand the multifaceted nature of the carceral regime upon Black life. While carcerality is usually associated with the physical site of the prison, the logics of carcerality bleed through all parts of state function: education, health care, welfare, social services, and public housing, to name a few.

The core mission of this book is to provide an intimate look into how the carceral state makes Black life precarious. Focusing on housing, education, health care, the nonprofit sector, and juvenile detention facilities, the aim is to depict the overwhelming nature of Black precarity in the twenty-first century. However, precarity does not define Black existence; thus, this book's core mission is also to describe the social visions of Black life that are immersed in radical freedom: being free of the carceral state, free of violence, free to dream, free to live in laughter and joy. What is also clear is that there is not just one way to attain such freedom, nor does freedom come easily. It requires listening to those whose existence has been marked as illegible and taking seriously the demands of those people whose vision of the world has been labeled as idealistic or far-fetched.

This book also borrows inspiration and a framework from Octavia Butler's books *Parable of the Sower* and *Parable of the Talents*. Written in the 1990s and set in the 2020s near Los Angeles, the *Parable* series follows the life of a young woman, Lauren Oya Olamina, whose gift of hyperempathy allows her to feel all of the raw emotions associated with life on the brink in a dystopic future where society is collapsing. The *Parable* series is loosely broken into a format that can perhaps best be described as narrative and vision. The narrative takes the reader along the perilous journey that Lauren and the burgeoning Earthseed community endure, while the visions relay bits of wisdom and experience learned through a trying time.

Utilizing Butler's framework, *Joy and Pain* can also be read along the narrative/vision schematic. The A side is ethnographic and follows Marley and the journey that unfolds as he makes his way through a society that is immersed in and indebted to multiple forms of violence. This B side draws on archival collections, Coalition Against Police

Abuse (CAPA) and the Urban Policy Research Institute (UPRI), housed at SCL, to recount the history of a time and place. The archival work presented on the B sides reanimate the ethnography on the A sides, together providing a foundational political impetus that governed much of Black life in the neighborhood. As in the visions in Butler's *Parable* series, the archives are both historical and prophetic, functioning as guideposts and harbingers of disaster to be unleashed by a state apparatus governed by the logics of carcerality.

ARCHIVE AND ETHNOGRAPHY
AS GENERATIVE THEORY

It is at the locus of the A side and the B side that the visionary aspects of Black struggle and world-making undo time boundaries of past and present. The CAPA and UPRI archives reveal the painstaking detail that radical-based organizations undertook in order to strategize against forces that encroached upon Black life. There are thousands of pages of state-based documents ranging from policy briefs and internal memos to detailed plans of real estate development that sought to remove Black people from their neighborhoods. It is evident in culling through these archives that study and planning was key to much of the work that had to be done in order to fight against the carceral state. A major component of the study process was having a constantly informed sense of the "goings-on" within the relational structure of the carceral state. While so much attention is paid to the policing apparatus of the carceral state, a core question that was asked by organizations such as CAPA was, what forces put the police into motion? Such a question required a multifaceted response in order to understand nuanced characteristics of the relational aspect of the carceral state. As a result of this robust approach to study, these organizations collected as much information about the state processes as they could in order to understand the mechanizations that fueled carceral-based relationships.

As stated and restated to me several times by Yusef Omowale and Michele Welsing, political education and study were and continue to be the critical junctures of organizing efforts against the carceral state. In this vein, the work of Marley and of organizations that used the library space was in conversation with a genealogical tradition that rigorously approached study as a foundational component in organizing against the carceral state. Utilized via workshops, organizing sessions, and political education courses, the archives that are detailed in the vision section represent the knowledge passed down from community organizations, lifelong residents, and community scholars who sought to create new ways of being. Marley and his fellow organizers utilized the archives on a consistent basis to inform their organizing strategies and political orientation to manifestations of carceral state power. By drawing on the archives of the Coalition Against Police Abuse and the Urban Policy Research Institute, the B side should also be read as providing needed context to the social, political, and economic milieus that set the stage for Marley and his comrades to organize with each other and against carcerality and its many manifestations and interlocuters.

The result of the interplay between the two sides is the generation of sets of theories that are informed by a specific Black intellectual praxis. This praxis in turn is temporally situated in the past, present, and future and should be understood as the primary and dynamic foundation of liberation struggles, social movements, and acts of insurgency against the liquidating violence that emanates from the many dimensions of carcerality.

MODELS OF THE ARCHIVE

There is a rich body of scholarship that details the interplay amongst archives and power. Two texts that have been very influential in the structuring of this book are Avery Gordon's *The Hawthorn Archive: Letters from the Utopian Margins* and Deborah Thomas's *Political Life in the Wake of the Plantation: Sovereignty, Witnessing, Repair.* Gordon's text provided a model to engage with material that was relational to each other, but did not fit into neat, preassigned categories. In addition, Gordon is very clear that radical archival formations do not belong to any one person, but rather are home to a tawdry collective whose desire is to construct social arrangements that value life rather than logics of gross exploitation. Deborah Thomas's *Political Life in the Wake of the Plantation* was very helpful in thinking through experimental ways of designing the interplay between ethnography and the historical archive. In this beautifully structured book, Thomas effortlessly transitions between multimodal ethnographic narratives pertaining to the tension between sovereignty and violence in Jamaica and the historical record that she labels as "Interludes" that provide the historic basis of said tension.

Indebted to experimental and collective models established by Gordon and Thomas, the goal of *Joy and Pain* is to pivot away from a conventional formal theorization of the archive or an analysis of lived experience through ethnographic engagement. Rather, in a very intentional manner, the theorization and framing of Black life and the carceral state emanate from Marley, SCL, and a collective read of the CAPA and Urban Policy Research Institute archives. Within such a paradigm, the citational practices draw directly from the archival material and ethnographical narratives and are done in a manner that reflects back upon the contributions of the collective struggle lobbied against carceral state.

UNFINISHED WORK

The stories and archival histories documented in this book are more than ten years in the making. Through this time, I have shared moments of celebration as well as moments of sheer agony with Marley, SCL, and the surrounding community. It is of note that during this time period there were many public-facing movements such as Black Lives Matter (BLM) and other nonprofit/state-partnered campaigns that gained popular attention. Quite striking, many of these movements (and perhaps most notably BLM) did not gain traction within many Black communities in

Los Angeles. One of the most consistent and poignant articulations of why many of these initiatives failed to mobilize the masses of Black Los Angeles was a differential set of politics with regard to the carceral state. While nonprofit campaigns and Los Angeles–based BLM organizing primarily framed the carceral state as mortal acts of police violence against Black subjects and primarily engaged with the formal political system, the conceptualization of carcerality for many within Black Los Angeles communities was informed by carceral state violence being animated throughout the many tentacles of the state apparatus (such as schools, housing, health care, and everyday forms of violence). As Marley told me on one occasion, "I am more likely to die because of diabetes or heart disease or something like that than to be killed by the police. But I am more likely to die of diabetes or heart disease because of the police. When they shut down a hospital or a clinic and that money then is transferred over to build up a much bigger police precinct which needs more police officers, that means trouble." The trouble was less about the police causing imminent physical violence than about the mounting causes of premature death—most notably, the myriad of treatable health ailments and calamities such as heart disease, hypertension, and diabetes. Further, there was an immediate connection made of the lack of housing, draconian punitive formations of public education, and complete void of health care to the rampant buildup of the carceral state. As articulated through a lack of participation and voiced critique, the core political strategies of many state-based and nonprofit-driven campaigns did not resonate with the lived experience of Black Angelenos and thus did not configure into sustained political knowledge.

As a means to document the political knowledge of the neighborhood, the book is intentionally void of my analysis of particular situations and instead presents narratives that give life to the voice and intellectual life of a collective process that was constantly working through the multiple positions that people held. The forging of the collective process was an arduous task that demanded, as Yusef once told me, "the constant struggle to be clear on what we had to offer, from our different positions, do the work to try and get to a place where we could share and articulate that, and that we are all implicated by and have responsibilities to undo, these violences of the carceral state."

I am aware that it is impossible to completely remove yourself from a story you tell, and, to that end, my place in the story is to mark a distinction from the day-to-day lived reality of Marley and his peers. Although I was born and raised throughout the area, their reality is not my lived reality. To an extent, my relationship with SCL helped to bridge that divide, but the divide itself exists. From a young age Marley grew accustomed to various agents of the state masked as patron saints who inevitably made life quite miserable for him and his family. Simply stated, you would be a fool to go through life as Marley and trust anyone who did not understand the core tenets of their struggle.

Casting a wide view over the past ten-plus years, the basis of Marley's skepticism was located in the relational nature of how the carceral state sought to forge relationships among people. According to the governing social script, someone in my station in life was cast as the mentor/savior in relation to Marley's wayward lived experiences. However, neither Marley nor his peers wanted any of these type-cast roles, and had a rather stern rebuke of the carceral state's attempts to situate their lives as illegible/inconsequential. Thus, the result was not only a rational distancing from people such as myself, but also an exposure to the contradictions of a set of politics that sought to separate charismatic and key members of Black communities from their neighborhoods and families. The exposure of such tensions places into question the very assumptions that are at the heart of much state-based (often foundation- and nonprofit-driven) reform work that reproduces harm back to Black communities through a castigation of Black knowledge formation, cultural production, and social visions as illegible, violent, and criminal. Through rigorous study, in-depth conversations, and many tense moments, what has formed over the years is a level of mutual respect, trust, and admiration for a commitment to the work that is yet to be completed.

ALBUM I

Hidden in Plain Sight

A Place Called Home

San Pedro, California, is many things, but close is not one of them. For people who do not live in San Pedro and do not have a day planned in the Port of Los Angeles, it might as well as be in another time zone. Although much of my immediate and extended family and friend network lived relatively nearby, it would take an unforeseen act of nature to get people to visit. But it is very affordable, and it is close to the ocean. Thus, while living in such a beautiful place, I put more miles on my car in a very short duration than I had ever thought possible. The result of all that driving also meant that I had to figure out the shortcuts and have a farmer's sense of time to know how to avoid the traffic lulls that could turn a thirty-minute drive into an hour-and-a-half-long commute. While Gaffey Street could get backed up, it was the Harbor Freeway that was always a dicey proposition.

Thus, when I woke up in the morning, I was in no particular rush to be stuck in traffic. There was a sweet spot that started right around 10:00 A.M. Getting a full night's rest, I ate a quick breakfast before heading out the door. Learning from the adventures in paradise, I bypassed Gaffey and headed down to Pacific Avenue driving north to the Harbor Freeway. Within a very quick amount of time that surprised even me, I made my way through the South Bay cities of Wilmington, Carson, and

Gardena before traffic started to back up along the border of South Central Los Angeles.

It was only then that the butterflies started to kick in. It was unexpected as I felt good about my meeting at the Southern California Library, but I also felt nervous. I had first learned about the Southern California Library by reading an edited collection that focused on the multifaceted nature of carcerality. I soon learned of the pantheon of scholars who had perused its hallowed archives and the litany of activist organizations that had relied upon the Library as an organizing and thinking space. These cumulative moments firmly entrenched the Library not just as a site of knowledge accumulation and transference, but also as central to the activist and organizing history of Los Angeles. The gravity suddenly hit me as I sludged my way through the muddy trough of traffic. Exiting on Gage Avenue, the butterflies in my stomach fluttered at a feverish pace as I tried to focus on not making a complete fool of myself.

Yusef Omowale, the Library's director, and Michele Welsing, the communication liaison, had reached out to me about assisting in the development of a grant project focusing on the relationship between Black boys and men and the carceral state. In this multiorganizational effort, Yusef and Michele were charged with helping to frame the basis of the project and requested a meeting to see if I could be of any assistance. Given that I had experience with writing grants, I jumped at the opportunity as I was eager to learn more about the project, but also to assist in the program development of the Library as a whole.

I turned south down Vermont Avenue from off of Gage and soon approached the Library. I scoured the street for parking immediately in front of the Library, but quickly learned a lesson about the density of the neighborhood: if you find a parking spot anywhere near the Library, take it. Turning the corner and driving around the block, I failed to find parking immediately adjacent to the building and instead found a spot across the street next to a small strip mall that was home to a liquor store and laundromat. I crossed the street, took a deep breath, and walked through the metal gate, double doors, and dark curtain that led into the lobby of the building. I received a warm greeting by Michele, which then was followed by an equally warm greeting by Yusef. They offered me a tour of the cavernous space, which I gladly accepted.

Michele led the tour, and the dry, slightly dusty aroma of paper, boxes, and magazines mixed with the burning of incense filled the air of the building. Michele ushered me through file cabinets full of reports, newspaper filings, and special topics. From there we went upstairs, and I was blown away by the enormous collection of newspaper holdings from the *California Eagle, Los Angeles Sentinel*, and *Los Angeles Watts-Times.* Michele was an immaculate steward of SCL, as she seemingly had an origin story that accompanied each and every collection. We then walked through the aisles of holdings that held all manner of collections ranging from the International Oil Workers Union to *Ebony* magazine. Moving back downstairs, we passed through a door and into a slightly darkened room that held an impressive collection of files including archives from the Los Angeles chapter of the Black Panther Party and the Coalition Against Police Abuse. Michele went into great detail about the long-standing relationships with organizations and activists and how those relationships were instrumental to SCL housing these collections. She further explained that the importance of the relationship between SCL and the neighborhood was embodied in the struggle and history documented in the collections. The tour lasted close to forty-five minutes, and I was slightly overwhelmed by the enormity of the collections held in the space. I did everything in my power to suppress the return of the butterflies. Taking a deep breath, I calmed myself as we exited the last room and sat down at a table in the middle of the main room to discuss the project.

We moved to a medium-sized table that was situated alongside other tables. Once we were seated, Yusef explained to me that the Library had been in conversations with a few other organizations in Los Angeles and they were looking to intervene in the prevailing wisdom pertaining to "mentoring" of Black boys. Counter to the respectable politics that called for Black boys to "pull their pants up" and learn the value of hard work and discipline, they were explicitly approaching the project within a capacity that would challenge the class and sexual dynamics in the construction of young Black boyhood. I was thoroughly intrigued by the idea as, while I was very much in favor of the push, I wondered how such framing could be situated within the confines of a grant proposal, which very often is predicated upon prevailing wisdoms. As soon as Yusef went over the groundwork of the project and the slow development that had led to this point, I knew that all prevailing wisdom would be cast aside, as they were adamant that the integrity of their political stance would not be compromised by engaging in a paradigm that castigated such a large swath of the Black community.

Based upon my initial conversations with Yusef and Michele about the project, I immediately thought of unconventional ways to draft a working model. Unconventional in the sense that they would not align with the very self-serving and righteous notions of the saving of a particular type of Black masculinity as intimately linked to the plight of the Black race. Unfortunately, such models were prevalent everywhere, and with Barack Obama's administration in full gear, they seemed to be everywhere all the time. To counter the weight of such prevailing models, I turned to the Combahee River Collective Statement (CRCS) to better parse out the tensions between the production of various types of Black masculinity within Black communities and the production of state power through state structures such as limited access to housing and health care, the impact of incarceration, and a woeful education system. Modeled upon the same didactic and straightforward approach as the Combahee statement, I incorporated historical and contextual details that are very often absent from a grant proposal. I then sent the draft over to Yusef and Michele and awaited my fate.

Sitting down at the table, I prepared for the worst, but instead, what I received was a message that I was not prepared for. While they very much agreed with the thrust of the piece, two things were quite apparent: (1) it did not go far enough, and (2) it would be better served, rather than use this as the grant proposal itself, to utilize the document as the organizing principle of the collective. To the first point, they explained that in order to fully grapple with what was happening to Black men and boys in the various neighborhoods and communities that the collective worked with, what would be needed was a further articulation of the concrete strategies, techniques, and processes that were of direct consequence. To put it plainly, I had missed with respect to my language and, as a result, the statement lost its push, cohesiveness, and power the further it moved away from the specificities of life for Black men and boys. As Yusef explained to me, everybody from progressives to very conservative politicians and policy makers utilizes terms such as white supremacy and state violence. It is not the terms that were the problem, it was that their power had become diluted as the thrust of their meaning had faded away. There was a general consensus that these words could galvanize people, but what was really being discussed? What was the meat of the argument? What was the direct impact upon people and communities? Who was complicit? All of this was getting lost. Thus, what I thought was a fairly "radical" statement turned out to be a relatively tame document that needed much more nuance and directness to achieve the aims that the collective was trying to put forward.

The second point shocked me even more than the first. Yet, I would come to not be surprised as I was communicating with people who had been both working directly with and in constant conversation with a wide array of organizers who had been working in the neighborhood for quite some time. As a result, they knew how to salvage the "good" parts of strategies and techniques. Rather than condemn the whole document as unfit, they were drawn to the framing of the arguments and further to the "remixing" of the Combahee Statement as a means to develop a unifying front for the collective. It was from this vantage point that they understood that, rather than be the body of a grant proposal, the document itself could function as the basis of the collective and sections from its core could be incorporated and expanded upon to develop a coherent narrative statement for the grant. They were also very explicit about the grant process, as they informed me that they were not sure of the likelihood that they would receive the grant but were optimistic given conversations with program officers. However, what they were positive of was that out of this collective process, they would generate a new platform that would be used to organize around issues of Black masculinity in a much different manner than the commonsense renderings of mentorship and climbing the proverbial social ladder.

Over the course of the following days that turned into weeks, we thoroughly fleshed out the skeleton and then the framing of the document. A painstaking process, it was reflective of the process that was valued by the Library. In a space that housed tens of thousands of documents that archived decades of strategies pertaining to organizing, it came as no surprise that Yusef and Michele employed a very careful and methodical approach to any major undertaking. We went over countless drafts of the document to get it to the stage where it was reflective of the multifaceted nature of the communities that the Library was situated within. And right when I thought we were finished, that was when the real work began.

The final document became an amalgamation of two statements: the Combahee River Collective Statement and William Patterson's *We Charge Genocide*. Taking up the call to implore a very specific type of intersectional analysis issued in both statements, once the framing document was "up and running," the next steps were to draft comprehensive documents that focused on the areas of wage labor, education, and carcerality. It was at this point that I began to understand the rationale for the meticulous crafting of the framing document as it provided the necessary backbone to then ground the subsequent documents. We spent the better part of the next few weeks intensely researching data from several sites including online resources and archival information housed in the Library itself. From that information, we sought to develop the language that would both outline the generalities of the issues and simultaneously be situated in the specificities that made Los Angeles unique.

It is often said that the shortest pieces are the hardest to craft. That was definitely the case during this process. Akin to a white paper that provides the nuts and bolts of a large policy brief, the documents were designed with a two-page maximum limit. After spending hours trimming and cutting, we finally arrived at the point where they were presentable and ready for discussion. Yet, before all of that could happen, fate would intervene and change the course of the project while also providing me with a firsthand account of just how dedicated the Library was to abiding by its politics and methods.

THE INTRODUCTION TO MARLEY

The Southern California Library had not always had the best reputation in the neighborhood. That is not saying that it had a bad reputation. It was more like it had virtually no reputation. While it was well known among scholars, activists, and researchers, for much of its existence, it was virtually an unknown entity among the people who lived within the blocks immediately around the Library. In the days leading up to my initial visit to the Library, I informed my cousin who had grown up two blocks down from the world-famous institution, and she had no idea what I was talking about. She initially thought that I was talking about the John Muir Library, a public library that was part of the Los Angeles Public Library System. When I informed her where SCL was located, she thought I was joking.

As I will expound upon in chapter 3, Michele and Yusef were quite aware of the problem that the Library had in the community, but even they were shocked by some of the responses from their immediate neighbors. Ranging from thinking it was a county building to a policing infrastructure, many people in the neighborhood had a somewhat standoffish relationship with SCL. Yusef and Michele, both being Black and having spent over two decades in Los Angeles, understood the often tense dynamics between Blackness and progressive mobilization in the city. Yusef informed me that much of this had to do with the general ethos of the Library, which, while being situated within a leftist politics, had a hard time bringing the academic conversation to the racial politics that the entity was directly immersed within. However, he was also aware that, while neighborhood residents may not have had a dynamic working relationship with SCL, they did respect it as a place of value within the neighborhood. This was perhaps best immortalized in a photo that was taken in the wake of the 1992 Los Angeles Rebellion. The photo, taken directly across the street from the Library, shows the Library standing tall among several other buildings that had been burnt to the ground. The photo spoke volumes, as one of the misconceptions about the 1992 rebellion was that Black people were burning their own community. However, what is left out of any superficial read of the '92 rebellion was the fact that the buildings and businesses that were burnt and/or targeted were those that had a reputation for being highly exploitative of and violent toward the community. There were several Black-owned businesses, mosques, and entities such as SCL that not only survived during the rebellion, but were strategic meeting places during the rebellion. Building upon this bit of history, Yusef and Michele decided to further that relationship and establish firm ties with the local community.

It was within this capacity that Michele was indispensable to the mission of the Library. Quite simply, Michele knew everybody in the entire neighborhood. Anybody who walked through the Library doors was seemingly an old friend whom Michele would greet with extreme warmth and grace. The patrons ranged from mothers and children looking for information on Black historical figures to houseless members of the community who often turned to the Library for various forms of support, and Michele balanced the art of listening with her vast knowledge of the archives and the city politics to assist people in navigating through a myriad of questions and issues.

Given that she had a pulse of the inner workings of the city and was in tune with mechanizations of the neighborhood and surrounding community, Michele was also keenly tapped into perhaps the two most vulnerable populations within the neighborhood: women and young people. Michele was acutely aware of the precarious nature that Black women faced within the neighborhood. Michele possessed a very calm and welcoming demeanor; however, her disposition would instantly change with the invocation of prisons, jails, police, or "the system" as designed to target a specific rendering of heteronormative Black masculinity. It was through my many conversations with Michele and subsequent introduction to several key members of the neighborhood that it was readily apparent that the "hidden" demographic that was impacted by the buildup of the carceral state within the community was that of Black women between the ages of forty and sixty.

Given her close relationship with the community, Michele had synthesized the odd predicament that Black women in the neighborhood found themselves in. She posited that, on one hand, Black women comprised a large percentage of the houseless population, had experienced various types of punitive institutionalization, and were in large part left to fend for themselves absent more than very limited communal resources. On the other hand, Black women had the social and political expectation of being the caretakers and nurturers of the young people in the community. This untenable position was situated within a milieu where the focus and energy pertaining to social spending, policy investment, and public discourse were centered on the construction of a particular type of Black man. Having this knowledge, Michele did not suffer the rhetoric that placed Black men at the center of the conversation lightly. Through programming work and crafting space within the community that focused on the needs of Black women, Michele consistently pushed for radical love and honesty as the centerpiece of the SCL project.

The political will and investment into the construction of a proper Black masculine subject was easily found in youth-based funding streams of philanthropic and state agencies throughout Los Angeles County. As Michele often lamented, so much energy and work was going into projects that would ultimately reproduce harm back onto the young people. We would talk at length about the sheer brilliance and energy that kids from as young as ten and eleven years old brought to the Library. They were eager to learn, eager to engage with each other, and, most importantly, they just wanted to be kids. It was important for Michele that the Library never lose sight of the fact that the city and virtually every other entity outside of their family-and-friends network treated them as a menace or a threat. She made it a point that regardless of how insightful they were and no matter how much their experiences had led them to appear to be much older than their age, they needed to be afforded the luxury of youth. They needed to enjoy making mistakes and to know that the process of learning was in fact being able to make mistakes within a safe and loving environment.

The energy and spirit that Michele facilitated through her relationships was the driving force of virtually every program and event that SCL hosted and initiated. It was within these spaces that Michele provided the space for truly organic community building to take place. It was also through these early program efforts that Michele became aware of the precarious position of Black youth and women. Their precarity was intensified because they were also two of the groups that had a clear read of the interpersonal dynamics of not just the neighborhood itself, but how the city positioned the neighborhood in relation to the formal and informal political infrastructure. These two groups, for somewhat related but often very divergent reasons, firmly understood the implications of city policy upon the neighborhood. From efforts to shut down motels and liquor stores to the lack of affordable housing despite the increase in Section 8 housing, they understood both how the policy was pitched to the public at large and what it actually meant once it was implemented.

It was from this first group that I met a young Black man, Marley. In many ways Marley was at an interstice of precarity that existed between Black women and young people in the neighborhood. As will be discussed later in the book, Marley's mother, who was his primary caretaker, lost her job when Marley was not yet a teenager, and this led to her and her family subsequently becoming houseless. It was during one of these moments when Marley was facing extreme precarity and needed

assistance with paying rent that he was pushed by his friends to turn to
Michele and SCL for help. His pride initially prevented him from asking
for assistance. However, at the insistence of his friends, he was convinced
to reach out to the Library. Similarly to what SCL had done for several
others in the neighborhood, Yusef and Michele offered what limited
resources they had with no strings attached. Such a mundane but powerful act of unconditional support went a long way to building trust and
rapport with Marley and reaffirmed what his friends had described as
their experience in engaging with the Library. Marley lived with family
members, friends, and spaces in between. It was through these experiences that Marley, from an early age, became highly attuned to the complicated and nuanced relationships between Black people, city officials,
nonprofit organizations, schools, and police. His insight and experiences
would forever change my outlook on a city that I thought I knew.

MARLEY

We sat in in the cozy confines of a Starbucks located in Inglewood, not
too far from where the Los Angeles Lakers had called home during their
reign atop the basketball landscape in the mid-1980s, outside underneath
a green umbrella that moved ever so slightly with the passing of a strong
breeze. I had met Marley a few years prior, but I will save that for later in
this chapter. As for now, we had grown quite accustomed to one another.
It did not start out that way by any stretch of the imagination. It took
quite a while for Marley to determine if I needed to be talked to, but as
we sat now, that seemed like another lifetime and we conversed in a
fluid banter as if we had known each other since birth. That was all Marley. His charismatic nature, quick wit, and disarming demeanor could
pull the shiest person from out of their proverbial shell. He had an ease
about him that relaxed a room, whether it had a hundred people or only
three. And so we sat there at Starbucks, Marley with a cup of tea. He was
usually open to trying new things, and on this day he had a fruit-herb
blend and was raving over his perfect choice.

The conversation shifted to Black organizations in the city, and we were questioning why certain groups were given the moniker of "gang" while others had more "official"-sounding names. He was confident that it was all a part of a greater scheme to discredit Black organizing efforts. Marley was a member of BRIM, one of the oldest Blood sets in the United States. He was very proud of his organization and what it meant to him. As it was told to him, BRIM was an acronym that stood for Black Revolutionary Independent Mafia and had developed during a time when community organizing in Los Angeles was pushing to radically alter the lived conditions for Black Angelenos. As he navigated through the world, Marley held onto this particular historical rendering of BRIM as a means to push forward. The Los Angeles that Marley had grown up in was a far cry from the multiracial picturesque utopia that is often associated with the city.

There was an intense, palpable disdain for Blackness in the city. You could see it in the administration of public infrastructures ranging from health care to public education. You could also see it in the intentional abandonment of public infrastructures that very often meant that Black people had to rely upon each other to fill in the void. As Marley once told me, "It is clear that they don't want us here anymore. You got all these folks who talk about, 'Oh, we need to bring some change to the community.' 'What we need is a better environment for our kids to be raised in.' What all that is really is code that says, 'We want these niggers out of here.' 'We want all of these Black people who live all up in this neighborhood out of here.'"

It was within this void that Marley understood the radical potential of BRIM. BRIM's power was in its multidimensionality: it functioned as an intellectual, social, emotional, metaphysical, economic, and political hub of Black being while also posing a serious threat to the long-range plans for the powers that be within the City of Angeles. Marley connected policies that seemed to be advancing the social bettering of the city directly to attacks upon organizations such as BRIM. As stated by Marley, "We protect Black people in the neighborhood, even those who don't even know that they need our protection from the craziness that goes down. When folks want to talk about who is hanging out on the block and who is a menace, man, all that is foolishness. Look at what they did when they passed that law that closed up all the liquor stores and stuff. They were targeting us. That is where we hung out at, that is where we met, held court, you know."

Marley was adept at pointing out the hidden contradictions embedded within city plans. The city placed the locus of general waywardness upon organizations such as BRIM through the utilization of rubrics of safety and well-being. Relaying it in a very matter-of-fact tone, Marley explained, "So, the irony of all that is that they want to lock us up and put us in jail because they say that we create an unsafe environment, but the safest place to be is right where we are. I say all of that to say, is that despite everything that is said about BRIM is that we bring stability, peace, and order to a place that without it would be ripe to be taken off the map."

Rather than an exceptional voice, Marley was echoing a common sentiment that had been expressed by many Black collectives and individuals. Black Los Angeles is situated on some of the most valuable real estate in the world. It is centrally located—close to the ocean, to major thoroughfares, and to the airport—and is envied as the future home for overpriced condos, luxury apartments, and houses. Such a vision runs directly counter to the ethos of organizations such as BRIM and previous generations of Black Angelenos who had a much different relationship with the land and the building of communities. Having migrated from the US South, Caribbean, and Central America, they expressed their relationship with the land through cultivation of food, artistic creation, and the nurturing of future generations. We closed our session with Marley's very poignant comments on the matter: "We came directly from the community and we protect the community ... This becomes the problem for the city and for those people who want to take all this and do something else way different with it, like bring in more white people, throw up a Starbucks, and start charging a crazy amount of money to live here. But this is our land, this is our community, and we are for damn sure going to make sure that don't go down."

We left Inglewood and headed back toward SCL. Once at SCL, Marley was adamant that I understand the full scope of our conversation. As a masterful communicator, Marley was highly adept at providing explanations in various registers. Not quite satisfied that his words had the intended impact, we took a walk down Vermont Avenue. Marley wanted me to see, smell, hear, and feel why he was so passionate about his neighborhood. He looked on wistfully across the street to a strip mall that barely had any foot traffic. According to Marley, the entire block used to look completely different. As Marley spoke, the images he conjured up reappeared as a photo album where the vivid colors and textures of the neighborhood radiated through his baritone timbre. He spoke about the gathering of people from all over the neighborhood and how they engaged in joyful, playful, and serious conversations right here on the block. The strip mall that felt empty and cold was a bustling major thoroughfare of kids, bikes, and people coming to life. Someone even set up a couch, and Marley laughed as he spoke about the outdoor living room aesthetic that not only filled that one corner but radiated throughout the entire neighborhood.

He explained that all of that changed with a sudden increase in policing of the community. Seemingly overnight, there went from being the minimum policing that was annoying but infrequent, to multiple times a day, constant pressure upon the community. It was not out of the norm for the police to show up at the strip mall and demand that everybody lift their shirts to show that they did not have any weapons, drugs, or anything that they deemed to be illicit. The intensity of their presence fundamentally altered the community landscape. In a rather stark manner, the throngs of people who gathered, met, and planned suddenly became a slow trickle. The vibrant conversations and engagement amongst neighbors came to a virtual stop.

The irony of the intensification of the police was that it brought with it a decrease in safety to the neighborhood. Marley succinctly explained to me that BRIM was in many ways the custodian of the neighborhood, that the police had effectively removed a central component of the neighborhood, and that as a result things had begun to fall apart. As explained by Marley, "I mean, when we were out here, you rarely had drive-by's or just random shootings from other hoods, and random people getting shot because we were here."

In addition to the internal and external politics of potential neighborhood conflict, Marley astutely pointed out that it was very often members of BRIM who served as a buffer between the community and police violence. Walking along the gray parched sidewalk that was intermittently interrupted by dull green weeds, Marley, in a calm smooth tone, described the dynamics between BRIM and the police: "But then you also had us protecting the neighborhood from the police. I mean, nothing crazy is going to go down between the police and nobody in the hood when the police know that just right down the block or at the very most within five minutes you are going to have at least twenty dudes show up and now you have a real problem on your hands. We keep the neighborhood safe from the things that want to destroy it."

We continued our walk down Vermont Avenue and he stopped by the recycling center that was next to the liquor store. It was always busy with all types of people walking in and out. Its most frequent clients were Black men between the ages of forty and sixty who hustled the streets looking for recyclable goods. Often navigating with multiple grocery store shopping carts, it was not out of the ordinary to see a line of men with multiple black trash bags on top of multiple carts waiting to recycle the day's or week's haul. In front of the recycling center there was often a group of young Black men who would make their way back and forth, disappearing within the neighborhood, and then pop back at the recycling center. We walked down the block that was lined with a long metal enclosure topped with barbed wire. Undeterred by the symbols that were meant to limit mobility and freedom, Marley spoke about the ways that businesses such as the recycling center really shouldn't be in the heart of the community. Detailing the environmental impact upon his neighborhood, he was equally concerned about the economic considerations of those who were long since abandoned by the notion of a safety net or state governance outside of being arrested. However, always pragmatic, Marley was adamant that in the interim, while such businesses were in the community, they needed to be a true part of the community. As we rounded the block and crossed the intersection of Gage and Vermont, he explained that every business in the neighborhood needed to have an investment plan where its owners were responsible for the development and maintenance of the community in a manner that was beyond merely enriching their bottom lines.

Walking back toward SCL, Marley stopped and instructed me to look up and down Vermont. While our conversation began looking fondly upon the past, he now wanted me to follow him into the future. He mapped out the myriad of possibilities of what the neighborhood could look like. He painted in broad strokes, revealing a newly designed configuration where priority was given to people and bikes as opposed to cars, buses, and trucks. He talked about having open-air center spaces on each block where the neighborhood could come together, break bread, and bask in the constant pleasure of the temperate climate. His face then widened as he described his plans for the library. He mapped out a sprawling four-story building where each floor had a different function and capacity. One floor would be just for fine arts, a performance space, and teaching. There would also be a floor that served the immediate needs of community members who needed job training or a chance to better their skills in particular facets of life. Another floor would be dedicated to community planning and development. Lastly, there would be a massive space designated for the community archives, which would include even more space for growth over time. Outside, directly attached to the Library, he mapped out an entire area for the plotting and cultivating of a community garden project.

He went on for a while in great detail, talking about the types of vegetables and fruit that could grow and how it would be very important that people with an expertise in horticulture be brought in to assist with the type of soil that would be needed and when best to plant certain crops. Yet, right in the middle of that statement he caught himself as he remembered that a close friend of his was a master grower. "Man, you know Barnes. He has been growing since we were little. Any and everything you can think of under the sun. And with just a little space in the backyard of his family's house. And on top of that, this brother can cook his ass off too." Marley took a few steps forward and made a gesture as if he were turning the ladle in a giant pot. He continued, "He takes whatever he grows in the backyard and it goes straight into that kitchen and we would have a feast! Now think about what he could do directing a whole area, because he would know exactly where to plant everything and he would have the interests of the neighborhood in mind."

We started walking back towards the Library, and right when we passed Sixty-Second Street heading towards John Muir Middle School, Marley turned and looked and said, "Now this is just for this area; the other area that I really have plans for is the park. That is where I really want to see us be able to leave our mark in the neighborhood." He explained further that Harvard Park was like an oasis in his mind: a place where kids and adults could come together and just enjoy being in each other's company. He had designs for all types of recreational activities for children, ranging from yoga training to skateboard instruction. Then for the adults, he was big on fitness and making sure that your body was always active. He spoke about the need to make sure that the neighborhood had a place to eat, drink, and just be good with each other.

He stopped on the street just as we were approaching John Muir. He looked rather solemn and calmly said to me, "Man, look, the most important thing is for all of us to be able to live. Not just in terms of getting by, but to really enjoy life. We spend all of our time worrying about how we are going to pay for this or that, but what if the majority of that was covered already? What if you could just live and enjoy life?"

CONSISTENT POLITICS

The sentiments expressed by Marley were not something that occurred because of a moment that the proverbial light went off or a spiritual awakening. Rather, it was a constant sentiment that had been expressed by Marley and many of his peers from the first day that we had met, when Marley was sixteen years old during a summer course at SCL. The impetus of the course was to go into the root causes of the development of prisons in the State of California. A text that we used for the class was a graphic novel series that was produced by the Real Cost of Prisons Project. One of the first of the series that we used was a book called *Prison Town*, which discussed the connections between the building up of prisons in desolate areas and the effect that it had on densely packed urban cities. A section of the book, called "Million Dollar Blocks," detailed how much money and other types of resources (totaling in excess of one million dollars per block) was going to police and surveil individual blocks within primarily Black neighborhoods.

The text provided a perfect entrée to discuss the effect of money and policy upon neighborhoods and, importantly, what could be done with that money if it were given to local neighborhoods. As an assignment, the participants in the class had to come up with a plan of action that would provide a clear and distinct line-item agenda for how the money would be used. It was a very engaging exercise, and all of the participants took to it very quickly and developed clear models of action that were predicated upon the enhancement of their neighborhood.

Marley took to the assignment with a ferocity that consisted with his reputation in the neighborhood as a masterful organizer. He explained in painstaking detail how all of the resources would be spent. Similar to our time spent walking down Vermont Avenue, he was insistent on a complete buildup of the neighborhood. His plan for the development of the block focused on a community garden space that would be situated in the center of the new neighborhood design. He drew a map of how all of the housing, which were single-story structures, would be directly connected to the garden space. Around the perimeter of the main streets that bordered the block were to be what he described as neighborhood institutions such as athletic centers, art collectives, and education centers. He had also very cleverly mapped out how everything was going to be paid for with a shared resource system by which all who contributed to the building of the new facilities would have access to the food that was harvested from the garden.

Rather than anomalous from the rest of the group, Marley's presentation was in line with the spirit of collectivism and neighborhood unity that ran through all of the presentations. It also went counter to the notion of "making it out of the neighborhood" that ran through the common sense of living in Black communities. Perhaps most profoundly found within the logic of athletics and entertainment, there is a perceived idea that one has to make it out of the neighborhood in order to make the neighborhood better. Yet, what the presentations demonstrated was that there was a tremendous volume of resources that were going into these neighborhoods and that if those resources were simply transferred over to the community, there would be no need to flee from anything. Put another way, the presentations showed the perverse irony of the "making it out of the neighborhood" ethos: that it was due to the absence of the money that was being spent within their community on policing, surveillance, and the like that their neighborhoods were highly volatile, unsafe, and unstable.

While there was a monolithic ethos with regard to the love and care for their neighborhood, there was a diverse range of experiences, and very often this diversity produced creative tension that provided for moments of intense learning. One of the issues that resonated the loudest was over gender and sexuality. Dovetailing off of the graphic novel *Prisoners of a Hard Life: Women and Their Children* (Willmarth et al. 2005), we engaged in an in-depth conversation about how policy related to carcerality places Black women in even more unsafe conditions despite claims to the contrary. While much of this made common sense to the young women participants, it was a point of consternation for some of the young men, and Marley was a leading voice as the conversation picked up steam. The biggest point of contention was how Black women were dually targeted by the state and also as the victims of assault within the Black community. While there was very little objection to that analysis, it was when the Black women began to speak out about what it was in fact that they objected to, that problems arouse.

There was consensus among the Black women that walking down the street could very often be unwelcoming as they would be faced with a number of unwanted advances and sometimes violent threats if those advances were not met in kind. Marley immediately took exception to the line of thought that was being expressed. "You mean y'all don't want us to holla at you when you on the street. Yeah right, then the next thing you know, you will be saying that we are all soft and aren't no real men. You can't be serious right now."

The intensity of the conversation picked up as the young women in the group countered Marley's reasoning. They stated that Marley's statement conflated flirtatious banter with oversexed, demeaning, and often violent verbal attacks upon girls and women. There was a consensus among the young women that unless they acquiesced to verbal overtures they would place themselves in a tenuous situation that could lead to their being physically harmed. They explained that for them, the real issue was the pride of the boys and men who were involved. They articulated that everybody in the neighborhood was dealing with some kind of issue ranging from evictions, to lack of food, to desperate need of health care. One of the young women commented on how hard it was dealing with the stress of trying to find housing assistance vouchers when the living situation was not the stereotypical nuclear family. She explained that she lived with multiple family members including cousins, aunts, and grandparents, but most housing programs will only assist if you can state in clear terms who is your care provider and who are their dependents. In a joking manner she exclaimed that the whole neighborhood was her care provider. She went to on to comment how the stress of searching for housing, knowing that it could be the last day you had a roof over your head, was a lot to bear while still trying to hold it together and not break down.

Very often having to deal with one or all of these issues, as you walk up and down the neighborhood, you just don't feel like talking to anyone as you are "not yourself" and are stressed out. Then out of nowhere, someone yells out something and you just don't feel like talking. The problem is that the lack of response is very often taken as an affront upon the masculine pride of the person trying to get attention. They articulated that they saw this as the heart of the issue. Instead of letting the moment move on, there would be a reactionary verbal attack back at the woman or girl who was merely minding her business. In turn, that verbal attack could lead to other forms of violence that could invariably lead to other people getting involved.

There was a back-and-forth that took place and ended on one particular issue: vulnerability. What does it mean to be made vulnerable? How is that vulnerability dealt with within the community? As a means to explain that, we embarked upon a brief exercise where the gaze of vulnerability was placed upon the young Black men, and almost immediately there was objection. "Man, I ain't a faggot. That gay shit does not play around here," Marley calmly stated.

Yusef, who was also sitting at the table, spoke up and reminded everyone that while they were free to speak their minds in whatever ways they saw fit, it had to be done in a manner that was respectful of their peers. "I am being respectful, there are no fag-gay people around here. None." His face looked rife with indignation that such a question could even be posed.

There was a ten-second pause within the conversation as the tension became palpably thick. Sensing that the mood was turning in a nongenerative manner, Yusef did what was almost counterintuitive, which was to dig into Marley's comments. He began to probe into the logic behind the statements and what was real, versus what was simply male posturing. Without waiting for Marley to answer he then pivoted and connected that posturing to the question at hand, which was how Black women were made vulnerable and in particular about this issue of pride that was up for discussion. I was quite astounded: I had seen Yusef facilitate discussion before, but what he was able to do within a short amount of time was impressive. He recognized something that I did not immediately recognize from the conversation, which was that the anger that was being expressed most viscerally by Marley was the price of vulnerability. That is, while Marley understood at an existential level about violence upon Black women, it was not until he was confronted with the specificities of vulnerability that the true depth of what it was like to be made vulnerable sank in. In a reactionary manner, Marley reflexively turned to that which he had been taught and knew from experience would make him feel secure. Grasping onto fleeting power, he denigrated a nonheteronormative position as a means to assert his position as a particular type of man who was impervious to being made vulnerable.

The other members of the collective spoke up, but Marley's face and general body language were hardened in his chair. No longer vocal, he remained physically present, but his disposition changed. Arms slightly folded, his eyes appeared disengaged and his face retreated away from the conversation. Having all grown up together, the other members in the collective simply proceeded and gave Marley the space to process on his own. Yusef, while recognizing Marley's change in demeanor, also did not want Marley's voice to dominate the direction of the workshop. Building off the conversation pertaining to vulnerability, sex, and gender, he posited a question that homed in on the connections between the carceral state and notions of gender and sexuality.

The conversation was full of experiences of family and personal narratives about how various institutional sites ranging from juvenile detention centers to schools forced people into particular gendered and sexed roles. The discussion was intense and methodical, but importantly mapped out the key players within the carceral state that constructed limited conceptualizations of gender and sexuality. There was consensus that these concepts were central to facilitating and intensifying various forms of interpersonal violence within the community. One of the conversations built upon the dialogue pertaining to the stress that many of the young women in the collective carried around due to matters of housing, food, and health insecurity. It was noted that while the city, county, and state were noticeably absent in providing the most basic of resources, their presence was intensely felt in the form of police, judges, and prosecutors in order to adjudicate the interpersonal tensions (such as physical fights or verbal altercations) that were directly attributable to the lack of said basic resources. There was consensus that the issue was not about lack of money or resources, as there was plenty being spent on policing, incarceration, and the criminal court system, but about priorities, and where local and state governments chose to allocate resources and to whom they chose to allocate them.

Once these concepts were mapped out, Yusef turned his discussion back to the graphic novel as a means to connect gendered and sexed violence to the buildup and maintenance of the carceral state. Wrapping up the conversation with an assignment that pertained to further reading of the text, we sat there as members of the collective slowly gathered their belongings and milled around the Library. Similar to conversations that had occurred in the past and would occur in the future pertaining to race, citizenship, education, and issues that were pertinent to members of the collective, Yusef constantly framed the conversation not as a matter of wrong or right. Rather, the focus was to understand the points of origin of carceral-based ideas, policies, and practices and how those points of origin had a great impact on both the structural and interpersonal dynamics within our communities.

We both had an eye on Marley, who was conspicuously silent for the last part of the class. He was talking with his friends as I looked to Yusef and questioned if he was going to return the next day. Yusef gestured to me that he was not sure, but not for the reasons that I thought. He explained that the one thing that he found in working with the young people in the neighborhood was that they appreciated honesty, consistency, and transparency. He stated that Marley might not come back, but not because of anything related to the conversation that was had during the workshop. He continued that just because he had the appearance of withdrawing from the conversation did not mean he had disengaged. He said that Marley relished the idea of being pushed and that it was our job as facilitators to keep on pushing, but in a loving way that provided space for everybody to engage. I sat with Yusef's words for a while, and we eventually got up as I headed out of the building to make my way back home.

I walked into the Library the following day, and just as Yusef had predicted, Marley along with the rest of the collective all made their way back for the workshop. After having a night to mull over the conversation, we brought up the situation of vulnerability again that following day. Specifically, Yusef discussed the ways in which structural vulnerabilities created and exacerbated interpersonal vulnerabilities, which in turn impacted political mobilization. Marley was just as frank as he had been the previous day, but he also had a moment to reflect upon the events of the day. He opened the conversation stating that he had had time to think about the conversation and, in a very matter-of-fact tone stated that there were Black gay men all throughout the neighborhood. "Man, one of the homies is gay. A matter of fact he dropped me off here today. But we just don't talk about that. I mean, everybody in the hood knows that he is gay or whatever, but it just isn't talked about."

Yusef began to push back on the notion that it is not talked about at all. Part of his intention was to challenge Marley's assertion that the majority of Black men in the community were a particular type of man and also to let the collective know that just because the conversation is not happening in front of one person, does not mean that it is not happening. Yusef's aim was to shift the conversation to the impact of what happens when members of the community such as gay men are not allowed to be their whole selves. Yusef then linked the conversation to invisibility and the inability to be seen and the psychological impact that has upon a person. Broadening the conversation beyond the interpersonal, he discussed the political ramifications of silencing and thus making invisible members of the Black community. Framing the discussion in terms of the failures of the civil rights and Black Power movements with respect to gender and sexuality, Yusef discussed the importance of not allowing the structural conditions of the carceral state, which were bounded together by a severely limited construction of gender and sexuality, to facilitate the replication and reproduction of violence against nonheteronormative positionalities.

Marley, picking up on the invisibility theme, commented, "Well, we call them ghosts." Yusef and I looked at each other very confused as neither one of us had heard of the term before. Seeing our befuddlement, Marley stated, "We call them ghosts. You know, men who dress like women. Everybody knows that they are here, but folks act like they are not." Immediately we understood the context of the conversation, and Yusef began asking even more questions to get at the gendering process that was taking place. He asked if the same sentiment was applied to women who dressed like what men were thought to dress like, and Marley responded that it was not.

Some of the women in the collective responded that women dressing like men was more acceptable as it was thought of as having a particular type of toughness about it that one needed to survive the harshness of their reality. The conversation also hinted at a much broader discussion than was commonly had in the Library, where mostly youth discussed the general neighborhood acceptance of particular types of lesbian performance and pointed to the careful navigation that those who identified as lesbian had to traverse. Connecting the conversation back to the previous day where the young women commented on the burden of carrying multiple stressors, it was mentioned that dressing in a typical masculine aesthetic was also done as a form of protection from unwanted advances and potential threats.

Yusef then once again tied those points that the collective brought back up to vulnerability and how the very idea of transgressing gender norms was understood as a taboo in many ways because it was making one vulnerable in a way that masculine performance did not have to encounter. He went to the easel, where he wrote out all the ways in which the carceral state conceptualized gender and sexuality and asked two questions. The first pertained to the notion of invisibility and who would be made invisible if we followed the construction of gender and sexuality as prescribed by the carceral state. The conversation was methodical, and each of the participants talked about various constituents of the neighborhood who would be excluded or forced to adhere to a set of beliefs that belied who they were. Some relied upon personal anecdotes, others referred to the graphic novel, and some others brought in aspects from the group discussion. One of the key takeaways from the conversation was that the collective had identified the queer community and, specifically, those who challenged gendered and sexed norms as the most readily impacted and were made invisible by the carceral state's version of being a man or a woman.

Yusef then made a subtle pivot and posed a question about the state of gender dynamics absent carcerality. Specifically, he asked what the neighborhood would look like if the collective weight of those gendering norms were removed from the conversation. The mood in the Library was dramatically different from that of yesterday's session. Rather than the absence of disagreement, of which there was plenty, everybody was engaged in the conversation and felt comfortable to share their ideas. While it was clear that everybody did not readily buy into Yusef's logic, they were eager to engage in the framework that Yusef posed. That conversation then turned back to the graphic novel and how state-crafted policies with regard to prison building both fostered and also were fueled by the making of vulnerable bodies, most notably Black women, and how if they could construct a society that was absent such policies, it would assist not only Black women, but everybody in the neighborhood.

The aforementioned moment was emblematic of the type of space that SCL under the leadership of Michele and Yusef fostered within the neighborhood. While the specific details pertained to gender, it was illustrative of the many conversations that were held in the Library where harmful power was mobilized as a means to shore up particular insecurities or vulnerabilities. Yet, unlike what I had witnessed in the formal school setting, such instances were thoroughly engaged with as a means to provide a space where nuanced and difficult conversations would be generative for the community as a whole.

As explained to me by Michele, and as I witnessed several times at SCL, a major part of holding people accountable is embracing them with love, especially when they have said or done things that harmed others or themselves. It was hard work, required a significant amount of patience, and would occasionally take a major toll on people who were involved. However, the result was a complicated engagement with the community that situated love, respect, and accountability as the heart of the relationship.

Looking back on those days during the workshop, it is interesting to note that half of the participants had withdrawn from the formal school apparatus, and within a few years the majority would do the same. I state that not as a mark of their character or an indictment as to the lack of fortitude of them as individuals. Rather, to the contrary, it is an indictment of a school system that has been designed in such a manner that withdrawal is the logical choice to be made. The conversations that we were having pertaining to prison expansion, race, gender, and sexuality were conversations that take place across college campuses around the world on a daily basis. And yet, while that is the case, teachers within the public schools cannot even fathom bringing in a curriculum that would directly address the lived reality and experiences of so many of their students due to an arcane system of arbitrary standards and testing measures. Many of the workshop participants who identified as gay, queer, and/or gender-nonconforming spoke at length about yearning to be free of the multiple forms of surveillance that were all too prevalent in their schools.

Lest I digress any further, the larger point that I want to put forward is that the Library was a space for many things for many people. In the case of the youth during the summer, it was an educative place where they could engage with curriculum that was informed by their own knowledge systems. It dealt with the issues that they confronted on a daily basis, all while covering all of the "basics" that are central to education. Aside from reading and writing, it was a matter of economics, politics, sociology, urban planning, and statistics. Further, the structure of the course fostered a type of critical engagement that hit on all of the measures that you would want from a truly educative experience. There were team learning assignments, individual presentations, and critical inquiry learning assignments.

Yet, one of the things that Yusef and Michele would iterate time and time again is that they were not doing anything special or magical. Rather, in this case, the Black youth in the neighborhood had brought the knowledge and skill set to the table. They simply provided the resources to make it happen. For example, during the course, it is not as if we had to train the participants on how to do any of the assignments; they fully knew how to make charts and graphs and critically engage with the material. What was evident to me was that the Library had provided them with the space to further sharpen an already highly attuned skill set.

One of the key aspects of that summer was that I gained a new respect for the notion of framing. This was a critical issue for the Library, in the context of how knowledge is produced—that is, how we understand what we understand is often situated by the barriers that are around it. There is a picture that Yusef and Michele like to share from the Library when they are giving presentations. It is a group of three young Black boys who from one vantage point look to be engaged in dubious activities. However, when the frame is widened and they move to another still image of the boys at the exact same moment, you see that they are in fact being silly and making mean faces on purpose for the sake of the photo. Framing thus becomes vital, because our understanding of Black youth in many instances is stuck in a very myopic rendering of criminality and deviance. Such rendering belies any possibility for humanity, and thus we have the case of the Black youth during the summer. On the surface, taking a group of youth who have actively disengaged from school is going to engender many of the same tropes of laziness and deviance. Yet, when the full picture is revealed, a much more complex and nuanced understanding of their existence is revealed. The Library in many ways is a space where that fullness of the humanity of the people who live in the neighborhood can be lived. It might be for a few minutes, a few days, or a few weeks, and years for some; yet it remains a central hub of Black maintenance and being that is immersed within a neighborhood that is full of life and vigor.

Manufacturing a Problem

The elongated wood table has been our de facto meeting point for these weekly sessions at the Southern California Library. The beech veneer of the tabletop has been well lacquered on a continuous basis, something that only a church pew could appreciate. Resting upon its well-shined façade are a collage of well-creased file folders, older books that have been cared for in a meticulous fashion, slightly faded newspapers that possess a white and yellow hue, and bright white filing boxes.

The collective that is standing, sitting, and mulling around the table are here to analyze, deliberate, and delve into the nuances of the city-identified "War on Gangs" that Los Angeles has had. The young people gathered in the vast space of the Library have an intimate knowledge of this war and are able to recount countless stories of its ill effects upon their families and friends. The mission of today's task is to dig deeper into that history and understand the multiple factors that led to the war and develop strategies to organize against a long-drawn-out assault upon their community.

The action was a part of a larger political education process—an uncovering—that revealed the core tendencies and disposition of the city, state, and federal government and their partners who sought to suppress Black movement, being, and freedom.

. . .

The city of Los Angeles has had a gang problem for just about as long as the masses of Black people made their way westward from southern states. While Los Angeles has always had a modicum of Black people dating back to the turn of the twentieth century, it was the large wave of "newcomers," as they were called, who migrated between the 1940s and '60s, who presented the problem for the racial order. That racial order was held together by a tawdry sheath that bound together herrenvolkian ideologues, ardent capitalist fanatics, and religious zealots. With wave after wave of Black migrants who arrived by train and car into the city limits, the question arose of how to fit these unruly Black people into the order of things. The established Black class who had carved out a bit of success within a limited set of possibilities also found these "newcomers" to be bothersome. Adopting nouveau riche sensibilities, they found these Black folks in their overalls who raised livestock and sold and traded fresh fruit and vegetables from out of makeshift stands and enjoyed the nightlife a little too much to be a problem. The general sentiment was that these "newcomers" were going to mess up the little bit that they had carved out in their place under the sun.

The major problem was that the "newcomers" would not accept their place in the world. They were not acceptive of being forced to live in hurriedly built shanty towns and were equally dissatisfied with the educative, health care, and social offerings that the city presented them with. There was no veil of liberal multicultural racial fantasy that is oft associated with present-day Los Angeles; rather, politicians and city planners alike were fairly explicit in their utilization of the Los Angeles police force to keep these newly migrated Black people in their place. Ranging from verbal harassment to out-and-out assault, the police force operated with impunity. Having made the proverbial deal with the devil, even those within the Black middle class thought the blatant assault upon Black people was taking things a little too far.

Yet while the established Black class attempted to work within the civil process of elected officials and policy mechanizations to remedy the issue, the newly arrived Black folks had no basis for which to believe such assimilationist tactics would solve the issue. For unlike their burgeoning middle-class kin, they had experienced the absolute brunt force of the city: a depravity of basic human resources, a highly volatile police department, and being left open to attacks by white terror groups. Their response was to work collectively and form an organized communal response to not only combat the conditions of the city, but also develop institutions that would allow them to thrive.

It is out of these social and racial conditions that Black collective action was given various monikers, including terrorists and communist sympathizers, but the one moniker that has consistently been deployed and thus is charged with the collective weight of that deployment is the term *gang*. Long associated with common and highly fraught tropes of "deviant" and "criminal," the racially charged inflection of those terms has not been lost upon those Black communities who carry that burden. The reality of the situation is that framing of Black communal action as a "gang" was part and parcel of a long-standing concerted effort to make illogical the very rational decision to organize a better life in the face of obscene terror.

GANGS AND THEIR DISCONTENTS

The Welfare Planning Council, a conglomeration of Los Angeles–based civic-minded organizations, politicians, religious figures, and business owners, issued a report in 1961 that laid the groundwork for the gang framework to take hold. The abysmal living and general social conditions that Black people found themselves thrust into were quite simply appalling. Through mechanizations of urban planning, Black people were heavily concentrated into the Watts section of Los Angeles, and it is thus here at this point that Watts becomes a touchstone. On one hand, Watts embodies the essence of radical Blackness—resistance, manifestations of beauty through music, painting, literature and dance, the joy of daily Black life. On the other hand, Watts simultaneously embodies the pantheon of structural violence—planned austerity and dispossession of wages, land, and basic human rights.

In many respects the Welfare Planning Council was quite aware of structural violence in Watts, because many on the council's board assisted in the planning and implementation of its existence. Thus, it is not that surprising that the stand that the Council took was to deflect all efforts and blame away from the structural realties and instead create a framework that would lay bare the "problems" of the city upon Black people. The plan was quite simple—repackage the organized response to the structural violence as an affront upon the civic functions of Los Angeles and, importantly, upon the sanctity of the good and decent white people of the city. In this manner, the Black collectives who began to organize in the city were given the moniker of "Negro hate groups" in the report and were lambasted for their inability to engage with white people in a respectable fashion.

It is important to note that the inability to engage does not account for the fact that Black people were being firebombed out of their homes, attacked by white terror groups, and forbidden to live in certain parts of the cities through housing covenants. However, what the report does do is shift the focus of the problem onto Black people and how the city could control Black people through various civic processes such as social workers and other forms of surveillance. While the report does not mention gangs and utilizes the phrase "Negro hate groups," the groundwork was laid for *gang* to be transitioned to *Black youth*. It is worth noting that the term *gang* is used in the piece, but is only used to describe incidents involving directly racial clashes between Black and white youth. By the time the white youth were pushed back by Black organized collectives and encouraged to flee in the form of racially incentivized government housing programs and head to the outer edges of the growing urban sprawl, the moniker of *gang* was laid bare upon Black youth.

In a very short time frame, such action took place, and by the 1960s Black gangs were indeed the problem. Using the same allegoric recipe concocted to make "Negro hate groups," the rhetoric and policy initiatives transitioned to frame Black gangs as the locus of the problem in Los Angeles.

The touchstone event that galvanized the coalescence around Black gangs as the scourge of Los Angeles was the 1965 Watts Rebellion organized by Black collectives such as Dodge City, the Gladiators, and the Slausons. The city responded utilizing a two-pronged attack. The first was an attempt to parlay all forms of revolt and resistance into a city-controlled paradigm. This was done primarily by the slow incorporation of Black people into positions of nominal authority within the city governance and bureaucratic chain of command. Second and directly related, the city placed the locus of blame for the consequences of structural violence upon the very Black people who organized the 1965 rebellion. This was fueled by the development of a more robust Black middle class whose class position came at the expense of disciplining Black dissidents who sought a total restructuring of society.

The culminating event of this process was the 1973 election of Los Angeles's first Black mayor—Tom Bradley. A former officer in the Los Angeles Police Department, Bradley successfully galvanized Los Angeles's liberal base and became the longest-tenured mayor in the city, serving for twenty years. Once he was in office, one of Bradley's first endeavors as mayor of the city was tackling the Black "gang problem." In 1974, Bradley formed a gang task force that was charged with figuring out ways to successfully address the problem of "gangs" in the city. The task force held a conference in May of 1971, which defined the problem as the following:

> Juvenile crime especially as manifested in violent gang activities is impairing the quality of life for all of Los Angeles County and a coordinated thrust to the resolution of the problem is retarded primarily for the following reasons: 1. Communication; 2. Lack of commitment to a team effort (team spirit); 3. Funding; 4. Political realities of making hard decisions; 5. Targeting; 6. Turf (diminishing); 7. Lack of coordination commitment, capacity, and understanding the working levels; 8. Genuine demonstration of commitment through allocation of specialized and adequate resources; 9. A common agreement on the definition of the problem of success; 10. Conflicting priorities.

Having addressed the problem as Black gangs, the next step built upon the model developed by the Welfare Planning Council during the 1950s.

As a means to coalesce power, Bradley's gang task force sought to unify bureaucratic sectors of city governance to directly focus their energies upon Black youth. To this end, the task force became the unifying front that aligned the Los Angeles School Board, the Probation Department, and the Mayor's Office together in a holy trinity that would directly address the problems of gangs in the city.

Bradley had to walk a thin line in the implementation of his new gang task force. While he was beholden to the coalescence of a white power base, one of his unspoken directives was to be able to control the Black masses who attempted to burn down the entire city. Thus, Bradley knew that his gang task force could not come in with a heavy stick, as much of the discussion even among the Black middle class was laced with particular vitriol for police brutality against Black Angelenos. While they did not accept the means by which the 1965 Rebellion occurred, the majority of Black people were in agreement that the police force was a problem. Bradley, well aware of this dynamic, chose a method of "partnering" Black community organizations with the city bureaucratic structure. With an attempt to minimize police contact within the framing of the gang task force, Bradley intentionally sought to bring selected Black community members to the proverbial table. The result of this strategy was Project HEAVY.

Project HEAVY was one of Bradley's pet projects to which his administration dedicated countless resources in the face of strong consternation. Bradley in this sense had to walk a political tightrope. He was worried about alienating particular sectors of his base, who wanted to discipline the Black working class but without the optics associated with police brutality. Yet he was also keenly aware of the large power base that saw any inkling of coordination with the Black working class as a sign of cowardice and a waste of resources, time, and effort. Born into this milieu, Project HEAVY was destined to fail. However, while it eventually did fall, it set the stage for an even more draconian approach that has only intensified over time.

Project HEAVY was a mirror approach as delineated within the WPC report. Bradley coordinated resources with several county and city jurisdictions to address the issues of gangs in the city. Launched in 1975, the program objectives of Project HEAVY were the following:

A. To establish a process for the purchase of services to counteract gang youth activity which may minimize further involvement in the criminal justice system. Service would be purchased from existing community agencies and could include, but not limited to health, education, training, employment, nutritional, recreational, cultural, etc.

B. To identify which type of game news respond positively to services, be they hard-core or the more marginal participation.

C. To identify the most effective services to counteract the gang activity. A variety of services will be purchased in order to provide a basis for this determination. (Mayor's Office of Criminal Justice Planning, 1975, 3)

The term *purchase of services* references the utilization of resources from city and county offices that would be focused upon Black communities. The determination of how these services would be spent was left to the discretion of a "Gang Resource Specialist" who was responsible for a particular geographical jurisdiction. Similar to the WPC approach, the Bradley administration was utilizing the civil servant approach, which sought to further ensconce the bureaucracy into Black neighborhoods as a means of surveillance and to achieve "buy-in." A primary means that Project HEAVY sought to get buy-in from the Black community was working directly with Black organizations. The Bradley administration had received a $650,000 grant from the Department of Housing and Urban Development to implement the program. The gang resource specialist was charged with identifying community partners that would work with the city in order to facilitate the grant. These partners were very often from a burgeoning base of nonprofit organizations that were hastily put together in order to satisfy the terms of the grant. These organizations had connections of various types with members of Black communal organizations and would pay them money to attend workshops aimed at curbing "rising gang violence."

While all of this seems very straightforward, it is important to take a step back and look at Bradley's approach in light of the fact that something of this nature would be understood as illogical, halfway crazy, and political suicide today. Members of Crip and Blood sets were paid to attend meetings and workshops to discuss "gang violence." This is exactly how Bradley's political opponents viewed Project HEAVY as it was rolled out through the county and city. In less than two years, the attack dogs were out and Project HEAVY was on the ropes. An internal investigation led by city and county investigators led the charge in dismantling the program. They claimed that due to fiscal mismanagement associated with the paying of members of the Crips and Bloods, the initiative was poorly run and needed to be halted. The investigation focused on one particular organization called Project Long Table, which supposedly made "payments of the authorized $50 weekly stipends to nonexistent gang members" and drew excess funds that were not in the original program budget. The *Los Angeles Times*, which had long served as the mouthpiece of the anti-Black, crime-and-punishment politics, covered the story with the fervor of a mega-criminal blockbuster. Dramatically playing up racialized tropes such as "gang activity," "power play for area control," and "shotgun attack on rival gang members," the *Los Angeles Times* played into the easily registered stereotypes of Black incompetence and racial violence in order to demonstrate the gross problems with Project HEAVY.

By the end of the decade, Project HEAVY was no longer functioning and Bradley's grand initiative was shut down. Yet, in treading in the murky waters of "gang violence," Project HEAVY set the stage for much more vile policy measures that achieved three desired goals: (1)

phasing out any partnership/contact with Black communities, (2) increasing the surveillance power of the civil sector in the lives of Black Angelenos, and (3) dramatically increasing the formal police presence in the Black community under the guise of protecting those same communities from gang violence. It is important to keep in mind that the overall budget for Project HEAVY was a meager $650,000 and that budget, by and large, was diverted away from the formal police in the name of bolstering the civic sector. By 1984, the LAPD ran the gang task force and oversaw all matters of budgetary spending. In the same year, the LAPD sought $400,000 for the establishment of special gang teams within the department whose sole focus was to target gangs. By 1988, with special antigang units fully embedded within the LAPD, coordinated raids were implemented throughout South Central Los Angeles, all targeting Black youth. In 1992 the city was on fire again.

The brazen radical action undertaken in 1992 brought to the fore several critical issues that had long since festered in Los Angeles. By most accounts it signaled the end of the Bradley administration, as it would be tough for any sitting mayor to outlast a rebellion, let alone one who, in the wake of the 1965 rebellion, was in part put in place to make sure that something of this magnitude did not occur. It also marked the end of the LAPD's iron-fist tactics. The bloodied video and image of Rodney King beaten at the hands of white LAPD officers had traveled around the world and brought great shame and ridicule to a city that had forged its image on racial liberalism. Moreover, the 1992 Gang Truce marked a new day in the city with Blood and Crip sets uniting to effectively push the LAPD out of the city and develop a list of demands that outlined the scope of the problems in the city while putting forth solutions. Prior to the rebellion, city officials had the luxury of ignoring such offerings; however, with the world's gaze upon the situation, they had to take the demands very seriously.

One of the major points of emphasis that the truce placed forward was to restructure the role of policing in the lives of Black people in the city. While the demands were oriented to an approach that called for control of funds that were being spent on policing, the city tentatively agreed to the transformation of the policing apparatus. Superficially, it was a victory for both sides; however, the reality of the situation was that the city had to concede that, on the matter of policing, the LAPD had been publicly tried before a proverbial international court and the verdict was widespread condemnation. Ironically, in a move directly from Bradley's Project HEAVY playbook, the city invested resources into the civil sector and sought to minimize the relationship between the LAPD and Black neighborhoods. In a clever sleight of hand, the city bolstered the nonprofit sector through an infusion of money that then went into accounts of program officers, project directors, and grant writers. On the surface this appeared to be a good thing, but it is important to note that the 1992 Gang Truce demanded that resources be given directly to Black neighborhoods and specifically to the organizations that were vital to those communities. While the term *nonprofit* often registers as a grassroots, neighborhood organization, the overwhelming majority of Black organizations in South Central Los Angeles were not nonprofits and not formally recognized (outside of the criminal justice system) as sanctioned entities.

Thus, when the city developed its LA Bridges program in 1996, which brought over nine million dollars in resources in the name of violence prevention, it was headed by a gang czar who was independent of the LAPD. Further, the gang czar worked in tandem with a network of nonprofits that, while geographically representative of South Central Los Angeles, for all intents and purposes were merely façades for the organizations that made the 1992 Rebellion and Gang Truce a reality. The program was centered on middle school youth and identified eighteen middle schools that were seen as prime areas prone to violence. Middle schools were key sites, as older youth in high school were already cast as lost deviant causes, whereas middle-school-aged children could still be redeemed. The funding also provided resources to bolster the civil sector through the establishment of more permanent jobs within the city governance structure that focused directly on youth violence.

By the close of the twentieth century and leading into the twenty-first century, Los Angeles in many respects had come full circle back to the WPC report. While still being able to invoke gang violence as a major problem in the city, it was able to build up a civic infrastructure that elided the core demands of Black people in the city. All the while, the city has been a key cog in the largest prison expansion process in the history of the world. It houses the largest jail system in the world and is home to the largest county sheriff's department in the United States. In this light we can see how the civil process has been utilized to soften the blow of draconian, punitive measures that have placed in their crosshairs radical Black organizing that continues to posit visions of the future that are autonomous and independent of the structural forms of violence that have been at the core of social governance in the city of Los Angeles.

The Heart of Rebellion

A True Education

The light turned green at the Imperial Boulevard off ramp of the 110 freeway. As I made a right turn, the day was beautiful, and for a brief moment my mind drifted to what all of this looked like before these concrete edifices dominated the landscape. The massive columns supporting the freeway infrastructure intertwined as the 110 and 105 freeways met, sharing an amalgamation of steel, asphalt, and debris. There really is no way to beautify a freeway, and despite the best efforts, everything, even the foliage, always wound up being a dusty shade of grey disrupted by patches of even more grey that covered up graffiti along the long swath of passageways. Yet, in spite of all the overwhelming dullness, on this particular day, the beauty of the natural landscape muted the ugly grey tones. The sun was hiding behind a patchwork of clouds, and in the distance you could make out the faint outline of the San Gabriel Mountain range. I drove east on Imperial toward Watts and came to a stop light at San Pedro Avenue. Turning left, I soon made my way by the famed Alain Leroy Locke High School. A smile came to my face as I thought about the sheer brilliance that walked those hallowed hallways. I would have given anything to be a fly on the wall of the jazz band practices during the late 1960s and 1970s. I kept on moving down San Pedro, making my way to pick up Marley.

We were headed back to the City of Carson to help my parents move some fairly large cabinets they had bought. I had not even asked Marley to help, but he overheard me talking with my parents on the phone, and in typical Marley fashion he volunteered his services. At Marley's insistence, we took the streets south to Carson. "Man, the freeway is cool, but sometimes you just miss the life of the city when you're constantly getting on and off of exits, driving over, around, and through people's neighborhoods." "I feel you," I responded, partly joking, partly serious, "But when is the last time you drove from Watts to Carson on the streets? That has to be about an extra hour at least."

"Man, you putting way too much on it now. There ain't no way it takes an hour to get to Carson, calm down," Marley quipped, "At most we are talking like fifteen, twenty minutes. And you have a whole life to live, what is fifteen or twenty minutes in the grand scheme of that?" "Really," I replied, "You want to get all existential on me when talking about taking the freeway." He looked at me with a cold, serious stare and calmly stated, "What is the meaning of life if all you are doing is spending it trying to get to the next destination?" He erupted into a ball of laughter and said, "Man, get in the car, your parents waiting for us, and these streets is waiting for us." I shook my head and entered the car in disbelief that I was about to make this unnecessarily long trip.

I drove the car back toward San Pedro and headed south to Carson. "Man, this is crazy," Marley stated, looking blankly out the window. "Yeah," I quickly replied, "it is crazy we are about to take the streets." "Man, stop being a baby," he retorted. "What is really crazy is all of these schools that they are building on this one street." We passed by a fairly large construction site that was soon to be home to a high school. Snuggled in between Fremont and Locke high schools, it was to be the third high school on San Pedro. "This is kind of weird," I told him. "Man, weird ain't got nothing to do with it," he said with an incredulous look. "What I am tripping off of is the fact that they are building this school right in the middle of two rival hoods. I mean, what in the hell kind of sense does that make? Unless, what you really want is for shit to pop off.

You mean to tell me that no one who works in that office that plans where the schools are going to be knows where all the hoods are? Come on now. When you have the police working with the school district and the cops know where all of the hoods are, how are you going to tell me that the school officials don't know that same information?"

I stopped him in the middle of his explanation as I could see where he was going. Marley was prone to jump from thought to thought when he was relaxed and on a roll, and this was one of those days. Before he jumped to another thought, I wanted to understand his perspective on the dynamics between city planning and Black people in the neighborhood. In his rather cool demeanor, he explained, "Man, look where we are. We are super close to downtown LA, right here between all these freeways, so you can get on the 110, the 10, and even get to the 405 real quick if you need to. Then look how close we are to the beach. Just hop on the 105 and bam, you are there. Then we are right there by the airport, man, this is perfect real estate. But look what is around here, brother. You got the pj's [project housing] over there, and then in between here and the freeway, you got nothing but us, just trying to live and mind our business. We are the problem, brother, we are in the way of big-time money, so we got to go."

The car meandered, seemingly on autopilot, through the low-density industrial hub. The size of the street gave the suggestion that at one time, it was a flourishing part of the city. However, those days were long gone and now it was transformed into the preferable route of large eighteen-wheel trucks that were parked along the street side and filled the parking lots of the small- to medium-sized warehouses that lined the street. As we paused at a stop light, I told Marley that I understood the dynamics of housing speculation and Blackness, but what I did not immediately understand was the connection to schools and, specifically, the siting of public schools. I wanted to know why he thought that schools of all things would be used in that manner. Marley explained that, given that they wanted Black people out of their neighborhoods, schools were the perfect location as school is the one place where people have to be, since by law children have to be in school. The connection with removal kicked in as he explained that the siting of the school between rival neighborhoods gave the perfect cover for the police to be brought into the neighborhood and school under the guise of public safety. Then when something happened, as was inevitably going to happen, the police would be there to arrest in mass numbers. The ripple effect would be tremendous as primary caretakers would now have to invest limited resources into trying to get their loved ones from the clutches of the criminal justice system, and if that included a gang injunction, then that very likely meant being tried as an adult. These issues were further complicated by the laws pertaining to housing assistance and restrictions based upon criminal records and who can and can't live in a house if they have certain convictions. This would be followed by a further crackdown in the schools, thus turning the schools into de facto warehouses that were governed by matters of strict understanding of law and order. As a result, all of the tensions of the school would spill out into the neighborhood and create more problems.

Marley finished his thought, stating, "Then that is going to bring out the police in droves. I bet they even write about 'Violence Spikes in South Central' in the paper. Then both hoods will get put on lockdown because of an injunction or some new crazy policy they came up with. Then pretty much, we are getting moved out of here because all the folks are about to get swept up. And all of this cause of all of this is that new damn school."

As Marley was talking I realized that this route was not taking as long as I thought it would. We were driving through the border between Los Angeles and Compton when it hit me that we were less than fifteen minutes away from my parents' house. We moved pretty quickly through the broad avenue that had large warehouses on both sides of the street. Large eighteen-wheel trucks alongside smaller trucks with trailers were sparingly parked along the street curb. There was virtually no foot traffic, and the route did make for a speedy alterative to the density of the freeway. I thought for the moment that maybe Marley was onto something, but snapped back into reality as my car-culture sensibility would not let me think outside of the freeway paradigm.

Focusing back on the conversation with Marley, I pushed back on some of his theory about the location of the school as a means to displace people. "Man, I hear you and agree a lot with what you are saying, especially the issues of policing in schools and its intent. But what I am getting stumped on is the intent of teachers in the classroom. I mean, you make it seem like they are all in on the whole situation, from the school district on down, like there is some sort of conspiracy against Black folks in South Central." Marley was listening intently and before he responded, in his typical fashion, he let a wily smile as if this were a game of strategy and he had me right where he wanted me. "Man, nobody is talking about a conspiracy theory or nothing like that. What I am talking about is facts. No one is saying that the teachers have taken some sort of blood oath or nothing like that with the teachers. And there was no secret meeting with some secret group of businessmen in a room in the middle of the night. Although if that happened, I would not be surprised," he said with a loud laugh. We had talked at length about conspiracy theories and the number of them that flooded social media sites, and he also knew that I thought many of them were dangerous to coming up with genuine solutions, so he gladly took the time to laugh in my face. I found great humor in the timing of his joke, but played back along with the moment and held a stone face as he continued.

"What I am saying is to look at how the game works," Marley stated is a most convincing tone. "I don't know how many times I have had to sit in the classroom and listen to the teacher talk about some sort of European hero who did whatever, whenever, in 'Africa.' The whole time I am thinking, like, hold up, I know there were kingdoms in Africa. I know about Ghana and Mali ... I also know that these Europeans did not just waltz up into this big-ass continent and start wrecking shop like it was a damn toy store. But that is how history is taught, and that more than any conspiracy theory is dangerous, because we are really supposed to buy it as fact." His body language shifted as he ever so slightly lifted himself up in the seat as if to straighten up his back. Briefly looking out of the window, he paused for a moment and then relaxed, rounding his shoulders into the mold of the firm stitched upholstery. He continued with a mild intensity that was delivered in a matter-of-fact tone. "But anyway, I challenge the teacher and then *bam*, I am now a problem, because you know me, I am not going to let it go until it makes sense. So, here we are, at a standoff, because I ain't backing down and it may not be that time, but for sure it is going to be the next time when I disagree, and I am sent off to the counselor or campus security. They may even go as far as saying that I made some sort of terroristic threats or something like that to the teacher, depending on how bad the teacher thinks I disrespected them, and then I am gone into the system."

As Marley was talking, I looked up and realized that we were making the easy transition from Compton into Carson. There is no readily identifiable marker of a border; rather, much like the geography of much of the massive sprawl that is Los Angeles County, it is the subtle change of the street signs or the slightly distinctive quality of a particular type of housing track development. Building upon his last statement, I pushed Marley upon his views of teachers, given that he had very solid relationships with many of his teachers and he truly loved learning. Before he answered my query, he intensely looked out the window and stated in a cold tone, "Man, you would never know that this is some of the most unhealthy land in the whole damn county. It is wild, you have all these Black folks trying to make something, and lo and behold, they are living on a damn landfill."

Marley was referring to the fact that so much of the housing and commercial development in Carson was built directly on top of, or adjacent to, some sort of landfill or superfund site. Much of the sordid history of the illicit dumping and building practices had come to light and reverberated throughout all of Black LA.

He quickly pivoted back to my question about teachers. "No matter how much I think that a teacher is just the best ever ... what say do I have as the student to change how things are taught? I don't have any say at all in how my education looks. I mean, am I really just supposed to listen to them talk nonsense about my people? Come on now, that is

not education at that point, that is some sort of punishment or something. So, you right, it is not like a conspiracy theory; it is much worse."

He uttered the last sentence with a confident air of pride as if he had
just issued a checkmate. But me being me, I could not let it go, and
replied, "Well I guess we shall ask the expert about how she feels about
you disrespecting her profession like that." His face slightly tensed up.
"Man, why you got to bring your mom into the situation? You know I was
not talking about all teachers, I was talking about how the game works in
general. It's like in football, I can appreciate the fact that Cam Newton
was a bad dude on the field, but that does not take away from the fact that
I think football is a messed-up game that will wreck your knees, arms,
and head. The dude was a bad man, but the dude is not football." "We
shall see," I said with a laugh, "because we are about to meet with the
commissioner of the league, and she always has the last word."

We kept on talking about schools and sports as we drove to my parents' house. We drove into their driveway and my dad had already
opened the garage door in eager anticipation of us working. We both
got out of the car and my dad, always possessing that sixth sense of
when someone is at the house, came out the door and shouted, "It's
about time y'all got here, these file cabinets aren't going to move themselves." He laughed as he approached and greeted both of us. We walked
into the house and my mom was sitting in the kitchen eating some fruit
and reading through the newspaper. Marley looked at me as if I were
truly about to hold to my word and bring up the conversation that we
had in the car with Mom. Just to make him sweat, I looked at my mom
and said, "Hey Ma, we were talking in the car and Marley was all kinds
of confused about what he should do." "About what?" she inquired. "He
has to give a talk a little later at UC Santa Barbara and he is really nervous and does not know what to talk about." Most of this was a ruse, as
Marley was rarely nervous about anything and certainly not about public speaking. However, my mom was a great sounding board for ideas
and especially those having to do with education. She looked at Marley.
"Well just be yourself and tell the story that you know. Don't worry

about trying to be somebody else or trying to fit in with what you think they want to hear. Just be who you know that you are and your story will be amazing." "See, Marley, just like we talked about. All teachers aren't that bad, huh?" I replied in response to mom's advice. He looked at me now with a stone face and just shook his head. With that stated, we then got on with the business of moving filing cabinets.

GO NORTH, YOUNG MAN—SANTA BARBARA BOUND

The drive heading north to Santa Barbara is a beautiful one. But you have to navigate through the hellscape that is Los Angeles traffic before the beauty becomes apparent. I picked up Marley from a duplex that he was staying at with some family. He was looking his usually dapper self and eagerly got into the car. "You ready to go, money?" he said to me. He had picked up on the colloquial word *money* my friends and I had grown up calling each other and now loved to throw it back in my face as if I were an old man trying to stay cool. I looked back at him and said something to the effect that he needed to put his seatbelt on, but just not in that nice of a tone. We had a good laugh and started our way toward the madness.

While I knew traffic was going to be bad, I did not anticipate quite the level of madness that it was on this particular day. We made the quick trip to the 110 freeway, which took very little time, but then once we got on the 110, I soon regretted that decision as just about the time we approached Gage Avenue, the traffic slowly became a game of cat and mouse and I just resigned myself to the fact that it was going to be one of those days. Marley started talking to me about some of the music projects that he and his cousins were working on as we finally approached the 10 freeway. "Man, my cousin has come up with this dope beat, and the lyrics that I have are going to be so crazy on this track. You know how sometimes you hear a crazy beat, but the lyrics are average at best, or vice versa? Well this is none of those things. The lyrics and the beats are just ridiculous." I drove up the spiral transition to 10 West headed toward Santa Monica and the 405 freeway as Marley explained the finer details of the song. "What I really need to work on is my ad libs. Once I have those down, it is going to be a wrap." We listened to some songs that were on the radio and Marley began pointing out which songs had the best ad libs and how hard some of them were to pull off, given that the beat of the song and the ad lib did not necessarily match up.

The 10 freeway was a welcome respite from the 110, and we made good time as we smoothly made our way through West Los Angeles, but then we came to the paradox, wrapped in riddle, surrounded by a ball of confusion, that is the 405 freeway. One of the busiest freeways in the country, you never knew what you were going to get in terms of traffic, but you did know that it would not be pretty. Moving at a slug's pace, we crept between 10 and 15 miles per hour through the West Los Angeles traffic. We finally made our way near Sunset Boulevard and the traffic broke open. I have never understood the mechanizations of traffic, aside from an accident or major road construction, which were rarely the culprit. In most instances, like today, there was no sign of anything, just cars packed on the road until they were not, and magically, the road opened and we were granted passage through an invisible bottleneck.

Taking advantage of the situation, I drastically picked up the rate of speed and we hastily snaked alongside the multi-million-dollar homes of Bel-Air that bordered the east wall of the freeway and the Getty Freeway to the west. The radio was tuned to an "old school" hip-hop station that Marley commented was just the same as the "new" music, as "old school" was considered anything older than two years prior. The deep bass of Tupac's "Ambitionz az a Ridah" was pushing the car forward as we climbed up the last gasp to the top of the hill before we descended into the "Valley." Approaching the interchange between the 405 and the 101 freeways, traffic once again and quite predictably came to a stop. However, we were in luck, as traffic going away from Los Angeles on the 101 towards Santa Barbara was moving well and I was able to maneuver to a lane that sped by the cars seemingly parked on the side of the road. We made the transition onto the 101 and things were looking much better. No traffic on the road, we settled in for our journey, which would take a little more than an hour to complete.

As we hit Woodland Hills, Ice Cube's song "Why We Thugs" came on and Marley suddenly came to life. No longer leaning back in the seat, he popped up and immediately turned the music up. "Man, you cannot tell me that Cube does not come with it on this song. He must have really known some folks that went through it, because this song is really like it is." Ice Cube's voice in his typical deep bass gravitas tells a story that ironically questions the building up of the prison system in California. Detailing the laws and practices that placed armed weapons and drugs on the streets of Los Angeles, he eloquently poses the question: "Call me an animal up in the system, but who is the animal that built this prison?" Marley was in his element and began rapping with Ice Cube verbatim throughout the whole song. When Ice Cube got to the second verse, Marley turned the song up even louder, with the pronounced bass of the song now vibrating every part of the car. As the second verse ended, he turned the song back down and bobbed his head through the rest of the song. "Man, that is so true, what he spitting right there. That same thing happened to my big homie." Marley was referring to the second verse, where Ice Cube talks about the main protagonist in the song having to cope with the collective trauma of being sentenced to a lengthy prison term at a site much too far away for his family to visit while also having his family in the courtroom to watch the whole spectacle unfold. As the story unfolds, the gravity of the situation is too much for the young man to bear and he simply snaps. He reaches over his attorney and punches the district attorney before being wrestled to the ground. Marley's face at this moment was a mixture of awe and recognition. As Marley put it, "He summed up what happened so accurately. Like that really happens. Not like oh man, he knows what he is talking about, like what he is saying really happens." Marley went back into his zone as the music continued.

The song came to a stop and Marley was eager to share a story with me that resonated with the song. The story revolved around a close friend of Marley's who was facing an insane amount of prison time, in excess of three hundred years, in a courtroom that was packed with friends and family. Such a number may sound hyperbolic, but it was not uncommon for judges to issue sentences that carried either multiple life sentences or were highly punitive in nature and as a result were hundreds of years in length. Marley also described the courtroom atmosphere as being very tense, given that his friend was well-respected and well-liked in the community. The fear amongst everybody was twofold: not only would he be missed on an individual level, but his presence and gravitas in the neighborhood were critical for maintaining stability and peace. Removing him from the larger equation was going to have a profound impact upon the inner workings of the community. The problem for all the people in the courtroom was that the judge sensed the gravity of the moment and, according to Marley, wanted to make a grand statement. He issued the long sentence and "all hell broke loose." As recounted by Marley, "The judge came down with the sentence and brother, he [Marley's friend] just lost it. He jumped the desk or whatever that he was behind and immediately went for the judge. He was trying his hardest to get that dude."

Marley's face lit with excitement as he continued the story. "The sheriffs did not know how we were going to respond. They probably thought we had launched a planned attack and were about to set him free. They looked that kind of scared. You can always tell when the police feel like they are in control and have power versus when they are scared as shit. The look in their face is always a dead giveaway and [they] looked shook." Marley laughed in an incredulous manner as he told the story. The fact that the police really thought that there was going to be a violent takeover at a courthouse truly befuddled Marley. "Really, in the middle of the damn courthouse with all of these cops around the damn building and us!" Marley exclaimed and continued, "You know they got metal detectors and everything up there, so we are not even talking about a fair fight, but nevertheless, they saw all of us and just knew it was getting ready to pop off. But nothing happened.

We all had to leave, though, and with the quickness. I mean, like they did not even flinch, we had to be out of there immediately. In the middle of everything, they took the big homie out so fast that none of us even saw him, but that was a day that I will never forget."

Marley shook his head in seeming disbelief after he finished his story. Even though the story had happened a while ago, it stayed close to Marley. The incident caused him to reflect upon the buildup of the carceral state. Marley looked out of the window at the rolling hills that we slowly moved through and very calmly stated, "Even if you were really concerned about someone's well-being and really wanted to stop people from being violent to one another, just stop and think for one second. How in the hell is locking somebody up with hundreds of other dudes in cramped-ass setting, away from the people who mean the most to you, for hella long, going to remedy any of that?"

As we began a steady incline up a medium-sized hill, the intensity in Marley's voice also rose. "That isn't doing nothing for nobody and just making things worse. And a result, you are going to get folks snapping and losing it in court, and that to me seems like a very normal reaction to a very fucked-up situation."

Marley continued to stare out the window as we continued along the 101 freeway. The songs kept playing at a breakneck speed on the radio, and with each passing song Marley was further enthralled in the moment. Ranging from Outkast to NWA to DJ Quik, Marley seemingly knew every word of every song. He also could tell from the slightest intro beat what the subsequent song was going to be. He simply was in a zone, and while he was generally a very gregarious person, he displayed a level of joy that I had not previously seen from him. As the song played, Marley in a nonchalant and adroit manner analyzed each and every song. Whether it was about the rhythm patterns or rhyme schemes or discussing the political and social context of the song, Marley had a story for each one of them. We debated about who were the best emcees of the time with the conversation ranging from Lil Wayne to Kendrick Lamar to Andre 3000. Marley could remember when and where he was when he first heard certain songs or where a particular song was played and what it meant to him and his friends. He loved music, but he also loved sharing his love of music with others. This also made for a pretty quick ride in the car as our conversation carried us over hills and turns until we got to the steep pass going down into Camarillo.

The conversation did not stop as much as the music did. As we made our way up the steady incline, the little-"old school"-station-that-could began to give out and became a mesh of static, indecipherable talking, and unrecognizable songs. We had reached the outer limits of the station as we hit the peak of the pass. I switched to another hip-hop station that I knew we could pick up and gently let my foot off the accelerator, and the car rapidly picked up speed as the road declined down the small mountain. Once we reached 75 miles per hour, I began to hover my foot over the brake and gently slowed the car down. While we stayed in the second lane, cars seemingly flew by as motorists used the mountain decline as a slingshot to spring them forward.

The rolling hills quickly gave way to open road. Driving through Camarillo, we entered one of the many breadbaskets of the state that were home to large swaths of farmland—Oxnard, California. Dominated by neatly plowed rows, on any given day during the harvest season you could see fields full of migrant and resident workers who from sunup to sundown worked the land. Marley looked in amazement at the large open fields that were speckled on both sides of the freeway. "This is amazing. Like I am really amazed at what this is," Marley stated. Rarely had I seen him brought to speechlessness, but with his mouth slightly agape, he held a blank stare that encapsulated his disbelief.

The feeling slowly made its way back to his body and Marley slowly began speaking in a steady stream-of-consciousness-like cadence. "I cannot believe what this is. I mean, look at all of this land... Who owns this land, who gets to decide what is done with this land? Look at how long we have been driving and look at how much land we have passed. Look at how much land is empty. How in hell can we have this many homeless people in the city and state with all of this land...? Shit, this land should be for all of us to use, not just for some rich white dude to own the whole damn plot of it, pay Mexicans, Salvadorans, Nicaraguans, and all these folks pennies to work it and then to make a killing off of it while the majority of us suffer."

We drove for what seemed like an eternity, passing row after row of various stages of crops in process. The car took on the aroma of the surrounding environment, and suddenly we were immersed in the countervailing aromas of deep earth tones and bitter salt as we traversed between the vast Pacific Ocean and the rolling mounds of cultivated farmland. Unlike his normal affable self, Marley had not said much and remained pensive, looking out of the window. Breaking his silence, he began to process the connections between land, food, and the very basics of safety: "Can you imagine how South Central would look if we had access to this land? It would be a completely different situation. We could literally work the land ourselves and feed everybody in South Central. Once you begin to solve people's basic life needs ... everybody is cool. I mean, this literally makes no sense at all that we live in a place where you would rather lock folks in jail than to give them just basics of life. It is all connected. The prison system is connected to the school system is connected to housing, is connected to food. All of it is tied together, and you can see all of it clear as day out here."

There was a certain clarity that was afforded from being in a seemingly vast open space. The view out of the car window was something out of a movie set. The wide swath of blue sky juxtaposed against the faint trace of whispering white clouds was the backdrop of our journey. Transitioning from a pensive state to a little more introspective, Marley stated, "You know, driving out here, it also hit me that it's good that they don't let us get out of our little space too much, because once you get to see how it really is ... then all of the pieces come together. You know how I am always on the homies about growing our own food and got to have our own resources, but it was coming out here and really seeing all of this in its grand display that everything just gained another level of clarity."

As Marley continued on about the possibility of what could be done with all of the land and who should have access to the land, we made our way along the coast. As you drive through Ventura, the freeway breaks directly along with the ocean, and for many miles the drive is quite stunning. As far as the eye can see is nothing but coastline and water. Following the beach route, we passed through the smaller coastal cities before eventually making the final push into Santa Barbara. We drove through the city marked by its mission-style architecture and massive hilltop houses before making our way to the 217 freeway, which quickly took us into the city of Goleta and directly to the main entrance of the University of California, Santa Barbara.

Marley had been invited to come to speak and meet with student organizers on campus. Some of the faculty and graduate students on campus had reached out to me and asked if I knew of people from LA who could help students think through the carceral state, and immediately I thought of Marley. It was Marley's first time on the college campus, and he was taking in the layout of the campus and how students walked around seemingly without a care in the world. He was asking all kinds of questions about the campus and what the function of various buildings was. We slowed down as we approached the building where Marley was going to be meeting with students. It was not until this point that it dawned on me that Marley had not even asked one question about his talk or even mentioned anything about being the slightest bit nervous. As young as he was, I was often amazed at his grace and confidence in these moments.

We walked through the set of double doors and entered the room. After a brief introduction, Marley began his talk. He started the talk by saying, "Here I am, having not even graduated from high school, giving a talk to a bunch of college students at the University of California, Santa Barbara." He went through his own processes of why he made the decisions that he did with regard to withdrawing from high school and then began talking more about BRIM, the police, being incarcerated, and back to organizing within his neighborhood.

Following his lecture, which had the style of a highly interactive workshop, he took a series of questions. Many of the participants in the audience were from the Los Angeles area themselves and had several questions about the confluence between race, class, gender, and space. The conversation lasted for another thirty minutes before we transitioned to a meeting with some of the students who were members of student organizations on campus. Many had been pushing the college on a set of issues that ranged from the incorporation of more Black students on campus to the cost of living on and near campus. Marley took his time and engaged with all of the students, asking as many questions as he was answering. He was clearly in his element, as he truly loved meeting new people and finding out more about their backgrounds and how people came to make the decisions that they did. A few of the students had some questions about BRIM. He gladly went through the history of the organization and what BRIM meant to him, outside of the conventional image as a violent gang.

Specifically, Marley went through the history of the organization, how it started, and many of the aims that he had been trying to achieve through his involvement with BRIM. It was a clear and lucid understanding of how the organization fit within the larger structure of Los Angeles as a city that has been actively hostile to the Black population while still maintaining a façade as a liberal bastion of inclusion. His description was also nuanced, as there was no monolithic understanding of the future; rather, he emphasized the constant conversation and dialogue within the organization about how things operated. He explained that while at times this put him at odds with some of the established leadership, given that he had always been very opinionated from a young age, issues and problems were generally worked out in a collective manner. He was also very much a realist about his plans with the organization. Being a student of previous organizing efforts in the city, he explained that there was a strong likelihood that some outside force could very easily try to tear apart the collective fabric of the group. Whether it be through provocation of internal tensions or the arrest and incarceration of key leadership, he was very forthright about having to plan as if the next day, week, or month would be totally different than the previous.

He wound down his presentation, and the students in the room were still fixated on his every word. A master orator and an excellent motivator, Marley had the skill to make time move with the ease of his words and his ability to connect with everybody in the room on an individual level. He wrapped his talk and thanked everybody and was gracious in his welcome to the campus. We moved out to a courtyard area, where he took up a conversation with a group of student organizers. What was supposed to be a closed-door session in one of the campus buildings transformed into an outdoor collective session where Marley and the other student organizers discussed the politics of race and the university, the purpose of higher education in an era of austerity, and how to balance the demands of organizing and academic pursuits. Lasting a little over two hours long, Marley generously engaged with the students and asked as many questions as he provided answers. Building in a collective pursuit, they exchanged contact information and we walked back to the car.

Making our way off campus, we decided to grab some food in Santa Barbara before making our way back down to Los Angeles. "Ain't that crazy, a kid from South Central who did not graduate from high school giving a talk to a whole bunch of college students in Santa Barbara," Marley stated as we made our way back to 217. "Did you know you were going to open with that?" I asked him. Laughing in response, "Man, I had no idea what I was going to say before I got up there!" I looked at him with what must have been complete disbelief because he immediately responded. "That is just something that I like to happen naturally. You know, otherwise it feels like, you don't allow the folks in the room to be a part of the conversation. Because you wind up thinking, 'I need to get to this point' or 'I need to make sure that I say this.' And if you think like that, then you could really miss out on a crucial question that would have really gotten people involved in what you had to say. So, yeah, I had no clue what I was going to say."

He continued to laugh as the look on my face still did not change. "Man," I said, "to be real with you, I am just jealous as it takes me so long to prepare for the smallest talk and you can get up there and give an amazing presentation without even thinking twice about it." "Well, brother," he responded, "I appreciate the compliment, but I was just being real about what I know and I really don't try to do anything more than that. Also, don't forget, my whole life has been in preparation for this moment." I had no response for his reply and the look on my face must have remained the same, as he laughed the entire way to the restaurant. We pulled in and both looked forward to the good meal that awaited us.

Watts to the Future

It was maybe around the second week of our sessions that a reality firmly hit me. The majority of the young people that Marley introduced me to and whom I had been meeting with during the political education classes not only did not finish school, but had more than sound reasons and rationales as to why they disengaged from the formal school process. Some had abusive relationships with teachers and administrators while others quickly learned that what they were being taught not only was useless, but ran counter to the knowledge traditions that emanated out of their communities.

The tension/angst that I was feeling was how much the older generations of Black Angelenos had countless stories of their schooling experience. Schools such as Fremont, Jefferson, Locke, Manual Arts, and Washington were legendary in part because of the legends and myths that were associated with their names. I had been told countless stories about the jazz bands, gospel choirs, fine arts directors, community organizers, political leaders, and remarkable athletes who were trained and honed their skills within Black Los Angeles schools.

The overwhelming majority of teenagers whom I met not only did not have that connection to these schools, but in stark contrast, associated the legends and myths that pertained to these schools with particular forms of disdain and moments of intense pain. As a result, our job became a little more focused. We had to figure out: What happened? How and why did these sites, which were home to some of the most

*dynamic forms of organizing and cultural creative genius, become solely synony-
mous with violence and repression?*

. . .

WATTS 1965

In August of 1965, Los Angeles, California, was on fire. The cumulative
effect of a racial regime bounded by codified housing segregation, employment discrimination, vicious white mob attacks, and a deplorable education system were the kindle. The fact that these structural impediments
were held intact by the Los Angeles Police Department (LAPD) was the
spark that set the city ablaze. Given the unfortunate misnomer "Watts
Riots," the scope and scale of the collective action by Black Angelenos was
unprecedented for an urban metropole (Horne 1995). In the wake of the
1965 Watts Rebellion, there were several reports and treatises that sought
to provide analysis of the causes and solutions. The McCone Commission, headed by former CIA director John A. McCone, an assembled body
forged together by then governor Pat Brown, issued the most famous of
these documents. While the report pointed out the most obvious ways in
which the city was divided upon racial lines, it failed to address the
demands made by Black Angelenos leading up to and during the Watts
Rebellion. The report also framed the revolt in terms of a violent rage
without direction rather than a collective action. However, the method of
the Watts Rebellion demonstrated that it was well-thought-out and
informed by a calculated logic of insurrection against forces deemed to be
oppressive within Black communities throughout the city (Horne 1995).[1]

1. Historian Paul Ortiz, writing about the framing by the McCone Commission in
contrast to Horne's analysis of 1965, observes, "Churches, schools, libraries and residential areas were mainly spared while numerous businesses, large and small were targeted
for arson. However, 'In the larger stores, department stores and clothing stores the first
target was the credit records. These were destroyed before the place was burned.' As
the riot progressed, small businesses that had acquired positive reputations in their
neighborhoods seemed to have been passed over, but as the flames burned out of control, such fine distinctions were sometimes blurred. For these reasons, Horne

The McCone Commission, in conjunction with several other state-sponsored reports, effectively reframed the narrative of 1965 and, significantly, ignored the structural forces that were at the root cause of Black anger. In very carefully crafted language, the state admitted to fundamental problems in Los Angeles, but laid the burden at the feet of state and federal bureaucratic administration. If policies related to housing, employment, and education could be reformed, the problems that triggered the Watts Rebellion would be resolved. Thus, while the state was seemingly taking responsibility for the events that unfolded in 1965, the objective was to shore up the fissures of the frayed racial regime through a reassertion of the state as the body that would be the barometer by which justice was determined.

The central means by which the city was able to achieve this objective was to diminish, remove, and replace Black demands for a radical restructuring of the city, which included a removal of the LAPD from the patrolling of Black communities, with a series of accommodationist policy initiatives and system changes (Davis 2006). Given that the city was in the midst of racial, political, and economic crises and national fears of Black unrest permeated the covers of news media headlines, there was a scramble to gain legitimacy of the situation. While much was made of the fact that many of the McCone Commission's policy recommendations were not implemented, what is more important is that the commission constructed racial diversion models that would be replicated over the next sixty years (Fogelson 1967). One of the primary models developed was to absolve the structural violence of whiteness through the manipulation of the "Negro" and "Mexican-American." Through a sleight of hand, the commission positioned Black Angelenos as the noncivil, violent subjects who needed to be disciplined, and the

---

characterizes the Watts Uprising as '... no mindless riot but rather a conscious, though inchoate insurrection.' This contrasts sharply with the assessment of the Governor's Commission on the Los Angeles Riots (known as the 'McCone Commission') who claimed that 'The rioters seemed to have been caught up in an insensate rage of destruction'" (Ortiz 2000).

mechanism for such disciplining was the construction of the peaceful "Mexican-American." The Commission reported:

> When the rioting came to Los Angeles, it was not a race riot in the usual sense. What happened was an explosion—a formless, quite senseless, all but hopeless violent protest—engaged in by a few but bringing great distress to all. Nor was the rioting exclusively a projection of the Negro problem. It is a part of an American problem which involves Negroes but which equally concerns other disadvantaged groups. In this report, our major conclusions and recommendations regarding the Negro problem in Los Angeles apply with equal force to the Mexican-Americans, a community which is almost equal in size to the Negro community and whose circumstances are similarly disadvantageous and demand equally urgent treatment. That the Mexican-American community did not riot is to its credit; it should not be to its disadvantage. (McCone et al 1965, 6A)

It should be noted that the positioning of the fictive "Mexican-American" came on the heels of a vicious campaign levied by the LAPD against the very same community. LAPD police chief William Parker, who never hid his disdain for Black or Latino communities, made it his primary objective to make life a virtual living hell for Black and Latino Angelenos (Davis 2006). Parker's racial theory, and that which set the culture of the department, was informed by pseudoscientific concepts of race and culture. In his assessment of the high crime rates of the "barrios" of East Los Angeles, he attributed crime to culturally inferior bloodlines of Mexican people. Testifying before the United States Commission on Civil Rights in 1960 as to crime in Los Angeles, Parker explained that the Mexican and Mexican-descended residents of East Los Angeles were the root cause as they "were only one step removed from the 'wild tribes of Mexico'" (Davis 2006, 295).

The Watts Rebellion changed the rules of engagement of a racial regime that was predicated upon dogged violence and racial manipulation as a means to maintain economic and political power for the white landed and financial class and the trappings of safety for a burgeoning white middle class. The sheer size and scope of the Watts Rebellion exposed the inter working of structural inequality in Los Angeles in a most profound manner. The fear, by both state and federal officials, was that the moral imperatives of such dissatisfaction would become commonsensical and thus the act of violent revolt against economic disenfranchisement, horrid housing conditions, and lack of social infrastructure would become the logical response. Doubling down upon race, the shift in techniques was in essence the colonial strategy of manufactured ethnic and racial manipulation. While the reconstruction of the "Mexican-American" population as proper civil actors was a tool of deflection, it also afforded the state time to regroup in an effort to consolidate white political and economic power that had been thwarted by Black rebellion. The result as described by Gerald Horne was devastating for Black Angelenos. Horne commented:

> The Watts Uprising was a milestone marking the previous era from what was to come. For blacks it marked the rise of black nationalism, as blacks revolted against police brutality. But what began as a black revolt against the police quickly became a police revolt against blacks. This latter revolt was a milestone too, one marking the onset of a "white backlash" that would propel Ronald Reagan into the governor's mansion in Sacramento and then the White House. (Horne 1995, 15–16)

EDUCATION, RACIAL REGIMES, AND THE DROPOUT

In addition to general community occupation by the LAPD in the immediate aftermath of the Watts Rebellion, one of the first sites of police occupation was public education. The LAPD became central figures on Black high school campuses and taught courses under the guise of a program cosponsored by the Los Angeles school district and the LAPD (Sojoyner 2013). The goal of these courses was to surveil Black students and their families on one hand and attempt to challenge the ideological framework of Black resistance that students were bringing with them from home on the other. However, education was also important in that it was a central cog within the political economy machine of the city. There was an explicit connection made by city planners, policy makers, and influential business owners to link education to notions of jobs and work. The objective was to reinforce the broken logic that jobs, rather than structural change, would ameliorate the circumstance of poverty (Office of Urban Affairs 1966).[2]

A major problem within the city of Los Angeles during the 1950s and '60s was the number of Black students who chose to disengage from formal schooling. Given the numerous protests, formal complaints lodged, confrontation with the police, and overall dissatisfaction with the education process, Black education in Los Angeles was for all intents and purposes in a state of operational dysfunctionality (Sojoyner 2014). The Watts Rebellion solidified a general Black ethos of repudiation for the type of education being forced upon Black neighborhoods. Several of the communal organizations such as the Slausons, Gladiators, and Dodge City that organized during the Watts Rebellion were made up of Black youth who chose to disengage from formal education (Horne 1995). Each organization pulled from a distinct neighborhood and school, and collectively they beat back the LAPD. It was this fact—the radical realized potential of organic Black organizing, absent state influence—that sent the city into a panic.

In the aftermath of the Watts Rebellion, the Office of Urban Affairs under the direction of the city superintendent issued a report titled *Implementation of Ad Hoc Directives on Equal Educational Opportunity*, which directly addressed the problem of school "dropouts" (Office of Urban Affairs 1966). The report summarized the steps taken by education officials and business lobbyists to address the problem of dropouts in

2. In the report issued by the Office of Urban Affairs in Los Angeles in the aftermath of the Watts Rebellion, the agency made the direct connection between education and work, stating, "Another publication which has been given wide distribution within the District is the attempt by the California Fair Employment Practices to point to 'the way of skills' as the way out of poverty and poorly paying jobs" (Office of Urban Affairs 1966, 13).

school. Without any equivocation, the report tied acts of revolt to behavior commonly found in school dropouts. In a section ominously titled "Discipline and Dropouts," the following is the description given to students who have disengaged from school (described in the report as "A" pupils):

> Changes which have caused a rise in the number of "A" pupils are described as the result of increased urbanization and apparent civil disobedience and defiance; general characteristics of the "A" pupil are noted as academic inept- ness and poor conduct; definition of the responsibility of the public school with reference to the "A" pupil is called for; use of the Social Adjustment Center is recommended as a last resort. (Office of Urban Affairs 1966, 12)

While the document as a whole provides a fascinating glimpse into the vision of the statecraft response to Black revolt, the aforementioned paragraph offers insight into the mechanics of forced control that were foundational to the eventual white backlash. The explicit connections made to the reframing of revolt within a legal framework of civil diso- bedience and psychological rendering of defiance is a shrewd and pre- dictable maneuver to locate Black radical action as illogical and criminal.

Education being the procurement of civility and the structural force that reproduced the civil subject, it became the central apparatus to forge Black refusal as illogical. Black youth, understood as the genea- logical carriers of Black radical action, had to be contained. The proc- ess of containment worked on multiple levels. On one level, there was the ideological containment of Black action that positioned the radical act of refusal as counter to the civil process. The construction of the dropout in this manner had to be configured as a pariah that would harm the fabric of American existence. Education, understood as a hallmark of said fabric, was the countervailing weight to Black radical action. As argued in the McCone Commission report, the state would remedy all of the problems of inequities in education, not by addressing the demands of Black people, but through an emphasis upon the civil process—more strident policies and stronger laws. Removed from the social vision of Black communal expression, the state reified its own power through a discursive project that connected education to economic social mobility.

On another level, containment meant the physical containment of Black youth. After Black youth organized and pushed back against both white vigilantes and the police, the state responded by targeting Black youth who withdrew from, and refused, state-sanctioned education. With behavior modification training that culminated in the utilization of the "Social Adjustment Center," the education of Black youth became solely focused on the training of Black students to be docile subjects. Marked by a severe crisis, schools underwent a drastic change as the soft side of the state marked by a predominately white women teaching base gave way to the heavy-handed police wing who became the teachers of Black youth (Meiners 2007; Sojoyner 2013). Black youth, the embodiment of resistance against state violence, thus were reconfigured as the locus of state dysfunction and forced back into the grips of state authority via education. Articulated through a language of rehabilitation and progress, the state demanded subservience or nothing else. Thus, Black youth who withdrew from and organized against state-sanctioned education in Los Angeles during the late 1960s and throughout the 1970s and '80s were an interpolated social evil used to reinforce racial regimes and pave the way for a new economic, political, racial, and social order that would have a harrowing impact upon Black communities.

REBIRTH AND RETOOLING—THE 1992 REBELLION

In 1992, the City of Angels was once again in flames. As the flames leapt from building to smoldering building, white backlash came tumbling down. The revolt of 1965 forced the state to reimagine a social arrangement that would both punish Black radical action and further ensconce petulant forms of structural racism as the modus operandi. The result was roughly three decades of pure economic and political insanity that rendered much of the working-class Black population of Los Angeles without food, jobs, or housing. The equation of Black misery was balanced by one of the most virulent forms of wealth accumulation in the history of the United States. Such a delicate balance was held intact by a police department that was given carte blanche to attack the Black population with a relentless and unforgiving force hell bent on squelching the earliest seeds of dissent. The response to such a draconian operation was the smashing of the scales of state-sanctioned justice under the collective weight of Black anger.

Following the acquittal of four white police officers who savagely beat Rodney King, Black Angelenos declared that decades of violent white backlash had reached its zenith. King, a twenty-six-year-old Black man, was detained by police officers on a charge of vehicular speeding. Surrounded by ten members of the LAPD, King was mercilessly wailed upon by a barrage of batons while his body was continually jolted with the shock of electric tasers. Unbeknownst to the officers, much of the beating was caught on tape by George Holiday, who upon witnessing the commotion from his bedroom window had grabbed his personal camcorder to document the harrowing spectacle. When the video was picked up by news outlets around the globe, the world was given a small glimpse of the racial terror faced by Black residents of the city.

To the casual observer, the video-documented evidence of King's beating seemed like solid proof as to the guilt of the police officers. However, what the amateur videotape could not reveal was that the LAPD was the enforcer of an economic and political fantasy that demanded Black subservience. The very court system that was constructed to uphold the state-sanctioned civil project was never going to condemn the structural force—the LAPD—whose job it was to protect the material extraction that undergirded racial violence. Simply stated, a guilty verdict of the police officers would have been an indictment against the grand social vision of a racial regime predicated upon obscene accumulation and rapid abandonment that informed the political economy of late-twentieth-century Los Angeles. Black people had had enough and revolted against a plan whose intent was to extract blood from a turnip until it was dry at the core.

EDUCATION AS A TOOL

Following the 1965 Watts Rebellion, the city reorganized the economic arrangement of the infrastructure. The white backlash as described by Gerald Horne paved the way for Ronald Reagan to become governor of the state. A former B-list actor, Reagan was marketed as a communicator who would be able to restore civility to the state, namely the urban centers of Los Angeles and Alameda Counties. While much has been written and discussed about Reagan's administration as president, what cannot be forgotten is that Reagan's governorship was utilized as a model of Black revolt management that was then exported nationwide (Horne 1997; Davis 2006). As a primary means to achieve this goal, Reagan immediately seized upon education:

> Later that year [1970], Roger Freeman—a key educational adviser to Nixon then working for the reelection of California Governor Ronald Reagan—defined quite precisely the target of the conservative counterattack: "We are in danger of producing an educated proletariat. That's dynamite! We have to be selective on who we allow to go through higher education." (Franklin 2000)

Reagan specifically chose to attack pathways to higher education, as such routes were the organizing strategy of several Black radical organizations. The case of Bunchy Carter is perhaps the most iconic of this strategy. Carter, a former member of the Slausons, became an instrumental member of the Los Angeles chapter of the Black Panther Party (BPP). In recognition that postsecondary education was under attack by the state, the BPP developed a strategy of both organizing

Black students on college campuses around the state as well as opening access for Black youth who chose to flee from the confines of public education. Carter, who in following the strategy became a student at the University of California, Los Angeles, was vital in recruiting members of the Slausons to the BPP, and his charismatic leadership style was able to draw many youth who had fled from public secondary education (Sloan 2005). Symbolic of Carter's success, the result of the Black organizing strategy was powerful, as Black students led campaigns and actions across the state demanding radical change of the university environment (Biondi 2012). Reagan and his advisors very well understood the magnitude of the situation and, under the guise of a monetary fee structure, circumvented the rules of state charter to add a financial cost to higher education. The University of California network had been established as a free system, but in 1970, then governor Reagan added fees in lieu of tuition (which was not allowed), preventing access for the very Black population that the BPP was organizing (Franklin 2000).

The racial educational tax that was levied against the Black population was emblematic of the economic strategy that accompanied the civil project. Reagan's gubernatorial tenure and eventual reign as president ushered in an economic regime that decimated Black Los Angeles. Under the framework of government deregulation, the financial sector raided the public coffers, culminating in massive fraud and bringing horrendous consequences to a population that was already on the brink of disaster.[3] In addition to the massive deregulation, the state provided

3. Cedric Robinson, commenting on the effects of the Reagan presidential administration stated, "In the last months of the Reagan administration, the yield from the debauchery of an unfettered capitalism and political and bureaucratic corruption surfaced with a vengeance: The junk bonds, corporate mergers, and financial mismanagement facilitated by deregulation occasioned the multi-billion dollar Savings and Loan crisis. The unprecedented growth of war production and the anarchy of capitalist development submerged the economy into a depression and massive unemployment .... Between 1977 and 1989, according to the Congressional Budget Office, the wealthiest 1% of American families amassed 60% of the growth in after-tax income while the

tax subsidies and shelters to companies in order to build up predominately white suburban enclaves and simultaneously exploit wage labor through the manipulation and eventual annihilation of the Mexican economy:

> South Central Los Angeles—the traditional industrial core of the city—bore the brunt of the decline in manufacturing employment, losing 70,000 high-wage, stable jobs between 1978 and 1982. At the same time that well-paying, stable jobs were disappearing from South Central Los Angeles, local employers were seeking alternative sites for their manufacturing activities. As a consequence of these seemingly routine decisions, new employment growth nodes or "technopoles" emerged in the San Fernando Valley, in the San Gabriel Valley, and in El Segundo near the airport in Los Angeles County, as well as in nearby Orange County. In addition, a number of Los Angeles–based employers established production facilities in the Mexican border towns of Tijuana, Ensenada, and Tecate. Between 1978 to 1982, over 200 Los Angeles–based firms, including Hughes Aircraft, Northrop, and Rockwell, as well as a host of smaller firms, participated in this deconcentration process. Such capital flight, in conjunction with the plant closings, has essentially closed off to the residents of South Central Los Angeles access to what were formerly well-paying, unionized jobs. (Oliver, Johnson, and Farrell 1993, 122)

In conjunction with the high rates of unemployment and government deregulation schemes that exploited mostly poor and working-class people, there was a massive attack upon the social infrastructure. Health clinics that had been established by the demands of Black residents of Los Angeles housing projects were shuttered under the name of budget cuts (Holland 1994). Due to the closure of the auxiliary clinics, the largest health provider, Martin Luther King Jr.–Charles Drew

---

poorest 40% of families experienced actual income declines (the 'superpoor,' the bottom 20% of families, suffered a 9% income loss). In the same span of time, chief-executive salaries rose from 35 to 120 times the average worker's pay, and the number of (primarily corporate) lawyers doubled to 740,000. These trends in the concentration of wealth at the top, documented by economic historians as having begun in the 1960s, accelerated in the 1980s" (Robinson 1993, 75).

Hospital, became overburdened by an overwhelming poor, Black residential base devoid of health insurance. While the social infrastructure was being gutted on one side, the public safety realm of the social infrastructure apparatus was being fattened. Under the guise of anticrime legislation, the LAPD under the direction of police chief Daryl Gates operated with impunity against Black residents of the city. With funding coming from the federal and state budget, the LAPD was able to develop violent campaigns such as Operation Hammer, which surveilled, harassed, and promoted the beating of Black Angelenos (Kelley 1996). However, in April of 1992, the white backlash had reached its peak and a racial regime predicated upon political and economic extortion was violently rebuked. The city was once again in flames.

RECONFIGURING RACE TO MAINTAIN POWER

In the wake of the 1965 Watts Rebellion, the city power brokers had effectively devised a racial regime that legitimated the levying of multiple forms of violence upon the Black population. A toxic combination of criminality and the reinforcement of personal-responsibility politics provided the means to gut social infrastructure, incarcerate Black people, and siphon away the public tax base in order to benefit the corporate and financial sector (Kelley 1998; Gilmore 2007). The 1992 Los Angeles Rebellion quickly exposed the fallacy of that argument. A rebellion that was started by Black anger quick grew into a multiracial alliance against a perverse governing structure. Similar to 1965, there were several reports and analyses that provided supposed insight into the problems of the city. However, following 1992, the city utilized a different strategy to craft a new regime that would mask the gaping holes left by the '92 Los Angeles Rebellion. Utilizing the *Los Angeles Times* as a propaganda machine, the city repackaged race in order to regain power and control.

A major problem that the city faced was that splattered across television sets around the world were not just Black people rising up in the city, but a broad spectrum of actors including whites, Asians, and Latina/os. Although led by the Black organizations (the 1992 Gang Truce having a major effect), the city could not easily spin the narrative as it had done in 1965 as a Black-versus-white issue. However, what the city constructed was a model that was in many ways much more insidious that the 1965 plan. Very cleverly, article after article ran in the *Times* putting forth a new strategy based upon a liberal conception of multi-racial politics (Costa Vargas 2004).[4]

Under the cover of liberal racial harmony, the new racial regime bared its fangs, exposing the governing philosophy of the new model: a virulent form of anti-Blackness. The basis of the plan was threefold. Through a castigation of Blackness in the form of Black revolt and rebellion against the civil project, the discursive and structural realities would promote and reward the civility of non-Black subjects. Second, the city was able to incorporate the Black middle class as a junior partner to condemn the actions of their poor and deviant brethren.[5] Last, the city devised a plan to manage dissent through the institutionalization of politics that would be controlled by city managers and

4. "The portrait presented by the *Times* at this stage is again—as it was at the very beginning of the rebellions—polyphonic and multiracial. The narrative tone now apparently switches from one that emphasizes black irrationality to one that focuses on the larger, multiracial composition of the metropolis. Persons of all races are given voice and opinion.... In this model, blacks and whites constituted the extremes: they embodied most of the conflicts that gave rise to the civil disturbances. Latina/os and Asians occupied intermediary positions in the continuum formed by blacks, on one end, and whites, on the other; and their depiction served not so much to assert the *Times'* commitment to present a multiracial city, but mainly to confirm the responsibility that was increasingly given to African Americans for the looting. Thus, when non-black persons appeared in the pages of the *Times* as models of citizenship, they, as if by default, centered the readers' attention on blacks, deemed responsible for the looting and burning" (Costa Vargas 2004, 216–17).

5. This was perhaps best articulated by the president of the Los Angeles Urban League (a Black business-oriented organization) who lamented during the rebellion: "My fear is that all that we've worked toward could be lost if people let their basic instincts take over" (Costa Vargas 2004, 216).

budgets. The goal of the last prong was to make Black revolt illogical and, connecting back to the post-1965 strategy, noncivil.[6]

The discursive strategies of the new racial regime provided the cover to inflict further material damage on the Black poor and increasingly shrinking working class. As an example, the only solution provided by the federal government in the aftermath of the '92 Los Angeles Rebellion was a $19 million bill that was dubiously referred to "Weed and Seed," with a main stated objective to "help weed out drug dealers and criminals and help seed education, employment and social services initiatives" (Costa Vargas 2004, 226). The not-so-subtle racial undertones of drug dealers and criminals were a foreshadowing of the manner in which law enforcement would be at the forefront of both the weeding and seeding within poor and working-class Black communities. The new racial regime also provided cover to launch a secondary attack upon Black education in a most profound way. Utilizing new strategies that would be adopted across the country, Los Angeles embarked upon a process that would permanently establish Black schools as sites of containment and obliterate any notion of educative progress.

6. Culling the *Times* archives, Costa Vargas surmises that "Blacks, again, were described as the most likely to revolt. With this narrative strategy, the *Times* not only relegated the rebellions to the realm of irrationality, but also emptied them of political meaning. In contrast to the immediate calls for justice made in the streets, the *Times* argued that the solutions to blacks' grievances had to be necessarily processed *within* institutionalized channels" (Costa Vargas 2004, 218). He explains further that the suppression of Blackness in this manner was directly linked to the city being able to coalesce power: "This notion of politics is a leader- and specialist-managed activity, dislocating it from everyday practices to institutionalized spheres. As well as operating through the de-politicization of conflict, the *Los Angeles Times'* politics proceeds from notions of stable, harmonic communities. It suppresses political voices that neither conform to the 'civilized' parameters nor relate to institutionalized, leader-oriented processes. It follows that social justice is a derivation of technical measures suggested and implemented by, and only by, officials, recognized representatives, and so-called competent specialists" (Costa Vargas 2004, 219).

EDUCATION: CONTAINING BLACKNESS

A little over twenty years after the 1965 Watts Rebellion, the city of Los Angeles's attempt to address Black disengagement from schools had failed. Oliver et al. make note that "for the Los Angeles Unified School District as a whole, 39.2% of all of the students in the class of 1988 dropped out at some point during their high school years. However, for high schools in South Central Los Angeles [predominately Black areas], the dropout rates were substantially higher, between 63% and 79%" (Oliver, Johnson, and Farrell 1993, 127). In essence, there was a mass exodus from a neoliberal form of education management that proved insufficient for Black youth. This presented a major problem for the city. However, the problem that the city faced was not one of an "uneducated" workforce, as was and continues to be the common rhetorical narrative in the face of Black disengagement from education. Rather, the problem that the city was up against was that the Black youth were becoming increasingly organized. In the wake of the 1992 Los Angeles Rebellion, in partnership with the Coalition Against Police Abuse (CAPA), the Crips and Bloods came together and formed what was called the "Gang Truce." Much more than a reconciliatory project, the Gang Truce laid out an agenda along with a list of demands for the city officials including a structural overhaul of public education (Costa Vargas 2006). Similar to the work of the Gladiators, Dodge City, and the Slausons nearly thirty years prior, the Crips and Bloods effectively organized Black youth and presented a potent challenge to a racial regime that demanded Black subservience. Once the 1992 Los Angeles Rebellion took form, the leaders of the Gang Truce were at the forefront of presenting an organized political analysis and forging alliances across racial and religious divides (Costa Vargas 2006; Gilmore 2007). The collective action of mobilizing Black communities not only exposed the fissures within the racial regime leading up to the 1992 Los Angeles Rebellion, but also anticipated the anti-Black multiracial political stance that the city would adopt following the revolt.

Such organic Black organizing had to be thwarted, and the city was intent on preventing the breakdown of the newly minted racial regime. To carry out its plan, the city implemented a partnership between the LAUSD and the City of Los Angeles District Attorney's Office. The basis of the partnership was the transference of power of truancy operations to the District Attorney's Office in conjunction with a plan that gave the LAPD (and later the Los Angeles County Sherriff's Department) unrestricted power to round up Black youth under the guise of truancy violations. The program, designated Abolish Chronic Truancy (ACT), became a model collaboration that was soon replicated across the country. The strategy was devastating upon the Black community in two profound ways. First, it gutted the limited financial resources of the community. The tickets, which were in excess of thousands of dollars and required court fees and time, were a most vicious type of racial tax (Schnyder 2012). Second, it forced Black youth back to the schools, which during the interim since the '65 Watts Rebellion had developed into little more than warehouses. The evisceration of curriculum through protocols of standardized testing/mandates and the militarization of school zones via several layers of policing (including police substations on school campuses) left the schools in Los Angeles akin to racial containment zones (Sojoyner 2016).

The power and resultant danger of Black withdrawal and organizing exposed myths that were critical to the maintenance of the racial regime that lasted from 1965 to 1992. With an intense focus on individual responsibility, the 1992 Gang Truce and Los Angeles Rebellion blew asunder racist explanations that masked structural violence. Further, the state had to now deal with an increasingly broad multiracial coalition that was increasingly adopting the politics of Black radical action. Rather than broach the notion of entering into good-faith conversations with members of the Gang Truce, the city doubled down on processes of racial terror and utilized the formal education apparatus as a means to dampen Black resistance. In the aftermath of the 1992 Los Angeles Rebellion and the attack upon Black communities, while millions of dollars have been pumped into the policing of Black youth and extorted from Black neighborhoods via truancy tickets, schools have all but abandoned the façade of providing an education. Yet, as a political stance, the commonsense drive is to stop dropouts/pushouts and force students back into the clutches of school. As a matter of praxis, there has to be a serious interrogation into governing methodologies when even the most "progressive" organizations have adopted the state civil ideological framework of education as a source of redemption and cast aside a radical tradition that has consistently exposed the fallacies of virulent racial regimes.

All That Glitters

Nonprofit Management

PLANNED CONTRADICTIONS

By the time I had gotten there, it was too late. Marley was gone. Physically he was there, but mentally he was somewhere else. I would soon be able to pick up on when Marley was in this space, but this was the first time that I had seen him in this manner. While I knew he was upset, I could not accurately gauge his level of anger. He looked not so much at me, but rather right through me. Not sure how to engage, I approached him, asking, "Hey brother, what is going on?" In a very curt and cold response he replied, "Man, I don't even want to be here right now." His face was devoid of all expression and his affect had gone eerily flat. At once looking a hundred miles past me, yet fixated immediately upon my brow, his eyes pierced into my line of sight. "This is some bullshit," he said. With the reverence of a preacher standing before the pulpit on a hot Sunday morning, his tone slowly rose as his story poured out into the echo chamber of Southern California Library's large cavernous design. A profound silence grasped the room as the rest of the participants gave their silent consent for Marley to bear his testimony for, I was soon to find out, it was theirs as well. A charismatic figure, Marley always knew when to add volatility to a situation and when to heed the winds of caution. This moment called for the former. "I put all of this work in, and for what? To have some dude who don't know what I have been through and what I have done to just make it to the office tell me that I won't be getting paid on time because I was late for one day."

His rage slowly began to burn much more visceral. This had been building for quite some time, and now the anger was to be revealed in its most concise form. "Look, I'm not mad at you. I'm not mad at Michele. I'm not mad at Yusef. But they just can't keep treating us like this. Just because we are from South Central and from the hood, they act like they can do whatever the fuck it is that they want to do to us. I'm tired of this and they are supposed to be helping us. What kind of help is this? This is some straight-up bullshit." I sat there listening, still trying to piece together the totality of the story. Marley, having a sense of when his point is not completely registering, cut off his rage mid-stream. "Never mind, man, just do what you got to do, but I am not staying here. Like I said, I am not mad at you or Yusef or Michele, it is the idea that somehow I am not professional enough and yet it is them who do not want to pay me for my time."

And with that, the anger, the rage, was vocally mute, but it had not disappeared. Rather, it turned inward. His eyes dropped slightly below mine, and while he was looking at me, Marley's face disappeared. His cold gaze was somewhere between disinterested and unadulterated anger. Save for me, no one was uncomfortable within the space. My own discomfort came not from awkwardness or fear, but rather from not understanding. There was a shared camaraderie within the space, and I was quickly drowning trying to catch up. I, who was supposed to be guiding discussion and leading conversation pertaining to critical issues such as the one that was happening right in front of me, was lost in a sea of confusion. Not quite knowing what to do, but knowing that I did not possess the skill set to bring the group morale to engage in any meaningful discussion, I thought it was in the best interest of everybody, but mainly myself, to give a five-minute break.

I walked over to the office space shared by Yusef and Michele, and immediately they could see my look of confusion/exasperation/loss. Yusef approached me and without my having to even ask a question explained the situation.

As background, the Library was operating its summer program in conjunction with a city initiative that aimed to "keep kids off the streets" during the summer. Very often programs such as these, run in coordination with the city, involved manual labor. Under the auspices of teaching "at-risk youth" the values of hard work, Black youth were hired to clean park benches and walls, sweep the city streets, and, in some of the more unfortunate circumstances, clean bathrooms. In alignment with a bygone era of industrial forms of education that targeted Black folks at the close of Reconstruction, the extraction of Black menial labor was both normal and profoundly violent. Seeing an opening, Yusef and Michele decided to take part in the program, but instead of paying Black youth to appreciate the value of mindless, laborious tasks, they set up a summer school and workshop. Bringing in instructors and facilitators such as myself, the goal was to engage the young people who lived in the neighborhood on a level that was beyond banal work tasks. Instead they were required to conduct research projects in the Library and take part in discussions that related to said projects.

The problem for SCL, however, was a similar problem faced by organizations that attempt to carve out space within the framework of a highly problematic structure. In this case, the participants in the program still had to engage with nonprofit organizations that were subcontracted out by the city to distribute resources to Black youth. These nonprofits would in turn contact organizations such as SCL that had the relationships with Black community members as a means to establish contact with actual people. It was at this moment of engagement that a series of profoundly absurd ironies unfolded and led to the moment of Marley peering through me and into another realm. Yusef explained that in order to formally be a part of the program and receive the benefits of the program (that is, money), the youth had to take part in scheduled meetings that were to reinforce the values of hard work, discipline, and respect for the nonprofit and the city. Most of the meetings started relatively early in the morning at 9:00 A.M. and were held at a different location, in a different neighborhood than SCL. If you were late to a meeting, then you did not get paid. Also, it is of note that many of these organizations purposely contacted more people than they had funds for as means to claim that their outreach was a success, but also meant that they did not have the budget to pay everybody. Thus, the first irony revealed itself: Black youth in South Central Los Angeles, as the city knows from data held in city databases, live in some of the most precarious of situations. Thus, getting anywhere around the city was already going to present a task, given the economic pains of public transportation or lack thereof in Los Angeles. The city was expecting those with the least financial resources to use those very limited resources to get to a building to receive their money.

This laid the groundwork for the second ironic situation: getting around Los Angeles during rush-hour traffic is a herculean task that even those who espouse the rhetoric of the Protestant work ethic cannot abide by. The coordinator, the same individual whose task it was to teach the values of hard work, timeliness, and respect, failed on two occasions to meet with Yusef and Michele at the agreed-upon time to go over the details of the program. Neither Yusef or Michele had any problem with him showing up late to the meeting; rather, they were perplexed that an individual who expected a level of human decency and understanding given the atrocious conditions of Los Angeles traffic and life circumstances could not extend the same level of care and attention back to those who desperately needed the financial resources.

The same official whose job it was to keep these aforementioned "at-risk" Black youth on the proverbial straight and narrow was also tasked with teaching the youth at the meetings about the importance of professionalism. According to the students, he stressed the need to always wear a buttoned shirt and tie, in the case of the men, as well as to be on time. Given that he had already faulted on the later, the third irony

presented itself as the city representative on both occasions showed up
to the meeting with Yusef and Michele without a tie or a buttoned-up
shirt and looked rather casual. Once again, Yusef and Michele did not
have any problem with him not wearing a tie, but rather questioned
what he thought of the Library as a site of serious inquiry and, more to
the point: why stress the need for a shirt and tie, when your own job
rarely requires a shirt and tie? Yusef and Michele would often point out
that Black people in the neighborhood were keenly aware of how to
present themselves depending on the situation. What they wore to
court when they were fighting a case or to church or to the park for a
memorial service was all context-specific. They did not need special
training to understand the logics of dress; instead, such training created a false dichotomy where successful people dressed a certain way
and unsuccessful/lazy people dressed another way. For them and for
many in the group, including Marley, it had very little to do with dress
and everything to do with moving away from that which was connected
to Blackness, which they knew was an impossible task.

In the face of all of this, the greatest irony revealed itself to be the tip-
ping point for Marley. Given the incessant demands placed upon the
youth to be respectful, professional, and abide by a set of ridiculous conditions to receive compensation, the nonprofit subcontractor did not
hold up to its end of the bargain. Upon the date that the participants
were to receive their checks, Marley was told his was not ready and it
might be a few days before it would be ready for pick-up. Marley had
met all the conditions that the city placed upon him. He found a way to
the office, he attended all the meetings, he came to the workshops and
classes at the Library, and yet the city demonstrated its complete disre-
gard for the precarity of Marley's life. I don't write that hyperbolically,
as the money that was earned by the students ($7.00 an hour) was a tre-
mendous amount of money considering the limitations of food and shelter in the region. But even more than the money was the time spent: the
time spent getting to the building, the time spent in the asinine training
sessions, the time spent participating in workshops and trainings at the

Southern California Library. This is all time that could have been used to attain vital resources needed for family and friends. While two or three days did not seem like an inconvenience for city officials, for Black youth in the area, two or three days very often represented the difference between living in a relatively safe space with light, heat, and a small modicum of food and trying to navigate through the maze of city-subsidized housing, paltry hourly-rate motels, and the streets.

There was no coming back for Marley. Above all else, Marley was an individual of principle and honor. These traits he held dearly, as his reputation within his community was largely based upon his ability to deliver upon his stated intentions and desires. Never one to back down from a confrontation, Marley understood that the best way to resolve conflict was to get at the heart of the matter through dialogue and conversation. In the proverbial book of Marley, once someone was demonstrated to be similarly principled, his level of sacrifice knew no bounds. He would place all of his energy to make sure that whatever was agreed upon would be honored. However, once someone was proven to be an untrustworthy partner, there was very virtually no coming back. Marley was also the walking manifestation of the Black axiom "they have been here before." By the age of sixteen, Marley had experienced life on a scale that was unconventionally profound, yet quite common among his friends within South Central Los Angeles. Having to navigate life within the most difficult of situations, he had become very adept in being able to quickly read the veracity of situations.

The problem with the case of the city is that Marley's fine-tuned radar had long ago told him that the city was not going to hold up its end of the bargain. Marley had been forged through the fire of the labyrinth that was the city bureaucratic system. From trying to help his family attain affordable housing to the gauntlet of the juvenile justice system to its latest foray in partnership with nonprofits, Marley understood very well how to read social scripts, and this endeavor with the city screamed fraud: not a literal fraud in the legal sense of the definition that resources were being siphoned away, but a fraud with respect to intent and matters of principle. As Marley once told me, "It is always the person who is talking the loudest about what they are going to do and how they are going to do it, that is the person that ain't going to do shit."

In this case, Marley was extremely weary of the ideological framing placed by the city of how to be a "productive member of society" and about timeliness and staking out a moral high ground when the city very rarely had proven itself to be trustworthy. Further, that ideological stance was being spouted very loudly and very repeatedly in a tone that was all too familiar to Marley: the tone that was just a little too loud, slightly lower in register, and rang with the harmony of condemnation and judgment. He had heard it from school teachers and administrators, police, judges and juvenile detention guards, and housing officials. He knew this tone, because he had been here before. He had ample reason to distrust this tone, but because of his relationship with the Southern California Library he had muted his intuition and gone down a road he knew was going to lead to disappointment and anger.

Once the city had proven to be what he thought it was, his anger was uncontainable. His rage was surely pointed at the fact that he would not be receiving money that he desperately needed to assist his family and at the city for proving to be the fraud that he knew it was. But perhaps most viscerally, he was upset with himself. He had allowed himself to believe in something that he knew not to be real, and he knew that hope was dangerous if not guided. He had allowed his intuition to be diminished, and after several hard-learned lessons, that was something that he had vowed long ago never to allow to happen. And in a moment of vulnerability, he had allowed hope to set in, and Marley had seen hope consume the strongest and most determined of people.

In that moment I reflected on one of our reading group sessions at SCL where the collective had warned me about the folly of hope. There was consensus that hope was not something that you could count on as it took control out of your hands. Marley had very strong feelings upon the matter and spoke passionately about the massive trap that was hope. After the session, I sat down with Marley in an effort to get a better understanding as to why there was such a strong sentiment against relying upon hope. I pushed Marley on the subject, insisting that hope was the foundation of the Black experience. Marley pushed right back: "Hope for what? Hope will get you killed. Do you know how many times someone had told me that something good will happen or that something will come through for me? If I just follow these steps and do x, y, or z, then somehow my life will be so much better? All that has led to is more work and empty promises. You can't live like that. I have to do it myself or it ain't getting done."

We sat on the burnt orange, slightly faded, but well-kept sofas in the lobby of SCL, and Marley could tell that he had me slightly off balance. He rather enjoyed this dynamic, whether it be a debate about sports, music, or politics; however, in this moment he took no joy. The profound insight of his words was matched by his sincerity. "You can't hope that the lights will get turned on or that someone is going to help you get a job or hope that the dude down the street has your best interests in mind. That is a dangerous way of thinking. I get it if you are a kid and don't know any better. Shoot, as a kid, you should always have hope, and in a way, I am mad that that part of me is gone."

Marley slowly rose from the well-cushioned seat and joined the others who were headed out the door. With a deep breath on his way up, his posture slightly relaxed and he said, "I wish I could be free to hold on to the belief that somehow, some way things will work out the way that people say that they will. That would be a beautiful thing and it is the way that things should be. It's like this: hope ain't nothing but a one-way street and for us, living here in this world, all the one-way streets wind up as dead-ends."

And that day at the Library with the city having once again proven to be a disingenuous partner, Marley had found himself in a world of trouble. He had to recalibrate his life. He had counted on the money for very specific reasons related to his housing situation, and now he had to quickly figure out what to do. However, his compass was in disarray because his anger at himself, the city, and the lack of money could not allow him to think straight. He also was quite aware of himself, and importantly, his tendencies when he got angry. He knew that he would act out of sheer emotion and that could lead to unfortunate situations.

We had spoken in detail about how he had had to learn to adjust the expression of his emotions at a very young age. Around his friends and family he sometimes got into heated conversations and debates, but it was in school where he very quickly learned that he had to watch what and, importantly, how he said certain things. Recounting his experience in school, he said, "It is messed up, because I feel like white kids in school, they get to be angry and go off and yell at and whatever. 'Get the fuck away from me, Ms. Suzy!'" he laughed as he imitated a white student in a classroom situation. "But for me," he continued, "that does not fly. I curse out a teacher and I'm about to be written up on some terroristic threats charges. I'm not saying that everybody should be allowed to curse out the teacher or law enforcement, but there is something freeing about being able to get that anger off your chest without fear of retaliation or being locked up."

Marley understood himself in a way and had a level of self-awareness that was astounding for a person his age. His natural disposition was to stand up for himself and not back down, and in particular in a situation where he knew he was right. However, he also had learned that such a disposition could lead to problems or, as he put it, "I don't mind confrontation, if you know what I mean. I'm not saying that I look for trouble, but if it comes my way, then well ... However, when I'm angry and upset, every and anything begins to look like trouble, even when it is not really trouble. And then someone or several people are about to have a problem. But the truth of the matter is, I don't like living like that. So, when I get really mad, I just go within myself and allow myself to cool down."

And so Marley retreated as a means of self-protection, but also as a means to not misplace his anger upon those who he felt did not deserve his rage. During the break, Yusef attempted to talk to him and convey that the Library would do everything it could to help him get the money. But he was too far gone. Marley had already made the cognitive dissociation with the here and now. In a stern, elevated tone, he stated, "Listen, I am not mad at you, I am not mad at Michele. But this situation is fucked up and there is nothing that anybody can do right now. They said one thing and did another. I knew this was going to happen. This always happens and now I am fucked." With that, he calmly turned around and, without saying anything to anybody, he walked out the door and disappeared into the bright sun. Feeling that there was a sense of solidarity among the group, I told them that there was not any need to proceed and we would convene the following week. Everybody milled around for a short time. Some took the opportunity to use the desktop computers, and some sat around Michele's desk talking in somewhat hushed tones.

I walked over to Yusef's desk and tried to piece together as best I could what had happened. "Man, I don't know what to do. These are the same folks who demand all sorts of respectable politics out of these folks in the neighborhood, but then turn around and treat them like this. To complicate matters, this puts us in a difficult situation with folks in the neighborhood who have come to trust us." Yusef was referring to the fact that under their stewardship, the SCL had made a concentrated effort to open its doors to the immediate community. For decades the Library had been primarily a research hub accessed by academics, journalists, independent researchers, and people who were looking to donate their archives. As the Library's directors sensed that the immediate neighborhood had very little clue as to what was happening in the beige building on Vermont Avenue, things began to slowly change. Yusef soon learned why it was that the pace moved as slowly as it did, as multiple people told him that they thought the Library was actually an unmarked branch of the Los Angeles Police Department. In hindsight, Yusef understood why that made perfect sense. With its tinted entry door and only a trickle of people walking in and out of the building at any given time, it had all the makings of a surveillance operation. Yet, over time, with dedicated programs such as the one that Marley was a part of, the relationship with the community began to change. That change, however, was in process, and Yusef worried that due to the city's negligence, that change would be stunted. What was particularly frustrating was that Yusef and Michele quickly recognized the dynamism in Marley's personality. His ability to organize and pull people together was quite phenomenal, and at a young age he was critical to the fabric of the community. Across the spectrum of age and to a certain extent gender, Marley was highly effective in getting everybody on the same proverbial page. It was by no means perfect or always smooth; however, he was highly effective. And now that presence had just walked out of the Library, and Yusef was rightly concerned that with him a part of the neighborhood would lose trust.

Complicating matters was the fact that Yusef and Michele were attempting to organize the community in a dramatically different way than most within the nonprofit sector. Through conversations and being a part of their planning strategy over the summer, it was clear that they were forging a new path. For SCL, the most important part was to organize with the immediate neighborhood and find pathways to build relationships outward. This style of organizing was quite effective, however dramatically different than most of their peer (non-church-affiliated) nonprofits throughout Southern California.[1] The forging of relationships in this manner allowed the Library to foster bonds with multiple people in ways that were complicated, fraught, tense, and highly fruitful. They spent countless hours listening to and engaging with people across the age, gender, and sexual continuum who, in the midst of chaotic situations, made the impossible reality. It was through these conversations and time spent that bonds were built that enabled them to transition SCL from the random building on the street to a part of the fabric of the

1. The distinction between church- and non-church-affiliated is critical as, while many of the ideological formations within the Black church in Southern California have moved away from a social justice focus that has an explicit critique at the intersections of race and capital, the primary organizing base is a local strategy that expands outward.

neighborhood. Through this shift in positionality, Yusef and Michele became adept at identifying people who were stewards of the community in very particular ways. Some people had a gravitas and charisma about them that could gather people with just a look. Other people rarely liked to be seen or heard, but would give their last dime and all of their energy to help their neighborhood. There were musicians, visual and performing artists. There were chefs and skilled artisans who could build bookshelves, lunch benches, and car engines just by looking at a picture. Then there were those who liked to have a good time, who threw the best parties and somehow always knew just the right words to diffuse potentially volatile situations. Yusef and Michele opened the doors to all of these people and allowed them a space to do whatever was necessary at that moment. Sometimes, it was just a moment to catch a breath on a couch and grab something to drink. Other times it was to develop a planning strategy to organize the neighborhood. The majority of time it was to just talk about the ups and downs of life. Through it all, SCL never positioned itself as the organizer of the community; rather, there was an unquestioned understanding that the Black residents of the community were quite astute at knowing how to make meaning and order out of a world that seemingly was on the brink of disaster. Using the energy of the community, the Library found ways to provide resources when needed to sustain communal functions.

SCL had become a key component of the neighborhood process, and now Yusef and Michele feared that the relationship that they had developed was on shaky ground. One of the key organizers in the community, Marley, a young man who was revered and, by the time I met him, had already developed legendary status, had justifiable reason to no longer trust SCL or the intentions (no matter how well-thought-out or planned) of Yusef and Michele. They understood the importance that Marley had as someone whose charismatic influence greatly impacted the work of the community and the Library. As Marley walked out the door, a bit of doubt swirled in the vast room and the silence that remained only served to reinforce that feeling of unease.

BROTHERS GOING TO WORK IT OUT

He was beyond ecstatic and had energy exuding from his pores. Barely able to contain his excitement, Marley was at his best in these moments. The planning was intense, and he had long since known to trust his preparation. He had sat down with Yusef, Michele, and several of his friends for the past few weeks to hash out the details that had been bouncing, skipping, and jumping through his mind. He had a vision of what was to be: a singular event that would launch mini-campaigns that in turn would galvanize his neighborhood. "Politics and food, politics and food." These were the phrases that Marley often uttered to himself in the weeks leading up to the event. In one of these moments of joy, Marley expressed to me, "You know how hard it is to get a good meal throughout the course of a day? I mean like a home-cooked meal that is full of nutrients and vegetables and just all that goodness that your body needs. Do you know how hard it is to get that around here? You can scrap your little dollars together and get some of that crap [referring to fast food], but that isn't going to sustain you long term. What you really need is something that will allow you to grow. Both physically and mentally."

Marley was adamant that food be a central part of the process. Marley himself had missed many meals throughout the course of the past few days. Aside from diligently working on the planning process, it was also a part of his daily routine to not expect to have food. He might be lucky to eat one solid meal a day, and the rest was just trying to figure out how to make it work. Yet, Marley also understood that he was not alone in trying to make a way out of no way. He had been in the same struggles with his friends, all sharing whatever money and resources they had to piece together a meal for the day. Referring to himself and his friends, he said, "And if we ain't eating, then you know our parents, aunts and uncles, and grandparents are really struggling, because they are not going to eat and let us struggle." Given this, he knew that one surefire way to organize his community was food and plenty of it.

Working with Yusef and Michele, he planned out a menu for the day. Chicken, hot dog links, hamburger patties and links. Green leaf salad, beans, and bread, lots of bread. Hamburger buns, hot dog buns, rolls and sliced bread. Juice for the kids and water and soda for the "grown-ups." For dessert, there was going to be a cobbler, maybe a cake and a pie too. Now that the menu was set, it was all a matter of gathering resources to make it happen. SCL agreed to help where it could, for which Marley was very grateful. However, Marley was also adamant about using collective action to forge together a plan. In his typical charismatic and endearing manner, Marley was able to get people from throughout the neighborhood to give what little they had in the way of resources to help out with the event. Mostly relying upon his long-standing stature as someone who was highly respected within the neighborhood and a person of his word, Marley, in conjunction with the donation from the Library, had put together enough in the way of financial resources to purchase all of the needed supplies.

However, while food was key to the event, what was paramount for Marley was to "nourish the spirit." Forged in the intricate dynamics of stated and unstated politics, Marley was very savvy about political thought and the potential of his neighborhood to be the one that could bring about systemic change throughout the city. He had a firm grasp of the city rules and legislation. On par with the best legal minds, Marley understood the loopholes, work-arounds, and stated implications of policies and laws. However, he also understood that just because something was written on paper did not make it so. He understood that the notion of citizen rights did not apply to him and his friends in the ways that it was commonly taught in schools.

In a planning session for the event, Marley was eager to situate a clear framing with regard to the politics of the event. Jotting down notes for the event, Marley made a clear distinction between what he deemed propaganda versus the reality. "You know how you learn about George Washington and the Bill of Rights, and all of this legal stuff about what you can and cannot do to be in protection of the law? Man, that is a bunch of bullshit. First of all, George Washington, Thomas Jefferson, all of them dudes owned slaves, so let's just put that out there first and foremost. They clearly were not thinking about the supposed rights of Black people when these glorious laws went into effect. Let's be real about that."

Marley's affect was palpable as he moved back and forth in his seat. He moved closer to the edge of the seat to make sure we fully got his point, "Now people want to say, 'Oh well, times have changed and we don't have slavery anymore, so everything is good.' True, we don't have slavery anymore, but tell me, did Black people get reparations after the Civil War? Were Black people given a whole bunch of land and I missed it? You and I both know what happened after that, there were more laws that were put in place that essentially told Black people where they could and could not go and how they damn near could not exist as a human being."

Marley was always good at sensing when he needed to shift the conversation away from some distant past to the contemporary moment, and right on cue he shifted his focus back. "There aren't laws that say Black people living over here in South Central, why our homes aren't worth nothing and why white folks in Beverly Hills, why their homes are millions of dollars. Or ... why in the hell does not everybody have a home regardless of how much money you make? You mean that is not in the damn Bill of Rights? Everybody should have a place to sleep, some food to eat and be able to get to the doctor for whatever reason that want. But if you put that into the Bill of Rights that is going to profoundly jack up the whole system. I mean, the whole thing is set up so that we don't have those things."

The particular type of politics that Marley wanted to infuse within the event was not the inclusive, diverse rhetoric that is fed throughout the school system or even shaped by typical nonprofit campaigns in Los Angeles. Rather, it was a political position informed by a tradition of knowledge that bubbled throughout his neighborhood. What shaped Marley as a charismatic leader was his ability to articulate a collective vision for change while also being able to tangibly make change happen.

Enough people had seen that Marley was true to his word in all facets of his life. Enough people had also heard enough of Marley's political stance to know that he was not going to back down whether talking to the police, a teacher, or any other contrived figure of authority. He was consistent and, more than anything, his consistency was what endeared him to people in the neighborhood. Marley's plan was now to bring the ideological basis of the communal politics to the fore and develop a plan of action to shape how the neighborhood would organize itself.

THE BEAUTIFUL STRUGGLE

The day started out particularly calm. In typical Los Angeles summer weather, a mass collection of grey clouds hovered above the cool morning. To an untrained eye, this seemingly would spell a recipe for disaster for an outdoor cookout, but summertime in Los Angeles is atypical of its oft-associated sunny climate. While the gloom of the overcast conditions would logically lend to a rainy forecast, Angelenos have long been known to dress in layers during the summer months as the cool clouds can quickly part and give way to a bright, open sun that in turn can bring with it sweltering heat. The cloud cover was perfect for Marley, as he and his cadre of organizers were able to do much of the heavy lifting under the brisk, cool sky. Moving the massive steel plated grill, carrying chairs, tables, pots, pans, and coolers full of ice, the natural shade provided needed respite from the laborious task at hand.

Once the grill was in place, Marley immediately went to work on making sure the grill was in pristine cooking condition. A blanket of charcoals and a small dosage of lighter fluid were the fodder for a tiny blaze that flickered between the perforated slits of the grill. Using the heat as an ally, Marley meticulously cleaned the head of the grill with a steel brush as debris fell beneath, adding another fuel supply to the contained fire. He then got to cooking. Having marinated the chicken in a blend of his secret sauce the night before, he carefully unwrapped each of the pieces, taking them out of a tin foil container and placing them onto the warm slits. Once full, he carefully closed the lid and exhaled. He immediately jumped to the next task and barked out instructions to everybody of what was to go where. Turning to Yusef, he laid out his thoughts of how the foot traffic should flow. Together they worked out a plan that would provide for constant movement.

Marley immediately returned to the pit, checked on the meat, gave instructions on when to take it out, and got back to directing the scene. Operating with a controlled fury, Marley was clearly in his element. He was excited about the potential of the day, but also worried about the possibility of complete disaster. While his tendency sometimes bordered on being a control freak, that was balanced out by his willingness to listen to others. However, this willingness had to be based upon merit and respect, which had to have been earned. And given that everybody was chipping in with the events of the day, while he was clearly in taskmaster mode, he also realized that folks were donating much of their energy and time in making the vision a reality. He showed his appreciation by carefully listening to the suggestions, questions, and comments that everybody offered and incorporating them into the development of the day.

This willingness to listen came in particularly handy when his frustration with unfolding events became a bit much for him to handle. While it was very important for him to make sure that everybody ate and enjoyed the food, what was paramount to Marley's plan was to have a neighborhood discussion and subsequent plan of action to build upon. However, he noticed that as people got their food, they quickly disappeared into the density of the block and were not necessarily staying in the cool confines of the SCL. This infuriated Marley, and, given the amount of work that he had put into the event, he almost lost his cool with the gathered crowd. However, two of his close friends who had been providing everybody with jokes and laughter throughout the day very calmly assuaged the tension. They assured Marley that everything was going to be cool and that they would handle the situation. While still frustrated, he trusted their better judgment and fairly quickly calmed down. The two then quietly slipped through the back exit of SCL's patio and made their way through the maze of people who had gathered along the sidewalk leading to the Library. Within twenty minutes SCL's main gathering space was enveloped with a mass of humanity. Upon taking a break from his duties and stepping into the Library's main entryway, he gave a big smile to Yusef and Michele.

Seeing the time was ripe, he made his move. Delegating the last bit of cooking duties, he gathered himself and made his way to the space of the gathered masses. He slowly moved to the front of the congregation and began speaking. "I want to thank Yusef and Michele for having us here in this space. They have been so kind to lend us the Library, and they have also let us know that this is our space and we should use it to make our neighborhood better. Now, to get to the specifics. So, we are here today to talk about the development of the community, how we want the community to look, and what we want the community to be in the future. But much of that is in our hands; we have to make things happen on our own. We have to make sure that we work together to make it happen."

The room was deathly quiet and Marley, who was great with reading a crowd, picked up on the desire of the audience to hear what it was that he had to say. He had their attention, but he knew that was not guaranteed to be the case. He strategically increased the volume in his voice and clearly stated, "They don't care about us here in South Central!" The crowd, a diverse age range, nodded in general agreement. Marley continued: "I mean, there is no reason why anyone here should not have food. Why anyone here should not have a place to live. All the money that comes into our neighborhood, we should have a say in what that looks like and how that operates. The recycling centers, the liquor stores, the restaurants, all of that money should be going to us if we want it to. All of those jobs should be had by us if we want them."

Marley, sensing that people did not want to be talked at all afternoon long, quickly concluded his thoughts: "But maybe, we want something else, maybe we want something drastically different, but whatever it is, we should be able to determine what that looks like." There was a silence in the room as everybody allowed the words to sit with them. Some people seemed to be seriously pondering his ideas, others seemed to be lost in their own thoughts, and others still appeared to be waiting on what was going to happen next. The silence was broken by one of Marley's friends, Rawley, who had come by several times to SCL but rarely said more than five words. Rawley was clearly annoyed and, in a very matter-of-fact tone, issued a counter to Marley's opening salvo: "Tell me this. It so easy to just say 'Alright, we going to lay down our past and everything is going to be alright.' There ain't no way that we will be able to work out this situation given the way that things are going down out here. And you know that. And, another question I have is, who made you leader of this whole situation? I mean, you think that you out here really running things now and that you can make this all happen on your own."

Marley became visibly incensed by the slight issued by Rawley. The room was packed and the tension was palpable in the room, and the questions that Rawley brought forth were legitimate in nature and needed to be addressed.

"First of all, did no one appoint me leader of anything," Marley started his rebuttal. "You know me and have known me for a long time and know what I am about. This is not about me trying to make any move and do anything for selfish reasons. This is for the community." Rawley immediately responded in a fairly loud and demonstrative tone. "I hear all that, but you clearly did not hear what I was saying. What you are talking about is way above your capabilities, any of our capabilities, and I think you just here wasting our time to think otherwise."

At this point, Marley lost his cool veneer and a switch was turned. He was not upset or dissuaded; rather, he understood that Rawley represented a particular train of thought that had to be addressed, but because of the nature of his attack, Marley felt there was only one way to handle the situation. In just as forceful a tone as Rawley had issued his proclamation, Marley, in a very clear, matter-of-fact manner, replied, "Well, it seems like the only way we are going to handle this situation is away from all these people and take this outside right here and right now."

I have no doubt in my mind that Rawley and Marley would have truly gone outside and engaged in some sort of more demonstrative conversation that might, but most likely would not, have led to a physical altercation, but what was also on display was a particular type of masculine bravado that, if left unabated, could have had the potential to derail the whole conversation.

Right on cue, a young woman with long braids who was sitting immediately next to me stated in a tone that was intentionally loud enough for the room to hear, "Here we go again. Every time we are about to have something worth doing, y'all want to act a fool." The words had the effect of waking Marley right out of a trance. His body went from moving with a deliberate intensity to a relaxed state as he seemed to realize that the whole room was looking at him and was more than likely going to take his cue on how to move forward. "You are right and we don't need that type of madness here," Marley said in a much more relaxed, yet stern manner. He continued as he attempted to defuse the situation: "Listen Rawley, if you want to stay and be a part of this, then you can stay, but no one is keeping you here ... You know that no one made me leader of anything and you know how I get down, so the choice is yours. But we got to push forward. We would love to have you, but if you choose not to be a part of it, there is no love lost between us."

And just like that the tension was sucked out of the room. Sensing the shift, Marley immediately moved on to the next phase of the program. "Alright, now what we are going to do is to break out into groups and have everybody lay down their issues very clearly." Marley then had one of his friends do a quick count of the room and broke up everybody into groups of ten people. Marley, using an easel and a marker, began going over the topics that were going to be discussed. He underlined each of the points that he covered to emphasize their importance. "As you can see here, we have a listing of topics that we think are important to the community, such as education, health care, and jobs, but what we want to do now is to brainstorm and figure out what is important to you guys and how we can go about getting what we need for our neighborhood. We are passing around pencils and paper; please have one person in the group take notes on what is discussed." With that, Marley set the marker on a table and informed everybody that they had ten minutes to develop a plan of action.

The groups quickly sprang into action. In true workshop fashion, some groups were strongly animated and dove head first into the project; some of the other groups were a little more reticent and needed a jumpstart to get the momentum going. Marley along with two of his collaborators, Juan and Mark, moved about the room looking for the groups that needed a little kindling to get the conversation moving along. The room slowly transformed from spots of intense conversation to a full-on cascade of dialogue. Seeing that the energy had engulfed the entire room, Marley extended the time ten more minutes and brought everybody back together twenty minutes after issuing the first set of instructions. "Alright everybody, we are going to come back together now and listen to what we have to offer as issues and solutions to what we see as going on in our neighborhood. Let's start with this group over here."

All Power to the People

The toll of the day had become evident on everybody's face. We were into the second month of the political education course and the long draw of the summer was intense. I met with Yusef and Michele after the course. We sat on a couch that was situated just outside of the office. It was an office mostly in name, as Yusef, Michele, and Raquel had positioned their desks in the main meeting space outside of the enclosed area. The office was perhaps the most recognizable design of the building for which it was originally purposed—a furniture store. Since it had been converted to a library, most of the tinge of the original aesthetic was gone, save for the office space.

I brought up the question to Yusef and Michele about the general mood in the class, and they were very quick with their response—food and shelter. The Library had become a way station of sorts for people in the neighborhood to grab some sustenance to make it through the day. However, even for the Library times had become tough and there was not much to offer. It was uncommon to see people come to the Library, sit on one of the couches, take a nap, speak with Yusef, Michele, and Raquel, and then depart.

The conversation pivoted to how much of the basics was needed for the majority of the community. Toothpaste, food, hygienic products—these were all in short supply. Not to mention a lack of access to stable housing and transportation.

With this conversation in mind, we dedicated a good chunk of time and Library resources during the course and meeting sessions to understanding the dynamics that governed the city's economic, social, and political abandonment of Black communities. Such a practice offered a brief conduit to understand how precarity became a normal part of the Black lived experience in Los Angeles.

· · ·

The popular image of the Black Panther Party for Self-Defense (BPP) is some iteration of gun-toting Black men wearing leather jackets and dark-rimmed sunglasses. While the Panthers were strong advocates for gun ownership as a means of protection against the constant attacks by the state, Black men with guns were not the major threat that they were conjured up to be. That distinction went to the countless number of Black women who staffed the numerous kitchens and classrooms that were the basis of the Panthers' Free Breakfast Program and Liberation Schools. The Free Breakfast Program in particular presented a major challenge to city officials in their attempt to counter the work of the BPP. While there might be some ground gained within the Black middle class and white liberal sympathizers on casting the Panthers as radical renegades who were on the verge of an armed rebellion against the United States, such a myth was difficult to push forward in the face of BPP chapters that provided food to people whom the cities had long since abandoned. Even the Black middle-class predisposition to a respectability politics that lionized a sanitized version of nonviolent resistance supported efforts to feed and educate the Black masses in cities across the United States. City officials may have been able to recruit public sentiment in de facto kill raids upon Panther headquarters throughout the country; however, the optics would have looked much different raiding a room full of children eating hot meals before they went to school.

With the growing sentiment in full support of the Free Breakfast Programs and Liberation Schools, the city governments utilized a different model of neutralization that sought to dampen the work that the Panthers did within Black communities: the propping up of racial capitalist allies that purported to have the direct goals and intentions of the Panthers. Such a model took various forms: in some instances it was a cultural event such as a music festival, while in others it was the increased funding of a city agency. However, by far the most effective and enduring model was the nonprofit/city partnership that funneled money—and ideology— into Black communities. The Panthers, understanding the logics of racial capitalism, very quickly saw what was afoot and spoke truth to power through its literary organ, the *Black Panther Party Newspaper,* and mass organizing. The following sections describe the contestation over community control and the impact that such struggle has had over the development of Black communities.

SEIZE THE TIME

"SEARCH and DESTROY" was written in big bold letters atop a December 1969 pamphlet designed by the L.A. Friends of the Panthers (L.A. Friends of the Panthers 1969). In the place of traditional bullets to mark new topics, there are renderings of actual bullet holes to draw the reader's attention to each new topic. Next to the first bullet is a brief description of the Los Angeles Police Department raid upon the Panther headquarters: "300 POLICEMEN ATTACK L.A. BLACK PANTHER PARTY OFFICE WITH MILITARY WEAPONS AND DYNAMITE." Directly above the bold capped letters is a graphic representation of the LA chapter headquarters riddled with bullet holes. While some of the imagery on the building is blurred, there are three distinct images that stand out. The first is the famous picture of Huey Newton sitting in a straw chair with two large guns on either side of him. The second is an Emory Douglas–style picture of a mother holding her child. The last is a relatively large sign that adorns the front of the building, which reads in bold letters: "FREE HOT BREAKFAST FOR SCHOOL CHILDREN MON.-FRI. 7–9AM." The sign is covered with bullet holes, indicating the indiscriminate manner in which

the LAPD launched into an attack against the Panthers. In a symmetri-
cal pattern, the bullet holes bleed down to connect with the "bullets"
associated with a brutal account of violence perpetrated against the
Panthers across the country. As the message flows up and down in a jar-
ring manner, the reader very quickly connects the violence against the
Panthers with violence against Black children and against those who
attempt to provide resources to the most vulnerable.

In contradistinction from a food pantry or church-led provision program, the BPP coupled hunger to deliberate acts of malfeasance on the
part of local, state, and national governments across the country. The
hunger experienced by countless people within Black communities was
directly linked to forms of state-sanctioned violence. It must be noted
that such a stance offered a biting counterframe to the well-funded narrative that was propagated through the halls of Congress, media outlets, and academia that Black people lacked key resources such as food
because of an innate desire to not work hard. A well-trodden myth, this
latest iteration of the 1960s and '70s gained momentum thanks to the
Moynihan Report, which in addition to degrading Black women also
situated the lack of material resources within the Black community as a
problem of the Black community's own making. Due to a lack of desire
to work and relying too much upon state-funded programs, the narrative posited that the primary focus of any solution should reestablish a
culture of hard work that abided by patriarchal norms of a mythical
United States nation-building project (i.e., the man is the breadwinner
of the house and the woman follows the lead of the man).

The BPP disavowed this framing and instead focused upon the manner in which hunger was intimately bonded to forms of historical and
contemporary structural violence. In a fundraising campaign for the
Free Breakfast Program, the LA BPP chapter connected the liberation
struggle of Black people to a lack of critical sustenance:

> One of the greatest forms of oppression is hunger. Children must be fed
> and the Free Breakfast for School Children is another key to the Liberation

by Halting the staunch form of oppression—HUNGER. One who looks into the face of a hungry child knows that his need is immediate. One can delay an asking face with a cold heart. A child does not understand hunger surveys made by the Government, but he can relate to a full stomach every morning. Black people are caught up in a vicious chain. They TELL US, you're hungry because you're poor … you're poor because you haven't got the best jobs … you can't get the best jobs because you're uneducated because you didn't learn in school because you weren't interested. And every time the teacher mentioned 5 apples plus 6 bananas, your stomach growled. (Black Panther Party: Southern California Chapter n.d., b)

While the Free Breakfast Program was focused on children, the Panthers established a more encompassing Free Food Program that was also in alignment with a praxis that connected processes of hunger to structural violence. With a focus on the Black community in general, but Black senior citizens in particular, the goal of the Free Food Program was to counter the exploitative tendencies of the state (both private capitalists and the formal bureaucratic machine that enabled the capitalists) with programs that would galvanize Black communities. Dubbed survival programs, there was an explicit understanding that these programs were not a revolutionary act in and of themselves, but provided the base for revolutionary acts to occur. In a memo that outlined the premise of the Free Food Program, the LA chapter articulated the importance of food as a critical aspect of revolutionary action:

The Black Panther Party's Free Food Program provides "free food" to Black and other oppressed people. The current high prices for food makes [sic] it very difficult for Black and other poor people to buy quality, nutritious food for their families. Huey P. Newton, leader and chief theoretician of the Black Panther Party, in explaining the Party's Survival Program says: "We recognized that in order to bring the people to the level of consciousness where they would **seize the time,** it would be necessary to serve their interests in survival by developing programs which would help them to meet their daily needs … All these programs satisfy the deep needs of the community, **but they are not solutions to our problems.** That is why we call them survival programs, meaning survival pending revolution. (Black Panther Party: Southern California Chapter n.d., a)

THE BATTLE FOR THE COMMUNITY

The connection between revolution and sustenance was a dividing line that was incompatible with the maintenance of a discipline-and-order regime whose primary resources allocated to Black communities were social workers and police officers. However, the Panthers were not deterred by the efforts of the state and city governments from accessing the public infrastructure to assist the public. While the Panthers were masterful at creating flyers, pamphlets, and media campaigns to elicit fundraising support, another key strategy was the utilization of public resources as a means to enact their programs. In the wake of the mass migration of Black people to California from the US South, one of the responses by the state, county, and city planners was to develop community centers within Black communities. Rather than a beneficent act, one of the primary goals of these centers was to monitor the actions of Black communities and Black organizing that was taking place in newly formed Black communities. Keenly aware of the pro-Black organizing that was happening among the Black youth, there was a concerted effort to establish a foothold in and near parks and schools.

One of the goals of the community centers was to serve as a hub for surveillance of the development of "Black gangs" that were galvanizing support in Black communities. Given that the living conditions, school conditions, incidents of police brutality, and overall quality of life were abhorrent, the level of anger within the Black communities throughout the state was palpable. Although the community centers were positioned to be a proposed solution to the myriad of problems, the Panthers were quick to realize that the city and county governments had ulterior motives. Rather than passively acquiesce to the buildup of state infrastructure within their neighborhoods, the Panthers adopted a strategy where they would position themselves as stewards of the community needs. In this vein, they would utilize these newly formed centers as a base of operations to implement their survival programs such as the Free Breakfast Program. A very shrewd strategy, it utilized the state against itself, as many of the centers were positioned in key locations with easy access for members of Black neighborhoods.

Yet the struggle over access to these centers was not an easily won contest, as illustrated by the case of Bobbie Watson. Watson was the director of the Campbell Village Recreation Center located inside of the Campbell Village housing project in West Oakland. Wilson held the position for two years before running afoul of city administrators. It was during the second year of her tenure as director that she was summarily fired by the city. While the city claimed that Watson did not act in accordance with city guidelines, it was common knowledge within the housing project that the tension stemmed from Watson's established partnership with the Black Panther Party. According to a *BPP Newspaper* story that covered the Watson's termination, "The city administration was angered by the presence of the Black Panther Party. This made no difference to Sister Watson because many of the parents of Campbell Village Projects had already voted their approval of the Breakfast Program's functioning at the Center. This is the case with all of the Center's programs" (Black Panther Party 1972, 9).

In addition to the relationship with the Oakland chapter of the BPP, the city was upset over Watson's insubordination in not acquiescing to police and city officials' demands that she inform on the activities being conducted on the grounds of the center.

> Sister Watson's refusal to push the city's program for "recreation" is not the only reason she has been harassed. She has refused to allow the center to become an arm of the police department. Before Sister Watson became director of the Center, the Oakland Police Department was frequently at the recreation center. When the city had complete control of the center, the staff and director were forced to inform the police of "all suspicious activities" by youth who came to the center. As Sister Bobbie said (of her refusal to inform on our youth), "This is not the probation department; this center is for the community." (Black Panther Party 1972, 15)

IDEOLOGY AND ECONOMICS

Cities in California quickly realized that they had a serious problem on their hands as the BPP proved to be savvy enough to utilize the public infrastructure to build momentum and organize large swaths of the Black community behind a plan of social revolution. As a means to counter the effectiveness of this strategy, formal governments teamed up with private capital to prop up faux Black empowerment organizations. Given that there was a campaign of massive spying and infiltration occurring within the BPP, there was an understanding of the rhetoric and strategies used by the Panthers in their organizing models. Armed with this information, these opponents waged a concerted effort to displace the BPP and social revolutionary ideology by flooding Black communities with organizations and programs that focused on Black assimilation into the state project. During the late 1960s and 1970s, Black communities were inundated with a plethora of organizations that focused on self-empowerment and cultural celebration, absent any analysis of state complicity to the degradation of material resources and cultural traditions.

Looking back at the 1960s and '70s, it is very easy to understand the military-style campaign that was utilized to neutralize the Panthers. In Los Angeles, similar to other cities, there was the brute force of war being waged against the Panthers in the form of assassinations and incarceration of key leaders and organizers. This was highlighted by the murders of Bunchy Carter and John Huggins on the campus of the University of California, Los Angeles and the kangaroo court conviction of Geronimo Ji Jaga. Yet similar to military strategies utilized during wartime, there was a very effective cultural propaganda campaign employed to impugn the character of Black revolutionary organizations such as the Panthers and supplant them with assimilationist, reform-based organizations that endorsed the logics of capital and exploitation. The city and national government employed these strategies hand in hand as police and informants did the work of planned assassinations and foundations, private capital, and the formal state apparatus found

Black junior partners in exploitation who were eager to make money in the name of "community progress." In the midst of the attack, the Panthers were very clear in their analysis of the situation. Being attacked from multiple fronts, they employed a strategy of naming the key agents as a means to inform the Black community of the larger plot afoot to counter a revolutionary-based platform.

In the wake of the Bunchy Carter and John Huggins murders, the LA chapter published its weekly newsletter, where it presented a thorough analysis of the two-pronged attack upon the organization:

> Last year, Bunchy, Alprentice "Bunchy" Carter—our Deputy Minister of Defense here in Southern California, who was assassinated last January—spoke at Will Rogers Park, right after the Will Rogers Massacre. The Massacre took place at that park on the final day of the so-called "Watts Summer Festival." He said that the Festival was a joke—a joke on the people—a joke with the people at the brunt of it. He said then that the so-called Festival not only did not serve the needs of the poor and oppressed people, the masses of people In Watts, but it was an insult to them.
>
> It was and is an insult because the people are used and exploited by the power structure and its black and white lackies [sic] in two primary ways:
>
>> 1. The sponsors of this Darkie's Day Parade see the Festival as a means of making money; i.e. Jim Randolph of KGFJ sponsored and produced this year a program at the Sports Arena and hoped to make a bundle from it;
>>
>> 2. That the people dance and sing over the graves and lives of the 39 people wounded and killed in 1965 [Watts Rebellion], the supposed commemorative purpose of the Festival—under the guise of showing how well Yorty's [mayor of Los Angeles] niggers in Watts are doing.
>
> Bunchy said this last year and this year we say that the dancing and singing in the slave quarters must cease forever. The people of Watts and, in fact, all of the true masses of people are not stupid ...
>
> Further—the people know that all the disguised government programs that exist on Poverty Program Row—also known as 103rd Street—like Westminster Neighborhood Association, Watts Labor Community Action Council, Neighborhood Adult Participation Program, and especially

Mafundi Institute, the nightmare of one Dr. Al Cannon—which has its fingers in everything and purports to have a Watts Cultural Center, an extension of the Watts Darkie's parade into a year-round maze—the people know the meaninglessness of these programs. And so we say that the people must openly challenge their existence.

And how do we know this? We—the Black Panther party—asked the people. We polled the Watts area and asked the people what they thought of the Yorty fiasco. The people responded and said plainly that they couldn't relate to it; that it meant nothing; that they didn't really care about it. The people said that they had not forgotten 1965, that they had not forgotten August 1968—the Will Rogers massacre—and they would not forget the sneak arrest by the Metro Squad and their criminal cohorts 77th division of the LAPD and others . . .

The residents, the people of Watts have seen the contradictions of a cultural center right in the midst of an area in which the people need and want a free hot breakfast program. The people of Watts want to talk about and act on controlling the police that have always run rampant through their community. The people of Watts woke up a long time ago and won't stand for any more madness being brought upon them. And we, the Black Panther Party, say and want to let the people know that we support their efforts to have a community control its police and itself, and to let all those of the power structure and their lackies [sic] know that people don't need their jive programs and will see to it that the games stop forever. All Power to the People! (Black Panther Party: Southern California Chapter 1969, 1–3)

While much has been discussed about the violent attacks upon the Black Panther Party at the hands of the police and the informants, there is a curious void with respect to the ideological, political, and economic attack via the establishment of private-public partnerships during the same time period that is referred to in the LA *BPP Newspaper.* In the wake of the 1965 Watts Rebellion, the federal government dramatically increased spending into the city in the name of community development and to assuage the concerns of those who participated in the rebellion. Yet, a consequence that continues to wreak havoc upon Black Los Angeles is the disentanglement of ideology from the promise of economic prosperity within a capitalist framework. Thus, while the

Panthers had a clear vision that their survival programs were intended to provide a stable ground to organize people against state violence, the government- and privately funded programs implemented similar-style programs with the intention of drawing people into particular hierarchal positions within the capitalist order. Thus, education programs were transformed from knowledge of resistance/rebuilding to the development of skills to become locked into a particular labor market. Free food programs were attached to cultural centers that framed "Black achievement" in terms of its contribution to the development of the United States, rather than framing Blackness as a measured check against US nation-building violence.

In its wake, during the 1970s and leading into the 1980s and '90s, Los Angeles further developed its public-private venture as the nonprofit sector exploded into the primary conduit of "social justice." Absent of an anti-racial-capitalist politics and ethos, many of the organizations became just that, organizations, and lost much of the community along the way. The BPP forecast the cruel reality that is now present within Black communities throughout Los Angeles—nonprofit organizations and government-funded agencies that flaunt the rhetorical inflections and program designs of Black radicalism, but are mere pipelines of capitalist exploitation and propaganda. Yet, as indicative of the work of Marley and communal organizing that is illegible to the state/private-funded nexus, the struggle continues.

ALBUM 4

Cruel and Beautiful

Shelter from Paradise

Over the past few years, I have developed a love-hate relationship with the summer months in Los Angeles. Aesthetically, they are simply beautiful. The brilliant sun over the slow-motion rocking of wind-induced palm fronds can often be taken for granted. The vast blue sky is highlighted by the tattered fraying of white clouds, which slowly gives way to an awesome amalgamation of purple, orange, and red hues as the sun moves westward. School playgrounds, parks, and recreational facilities are filled with the laughter of children who are participating in a variety of summer camps. Aside from a few outlying days, the extreme humidity that can often add an extra ten to fifteen degrees does not exist. Occasionally there are a few weeks where the heat can be particularly taxing, reaching into the upper nineties or even hundreds. However, during those moments I often think of cities such as Houston or New Orleans, where such climate is the foundation of the summer. In Los Angeles, when the summer days do become too much, the beaches become the de facto safe haven. The cool water of the Pacific Ocean is the perfect elixir to the burning heat of the asphalt-lined streets that dominate the city's massive landscape. Winds that accompany the jet streams from the coast are nature's air conditioner for the thousands of Angelenos who line the brown sandy beaches under polyester canopies and massive umbrellas. As the sun sets, beaches mirror the night sky as lit fire pits transform into stars dotting the darkened coastline. The cool air softens the warm sand and as the temperature drops somewhere between 65 and 74 degrees, there is an ease and peace that can lull you to sleep.

The beauty of this place, its sheer vastness of space and abundance of perfect days, is perhaps what makes it difficult to live here. For in many ways, the beauty is a façade that, when pulled back, covers another milieu that is equally abundant, yet much more sobering. The summer is a time of frustration and anger. The cursed bright sky is a painful reminder of the heat that is soon to come. The heat that boils among the flesh of multiple bodies sleeping in one bed in an apartment that was once part of a single-family home that has since been partitioned into four small one-bedroom units. The heat that rages in the empty stomachs of young children who play under nylon tarp–shaded backyards to keep their minds occupied from hunger pains. The heat of angered young men and women who have to cleverly navigate the sun's warmth, law enforcement, and sometimes each other in the search for the necessities of life. The heat is coming and yet there are very few places of respite. Those with the least have long since given up on the city to provide them with anything. There is not an expectation that anything will be handed out and that anything will be given. To the contrary, such promises are met with a great deal of skepticism and disdain. Thus, Los Angeles as a city is always on the brink. It takes a lot of work to provide so much beauty to so few little while simultaneously denying that beauty to the vast majority. I learned these lessons from Marley and his friends as they painstakingly told story after story of how at a young age he came to traverse a city that he knew he could never trust and yet he had to be intimately connected to.

A HOUSE IS NOT A HOME

A phone number can tell a lot about economic stability and precarity. I never realized the extent of this until I met Marley and his friends at the Southern California Library. During the first few months that I met Marley, he changed his number four times, and this number would mushroom in the subsequent years, taking into account the times he shared a number with friends and family members.

Bustling intersections such as the one at Slauson and Vermont Avenues were home to cell phone pop-up tables that tried to get people signed up to a variety of contracts ranging from a month to two years in duration. A very good communicator, Marley was always looking for a way to upgrade his plan and get a better phone. He also knew how to finesse a situation to turn a seeming disadvantage into an advantage. Not having a permanent address very well counted as a disadvantage; however, Marley also knew that he could open an account using an old defunct address and keep the phone operating without having to make payments for about two months. This was not an ideal situation, as it required getting used to the mechanizations of a new phone. Very often Marley was trying to figure out how to get his contact list from one phone to another. Venturing into the liquor stores that also functioned as cell phone way stations, Marley could simultaneously pay a small fee to transfer contacts from one phone to another and put just enough money on his bill to keep his phone up and running for a week at a time. Marley had also mastered the free-phone racket. He knew what city and county programs were offering free phones as part of a partnership with a cell phone provider and would use this information to help him and his family members and friends get as many phones as possible. Showing me one of the phones he had just gotten one day, he remarked, "These phones ain't worth nothing. I can promise you this thing is going to break somehow, some way in a matter of weeks." Built by manufacturers that I had never heard of, the phones appeared to be overstock that cell phone companies had on hand and were looking to unload in order to make way for new inventory. Perhaps being counted as a tax write-off while letting the city look magnanimous, these types of partnerships festered throughout the city. Marley took full advantage, and, knowing the poor-quality design of these phones, he was constantly on the lookout for phones.

Possessing an encyclopedia-like memory of the addresses where he lived, Marley knew which phones were associated with which address and which phones were live and which ones were defunct. While his memory was sharp, he very often misplaced or lost his phone, leaving it at a park, a friend's house, or his grandmother's house. Never too pressed by the situation, he would simply figure out a way to get another phone up and running with a different address. His ability to float through the digital spaces of cell phone providers and government bureaucracy also undergirded a very unavoidable fact—Marley was houseless. Specifically, he had access to housing for moments at a time, through the generosity and availability of friends and family, but from the time that I first met him Marley, who was then sixteen years old, did not have stable housing. Such a situation created gulfs in our communication, for while he was in between housing situations, his phone number would invariably change and I could not get ahold of him. This was not unusual during the time I knew Marley. There would be short durations where I would not hear from him at all. I would check in with Yusef at SCL, and, while I knew several of his friends from the neighborhood and I lived nearby, I was not from the neighborhood. While I was known by some people, the vast majority of people in the neighborhood did not know who I was and did not trust that I had the best interests of a beloved member of their community in mind. Thus, I very often did not know where Marley was until he popped back up either at SCL or, invariably, I would get a phone call from a random Southern California–based number on my phone. I very often hid my relief knowing that Marley was on the other end and we would catch up on what was going on in each other's lives. On one of these occasions, we made plans to meet at his new residence, where he was sharing a duplex with his extended family.

I picked him up at 10:00 A.M. and, as usual, he walked with a big smile to the car. He opened the door and before he was even seated, he started talking. "Man, I am grateful to be living there, but I need to get my own space. I mean, I don't even have room to think." Marley had been talking about maybe enrolling in junior college and taking a few classes. At his request, I gave him a few books to read, and we decided that we would meet at least twice a week with a plan for him to describe to me in detail the major themes of one of the books. "I have been going through the book, but you know, I just can't even think. Someone is always in the room, or in the kitchen. It does not matter what time of day either, as people are always up. I mean, I love my family, but there is no way that I am finishing that book there." I did not even bring up the idea of walking to the local library, as that would mean he would have to cross through neighborhoods that were feuding with his hood, and that would seriously put his safety at risk. With that charismatic smile on his face, he matter-of-factly stated, "I'm pretty much stuck here until I can figure something out. And I don't see that happening anytime soon. So, until then I pretty much just hang out in the backyard or catch rides with the homies and try to visit my family as much as I can."

We drove down the street and Marley inquired about which library we were going to. I told him that since the library that we normally went to was not open until 11:00 A.M., we could drive to one that was a little bit further away but would have ample space. On the drive over, Marley began talking about what he liked about his new home. "I mean, it is great to have a solid meal and to be with my cousins. It is great seeing them and hanging out, but man, I would really just like to be on my feet with my own stuff and not have to worry about sharing a bathroom with five other people. It is not that I am not grateful for what they have done for me, it is just I am tired, I miss just being at peace. You know I really like the quiet and I like being able to just think, but I have not been able to do that in so long, that it is almost like I forgot to," as he laughed into his hands. "The last time I was able to do that was when I was living with my mom, and that was a long time ago." I asked him about what happened and his demeanor ever so slightly changed. Not that he was uncomfortable, it was more that he was trying to make sure that I clearly understood what he was about to say. "Well you see, we pretty much had a great life for the early part of me growing up. I mean, my mom had a solid job and me and my brothers, you know, were living life as young kids should. We had an apartment and then we had a house over there near the Library [SCL]. But everything changed once things started to go downhill for my mom. She lost her job, got laid off for some reason or another and then could not really find work again."

Marley had always spoken with a particular reverence for his mother, whom he loved unconditionally, and his love extended to a very nuanced read of her as a parent. "My mom liked to have a good time with us, and I know not being able to do all of those things must have just been eating her up inside. With all the stress and everything having to do with us being around and needing clothes and food and trying to work and make sure we were good, she began to drink, and that pretty much ended the stability of having the house and a ready-made place to stay."

His affect became increasingly flat, but he still held on to his characteristic smile. "From that point on, we were on the move, a lot. At first we were just staying in apartments for a maybe a month at a time, but then it changed to shorter and shorter stays. I don't know where my mom was finding these places, and then one day I moved in with my grandmother. I did not know if it was going to be a permanent thing or what, but that is where I was."

The slightly longer-than-normal drive seemed to fly by as Marley was such a dynamic storyteller, and while he normally spoke with great enthusiasm, the contrast of him speaking just as passionately, but in a calm, somewhat sullen style was just as gripping. He continued: "It was cool, but it was nothing like when we were all together, and plus, that was when everybody was staying at my granny's house. More than just family, which is big by itself, but my granny has always had a big heart. She would open her home up to other folks in the neighborhood who just needed a place to sleep while they got themselves together. This all happened when I was around eleven or twelve, and ever since then, I've been pretty much sharing my space with a lot of people."

About a week and a half had gone by after our conversation. I had not heard from Marley and I began to worry. Yusef told me that he had not seen him in a few days and that when he did pop back in, he did not look too good. This was very unusual for Marley, who was a very prideful person. He always took great stock in how he looked and was very cognizant of how he presented himself to people. Recalling one of the downsides of living in a big household, he once said, "Man, that is the thing about living with so many people, you never can take a shower when you want to take a shower. And before I go anywhere I have to be clean. I mean, I can't just roll out of bed and get going, I need to be smelling good and looking good." Marley was particularly meticulous about his hair and needing it to look just right for the style he wanted to achieve. Regardless of if it was a bushy Afro, low-cut and faded, or in a mini-twist, he always kept a well-manicured shape-up around the perimeter of his head. On the off chance that he did not get an opportunity to "line up" his hair, he would be constantly bringing it up as a point of irritation that he needed to do something about his hair.

Then there were the clothes. Marley did not have an abundance of outfits, but everything was always pressed and well taken care of. It could be the tenth time that I saw Marley in a particular shirt, but each time looked like it was freshly taken off the clothing store rack. The crisp edges from the iron marks were evident as he liked tight creases and seams in his shirt lines. He always had on meticulously ironed pants, and even his shorts were sure to have received the heat treatment. And then there were the shoes. In the age of overpriced athletic shoes, where it was not out of the ordinary to pay over three hundred dollars for a particular type of shoe, Marley's fashion sense was informed by a political aesthetic that was extremely consistent. "Look man, what sense in the world does it mean to buy shoes made by Nike for two hundred dollars when they aren't paying their workers shit? I mean, they got kids working to make these stupid shoes and then you want to charge us some obscene amount of money for them," he demurred during one of our conversations that ventured into the relationship between fashion and economics.

Always searching out information, he went on to discuss a documentary on the athletic shoe industry. "I remember seeing that on a report that talked about Nike. They had the workers up in these horrible conditions making these shoes, and I'm sitting there watching, like damn! I almost had to laugh, because they were living just like me and the homies, struggling to try to make it and then they had to work all day in these damn warehouses." Ever present in making connections about matters of economy, Marley did so in a fashion that was never self-aggrandizing about how much he knew, but rather was in the context of the stark disparities that he saw all around his community. He continued, "They just pay them so little because they can, like something ridiculous like ten cents or twenty cents an hour, something crazy. I say it is crazy because look at how much they are making and how much it costs, and then look at the people who are buying these shoes, look how they are living. I am not talking about some dude like me or you and we have one or two pair of Jordans, I'm talking about folks who have over two hundred pairs of the shoes. The shoes have their own house, with temperature control knobs and all of this craziness. That is the crazy part. The shoes have a better home than the damn people who are making the shoes. I mean, who ever thought we would see the day where a damn shoe is more valuable than human life?"

By this point, Marley was incredulous, as from the look on his face he was truly perplexed by the situation. For him, the incredible gulf between what was not just unfair, but what was so brutally unjust, and the way that everybody seemed to go on with business as usual, was baffling. It was with this look of befuddled indignation that he continued: "Then the shoes don't last a damn anyway. I mean, I have so many homies who got the Jordans, and you know how much those damn shoes cost, and then within a year or two they are falling apart. So you tell me, at the end of the day, what are you paying for?"

And immediately on cue, Marley looked at me to signify that he was ready, and we went shoe shopping at the Slauson Swapmeet. It is a giant green building. There is virtually no other way to describe it. Now, it has not always been green, but for folks who live in South Central Los Angeles, the iconic structure sticks out for its bright green color with yellow and orange lettering. There are other places that are known to have better deals and more for negotiation, such as Santee Alley in Downtown, but for people who may not have access to transportation or don't feel like dealing with the hassle of large crowds, the Slauson Swapmeet has been a consistent part of the community. That is not to say that the relationship has always been an amicable one. While the history and lore of the swapmeet has largely been carried by the Black community, the primary business owners selling their wares are mostly entrepreneurs of Chinese and Korean descent. Given the history of the 1991 Latasha Harlins murder by convenience store owner Soon Ja Du and the 1992 Rebellion, the lingering friction is often unstated and, aside from personal relationships that have developed, there is a sense of slight distrust. While both of those incidents are over twenty-five years old, they have not faded away from the collective memories of Black Angelenos. As a testament to the power of the memory, Marley, who was not even born when either happened, was quite aware of their significance. From the perspective of Marley, "Hey man, you know me, I ain't got a problem with anybody. What I am frustrated with more than anything is what we could be doing if we had some money flowing into our community. I mean, could you imagine if this whole building [Slauson Swapmeet] was Black owned? What if the BRIM owned this whole building, and what we could do with it. Like we could build schools, buildings for music programs, art programs—everything we could need could be generated right from here."

His blissful optimism quickly faded to reflect what was a cold bitter reality—there were virtually no Black-owned booths in the giant warehouse. Commenting on this stark reality, he said, "Then there is the way that some of the storeowners, not so much here at the Swapmeet, but at some of the liquor stores, treat you. Like you know the liquor store right across the street from the Library. I swear the owners there hate Black people. Whenever we are in there, they are trying to get us to get out. They drop our change on the floor, and will yell at us for no reason at all. So that creates a feeling of anger, and you just don't trust the intentions of the folks who are right in your own neighborhood."

Adding to the level of distrust in the place is the constant presence of security throughout the entire swapmeet. Depending on the day of the week, it is not uncommon to see both armed private and local police manning several posts at key strategic points. Entering one of the main entrances of the swapmeet, upon immediately passing one of the security posts, you are taken into a world that has a bazaar-like quality. While each of the vendor markets itself is unique, the stores can be broken down into five general groups—clothing, shoes, beauty supplies, jewelry, and general household goods. There is also an assortment of restaurants along the periphery walls of the swapmeet, along with a handful of storefronts that sell art, movies, and music. The later is very important historically, as swapmeets were once the lifeblood of the Los Angeles music scene. The vendors are arranged in a series of walkways that intersect roughly every fifty to seventy-five feet.

And it is here within these confines that Marley made his magic happen. For those who have never been to a swapmeet, one of the first things that stand out is the plastic. There is literally plastic all over in all of the stores. The majority of clothes are in some sort of plastic covering, and the shoes, the athletic shoes in particular, are covered in plastic wrap. While you can clearly see the shoe, the aesthetics of the plastic wrap are definitely appreciated by those who have swapmeet sensibilities. Within the first five minutes of looking, Marley saw a pair of deep blue, almost black, casual athletic loafers that he really liked and immediately went to work. The initial cost of the shoe was $40, but Marley was confident that he could get it for cheaper. He spotted three other vendors that sold the exact same shoe and went to negotiating for the best price he could get. In his typical, charismatic way, he was able to push each of the vendors down in price without coming off as being too demanding. Always in a laughable tone, he struck the vendors with the retorts: "I know that you can do just a little bit better than that." "Oh, come on, you see me in here every week, how you are going to treat your best customer that way?" After about a ten-minute negotiation period, he decided against getting any of the shoes. "They didn't want to sell me those shoes today. But I am not worried, I just came on a bad day and time. You really need to get here right at closing and find out when they are getting a new shipment in, that is the key. Then they are ready to deal. But I'll get those shoes. They are good shoes and they won't break down on you." He said the last words with a wily smile as we had just had a conversation about my having purchased a pair of Nike Air Jordan shoes that cost $190. Walking out of the swapmeet, he remarked, "Since you just throwing money away, why don't you just give it to me?"

True to his word, a few weeks later when we were together at SCL, he was wearing those well-negotiated shoes. He caught me looking down at them and smiled. "I told you it is all about timing," he said. We sat down on one of the couches in the lobby of SCL and I asked him a question that had been on my mind for a while about where he had been during those weeks where he was off the radar. I also told him that I was worried as Yusef had mentioned that he was looking worn down and just really tired, not his usual self at all. "Man, I had some serious things on my mind and I just needed to process the best way to handle them." I pressed a little further, asking about if it had anything to do with his living situation and if there was any way that I could help. He sighed with a deep heavy breath, but maintained a faint smile. Taking a deep breath, he leaned back just a little against the sturdy wooden chair he was sitting in. Upon breathing out he explained, "So basically, I was staying with friends here and there for a little while. Things got kind of cramped at my granny's house and some things happened in the neighborhood that always go down, so I had to make sure that I was keeping myself on the low for a while." While Marley was usually very "stream of consciousness" in his tone and framing of dialogue, this was different. He was much more purposeful with his words. "To sum it up, being at my granny's house was not the safest place for me to be, because of some situations that unfolded, but I had to lay my head somewhere. So, I was staying with different folks and trying to figure out my next move. It was tough because people were helping out, but it is tough when you got to sleep in a garage and maybe eating one meal a day if you are lucky. So, it has been hard."

I did not press further as I had learned that there was much that happened in the neighborhood that was not meant for public consumption. On a basic level, even for people with the best intentions in mind, so much of life in the neighborhood had been criminalized and was under constant threat of being made criminal that good intentions often had bad consequences. I pivoted and inquired about the possibility of staying at a shelter or getting temporary housing through the city.

Immediately upon hearing my question, Marley positioned one arm over the chair and ever so subtly stretched out his legs. "Well that is even more complicated," he started. "Most shelters around here don't really like people who look like me to stay there for too long. They see the tattoos, they see I'm a young Black dude, they think they know the gang ties and they immediately become leery of having me around."

His facial expression quickly changed. The slight pressed brow that one gets from a moment of introspection was now positioned as a hard flat affront that conveyed a different level of intensity. Not anger, frustration, or pain, but slightly more serious in nature. He continued, "Plus, the truth of the matter is that being under eighteen is even harder because it runs the risk of placing my mom in jeopardy by having child protective services involved, and trust me, that is not happening."

He straightened his body in the chair and became more present in the moment. Marley lamented, "Aside from that, you really can't get housing from the city if you are in my situation, you need a parent or a guardian involved, and don't even get me started on how you have to go from one part of the city to another to try to get business handled. It is a joke, what it takes to just get on the damn list. But that doesn't even apply to me because of my age and my relationship with my mom."

While there were people coming in and out of the Library, the entire space, in all of its vastness, felt empty. Marley, with his usual magnanimous engagement, filled the space and without raising his voice conveyed his disdain for the city administrative hurdles and what was required. In a slightly exasperated tone he said, "It basically comes down to me having to snitch on my mom to the city on some b.s.—just to get a chance at getting housing somewhere. That makes absolutely no sense, because that day is never coming. You really think I'm going to send my mom to jail so that the city can say it was looking after my needs! That shit is a joke. The city knows what's going down and who does not have housing and who does. They could have put a program in place that would have helped us out a long time ago."

His voice began to increase in volume, not so much in an attempt to get loud, but more because he was reliving the story as he was retelling it and his anger against the city was rekindled. He ended his thought with a poignant comment: "And just the fact that you could lose your damn house is a joke. Come on, they want to preach about safety and talk about how we are hiring more police to keep the streets safe. Now, I am no expert or nothing, but it seems to me that one of the best ways that you can be safe is if you have a roof over your head."

Intrigued, I wanted to find out Marley's thoughts on the creation of housing in situations for people such as himself that were not always in the safest situations. I told him that the city was always going to fall back on the notion that people, not policies and laws, create unsafe situations. Getting at the meat of my statement, Marley went straight to the point: "While there are disagreements all the time, both between hoods and in the hood, the truth of the matter is that all of this is a joke in comparison to bigger issues like having a place to live, money in your pocket, and a good doctor. The levels to which it rises is a joke because it could easily be squashed if folks just had the basic necessities of life. I am not even talking like a million dollars, but we are talking about people who don't have anything."

Marley had a meeting planned with Yusef, and as Yusef walked over to the table where we were talking, Marley shifted his body to move closer to the long table where a series of folders and boxes were arranged. He concluded his thought by stating, "No job, no health care, no food, so then you want to wonder why things are so tense all the time. Anyway, I can deal with my situation in the hood, what I can't deal with on my own is the situation with the city, and that is what I have been trying to do with the homies. We got to put pressure on them, and the only way to do that is together, and that is what I really think scares the shit out of them."

THE BASIC NECESSITIES—FOOD AND HEALTH

"Man, don't even get me started on the food issue. It is crazy to even think about," Marley stated as we drove past a strip mall that was populated by fast-food restaurants. "This food that they have us eating is some of the grossest shit on the planet," Marley retorted to my comment about getting a quick bite to eat. We were heading north on Western Avenue in Los Angeles and it just hit me that in my haste to leave, I had forgotten to grab some nourishment on the way out the door. The dull pain of a simmering headache slowly crept through the back of my neck and rested behind my ears. While my invocation for food was about being hungry in that moment, for Marley it was a springboard into the problem of hunger in relation to the long-term effect of food practices in his neighborhood. Marley continued with his missive on food: "If you even want to call it food. It is more like something that was concocted in a lab down in somebody's basement."

Marley was always good for bringing levity to a serious conversation. He was also good at calling out the glaring ironies between what was in the best interests of people versus how people have to live. He continued along the lines of healthy eating and began to merge into the realm of living an overall healthy lifestyle. "They said that the cost of heart disease is going to go up by seventy billion dollars over the next twenty years," Marley explained to me. "And they are saying that all people have to do to save money and save lives is to exercise and work out a little bit. And Americans need to stop eating so much salt. Well, grocery stores need to stop selling so much salt, stop putting all this stuff on TV, 'We need to eat healthier and heart disease can be prevented by leading a healthier lifestyle.'"

The endless parade of strip malls gave way to single-family homes as we turned onto Century Boulevard. The well-manicured lawns, shrubs, and hedges were flanked by Jesse Owens Park, a massive green space that was once part of an incubator network of parks and recreation facilities for some of the prodigious baseball talent in the country. Marley, looking out the window, remarked, "How the hell do you expect folks to lead a healthier lifestyle when there is smog all in the air, y'all cutting down trees, and every time I hit a fast-food spot, there is grease dripping out of the bread?" Marley lifted his hands in the air and then wrung them in a vigorous manner to exaggerate the effect of grease being on his hands. "Grease on the hamburger bun," he continued. "When you squeeze out the hamburger buns, you got grease dripping off the hamburger buns. Then you turn around and say that the cost of heart disease is going up by seventy billion dollars. That is just cruel all the way the around."

We slowly approached a red light, and as the car came to a complete stop, Marley quipped, "There is no way that you can tell people that all they have to do is cut out salt and exercise, when all around them is horrible food options and nowhere to work out or be healthy because it costs so much money to go to a gym, or if you work out outside at a park or something, you going to die from asthma from how unhealthy the air is."

When the light turned green, I followed the extended caravan of automobiles as we approached the Los Angeles–Inglewood border near Van Ness Avenue. Designated as a mixed-living development, on the Los Angeles side of the border Century Avenue was marked by low-rise apartment buildings, various storefronts and miniature strip malls, and single-family houses. However, as we entered into Inglewood, the street changed. Already a broad thoroughfare, it seemed wider, slightly grander in appearance. The orientation of the houses changed from directly facing the street to now being set back away from the street set along the famous avenues that intersected Century in a continuous fashion in ascending order. A distinctive memory as a child growing up were the beautiful light displays that the houses along Second, Third,

Fourth, Fifth, and all of the avenues organized during the holidays. Not in too much of a hurry, we slowly made our way down Century, and Marley continued to connect the perils of food, the economy, and health. "And man, aside from the problem of these fast-food chains trying to kill us, I think there is a much bigger issue," Marley firmly stated. "That is, we can't rely upon these corporations to save our lives. This is not a conspiracy theory, but they are not going to save us when they are making billions of dollars by killing us. That is just simple math. But the truth of the matter is that it is not just the fast-food corporations, it is the supermarkets and everything."

In somewhat profound irony, once we passed through the avenues and crossed Crenshaw Boulevard, we came upon a giant development that contained an assortment of fast-food and sit-down restaurants as well as large chain grocery and convenience stores. Not fazed by our new surroundings and perhaps because of them, Marley continued, "I mean, what we really have to do is knowing where our food came from. I think we need to have our own homegrown food. In LA, people would be freaked out if they saw a real-live chicken," Marley said with a good laugh. He continued on the same theme. "I know people that would run if they saw a chicken, and I'm like, what the hell—that is supposed to be a natural resource, you are supposed to see that every day if you are eating it," he said as he continued to laugh.

I shook my head at his jokes as we turned into the massive development, and he leaned back into his seat after having a good laugh. "I really think that we need to go back to basics. Just start over and replan the way we live, and planning the way we live in the future. I heard that they are making plans to see what other planets are sustaining life. I am like, if we were made to live on other planets we would have been there already. We wouldn't have to construct and build like a big ole facility that looks like the damn Superdome."

I was not sure where Marley was going with his thought, as I knew he was a big fan of science and really enjoyed science fiction, so I was intrigued. I parked the car in a spot amongst several, and he continued.

"I don't want to live in no Superdome where you got to grow plants and all this stuff and nothing natural, we already living in a world where nothing is natural. Then people are going to start turning into herbivores and eat nothing but grass." At this point he couldn't control his laughter as he mimicked people who had turned into cows. He attempted to restart his thought, but his laughter broke up the words. As we got out of the car, he was able to pull himself together. "But I'm just saying … I think we need to take it back to the days when we had our own homegrown farms and stuff like that. We just got to go back to the days, it's too much pollution, it's not enough agriculture and forestation."

It was another beautiful day in Southern California. An ever-so-cool wind greeted us as we walked toward the coffee shop. Marley pressed on as we approached the doors. He looked at me and said, "People say that people come to California for the weather, but look at the climate and all the stuff going on in the world, we aren't going to always have good weather if this keeps going on. You can't expect a good thing to last forever. It's something like, you can only enjoy it if you don't abuse it. We can't enjoy this forever and abuse it." With that, we entered the shop and bought our outsourced beverages and pontificated upon various ironies of the world around us.

STAYING HEALTHY WITH NO HEALTH CARE

I drove slowly down the street looking for the address as I passed each house. The street was a mixture of both single-family homes and two-story duplexes. A common trend in the area, developers had started to purchase homes from families throughout South Central. They would then tear each one down and quickly build a multi-family home in its place, which could be used to charge more rent on the same small plot of land. Usually in the form of Section 8 vouchers, a developer could put two and sometimes three families in a newly constructed building. The issue for me, however, was that I was having a hard time seeing the street addresses. The addition of more families in a house also meant the addition of more vehicles on the street, which meant that seeing the addresses was particularly difficult when trying to look over, around, and through vans, SUVs, and cars that all lined the street. While the street was not small in its original design, it clearly was not planned to have both sides packed with cars and, as a consequence, cars had to do their best to navigate both directions without seeing each other. In my case, I was trying as mightily as I could to make room for other cars approaching in the opposite direction while still keeping a lookout for the address that Marley had given me.

I finally spotted the corresponding numbers and pulled alongside the two-story dwelling. The block was fairly quiet save for the barking of a dog that seemed to be annoyed by our presence. It was a beautiful day, and I called Marley from my car to let him know that I was outside. This was a new address, something I had gotten accustomed to from our time knowing each other. Up to this point, I had picked Marley up from several different addresses, and while each was in a different location of the city, they all had shared the common aesthetic of being in flux. This was a far cry from the South Central that my parents had grown up in and from what I had known as a young child until late adolescence. While it was not uncommon to have a multigenerational family living environment and in some cases quite desirable in terms of childcare and neighborhood memories, what was different was the constant change in the neighborhood. Gone were the days when families stayed in homes for longer than five years. With the sudden interest in real estate in South Central, the transitory nature of family movement picked up at a fairly fast pace. Yet, through it all, Marley was able to always quickly make friends. He came walking with his typical gregarious smile and shared a few words with a neighbor who came out of his house at the same time. Talking as if they had grown up together, Marley ended the conversation with a quick dap and gingerly jogged over to the car. "What's going on with you, brother?" he said as he sat down. "Everything is good, how about you?" I replied. "Ah man, every day is a blessing, you know. Just trying to get it together. The neighbor right there is having a party this weekend and I was chopping it up about what I could bring or whatever. You know I like to hang out and cook, but they said that they got it all under control. It should be cool, everybody around here is cool as a fan, so it should be a fun night."

"But man," he continued, signaling that the conversation was going to shift, "let me tell you, I really need to go the dentist." "Why is that," I replied. "I have had these braces on my teeth for a long time, but these things were never meant to be permanent braces. They were supposed to be temporary until I could get some permanent ones put in. The problem of course is that we could never afford it." "Wait, back up a second," I retorted, "I don't think you ever told me about your braces before. I mean, clearly I see that you have some in your mouth, but I'm confused about the whole temporary situation." "Well, you know it is because I make them look so good," he said, unable to keep a straight face. I started the car up and pulled back into the street as he continued. "But for real, I had to get these things when I was thirteen years old, but the problem was that we could not afford them. My mom's job situation was up in the air and it was not like any of my other family members could help out, so I was kind of stuck."

Marley pulled down the passenger seat visor and flipped open the mirror to check out his teeth as he was describing the story of his braces. "My granny only had so much money and everybody else is trying to make it, so I did not have enough money to get the real braces. So the dentist put these on just to stop my teeth from shifting and moving, but they were only meant to be a temporary fix, not at all a long-term situation. I wish I could take them off by myself, but they are on there with some kind of superglue type of stuff, so there it is."

Pulling away from the residential area, we continued down the street heading toward the freeway, talking about dentistry as a profession, oral hygiene practices, and an assortment of other health-related topics. We pulled up to a stoplight near the 110 freeway and I asked, "So when is the last time you have been to the dentist?" He looked away as I could see him counting the time in his head. "Come to think of it, I think the last time I have been to the dentist was when I got these put on. I may have gone one other time, but this was the only time I can remember," he replied. I approached the on ramp to the 110 freeway and Marley popped up in the seat. "I do remember I had a toothache that hurt like hell," he exclaimed as he had an "a-ha" moment. "I mean, you ever have one of those toothaches that hurt so much that you could just feel it throughout the rest of your body?" he questioned out loud. "Man, the whole time I was laying in my bed, just hoping that someone would come and take me out of my misery. I would have done damn near anything to make the pain go away," he recalled as he slightly squirmed about in the seat as the feeling of that moment reverberated throughout his body. "Drink a quart of oil, jump into a cold bath, anything to just stop that pain," he continued. "It just vibrated throughout my whole head. And there was nothing I could do, I didn't have any medicine. So I think that was the last time that I went. I basically was waiting around to try to see if the pain would go away, but it never did. So after a day or so with the horrible, intense pain, I was just like fuck it, I need to go to the dentist or else I can't take it much longer."

I felt the intensity of his pain. As he recounted his story, we transitioned from the 110 freeway to the 105 freeway going west toward the Pacific Ocean. "So how did it go at the dentist, were they able to fix whatever was wrong?" "Yeah," he replied, "It was something having to do with a root in my tooth that was bad or something to that effect. To be honest with you, I really didn't care what the problem was, I just wanted the pain to go away." "So was that covered by somebody's insurance or something like that?" "Brother, I wish," he replied. "There are some places around here that will take you in if you don't have insurance and they will work with you on payment plans, but some of those places you have to be careful of, because they know you don't have any money to sue them or anything like that if something goes sideways, so they can really get you, and I mean just like completely destroy your teeth and everything."

The massive 105 freeway was never not imposing, a "modern" freeway where certain sections feel as wide as they do long. I often thought about the mass displacement that took place during the 1980s and '90s to construct the monstrosity of steel and concrete. As we drove above two iconic housing projects, Nickerson Gardens and Imperial Courts, Marley described in more detail the travails of dental services. "I know some folks who were really, really jacked up and there was nothing they could do about it. So, I try to stay away from those places. There are some other dentists' offices that are like connected to churches or some type of hospital where they will give you services for free, you just have to know where to go and how to get on the list to be seen," he offered as stretched out in his seat. "But," he cautioned, "they are not always open, and sometimes they just pop up with a trailer or something like a big camper, but it has a whole bunch of stuff in there that a dentist needs, like a chair that reclines and all of the equipment. Basically, it is just like a dentist's office inside of a camper."

Describing the limitations of the dental office in more detail, Marley continued, "So, it is not like going to a normal dentist's office where you make an appointment. I was lucky as one of them was open over near John Muir or Manual Arts, I can't remember exactly. I went there, I was trying to hold back the pain, but they could kind of tell that something was wrong and they saw me that day. Like I said, I was lucky, but man, I was so happy to not have that damn headache."

We made our way down the 105 freeway and exited off of Sepulveda. Normally I would have been a little reluctant to take this route, as it also serves as one of the main arteries to the Los Angeles Airport. Given that public transportation is quite bad throughout the city, most people are forced to take some sort of vehicular transportation to get to and from the airport, and thus traffic is usually quite bad. However, I had found a sweet spot during the week and around the mid-morning where, while not great, the traffic kept on moving at a decent pace. We drove through the long tunnel under the massive configuration of hangers, runways, and parked airplanes and by the main entrance that funneled us to the Lincoln Boulevard–Sepulveda Boulevard split. Taking the Lincoln route, we eventually reached our destination of the Westchester Library.

We walked into the library and found some seats in the teen section, which was a little more lax when it came to noise and talking in the building. We spent the bulk of the next two hours going over flash cards and a GRE practice book. Marley, who had always been a thinker, was trying to plot out the next steps of his life. "Man, I have gotten about as far as I can in the hood doing what I am doing. If I am really going to be about the action I am talking about, I need to change some things up." We finished up at the library around lunchtime, and normally we would go grab something to eat at one of the vegan-friendly places near the library. Marley, who was a self-professed "carnivore," was very open to the idea of eating as many fruits and vegetables as possible. As a result, he was always interested in trying out new places, and, while he assured me he was never going to change over anytime soon, he was more than happy to explore the abundance of vegan fare that Los Angeles had to offer.

However, on this particular day, Marley was not so much interested in going to get some food as he was in going to the doctor. "Man, I would love to grab some food, but could you take me to the doctor? We can just grab some food to go, and if you don't mind we can eat it in the car on the way over." I assured him that would be no problem, and we took off to a nearby grocery store, purchased some ready-made items, and made our way back to the car. Turning out of the grocery store parking lot, Marley directed me to a county-supported health clinic in South Central. Rather than chance it with traffic on the freeway, we decided to take Manchester Avenue all the way east. Once situated in the car, Marley explained the need for him to go to the clinic. "So man, here is the issue. You know I have been with Tasha for a little while. And while everything has been good, you know occasionally we have our arguments, and look, I am not the easiest guy in the world to get along with, this I know. I am strong-headed and strong-willed, but she has put up with all of that. So, even though we were together, we also weren't during that time, and so I was out there with other women and she was doing her thing."

One of the things that I most admired about Marley was his consistent self-awareness. He very rarely framed the world as a static entity;
rather, he was aware of the myriad of possibilities and, importantly, his
role in shaping outcomes. In a somewhat muted and matter-of-fact
tone, he continued. "Well, we got back together and everything was
cool, and then she told me she contracted an STD from this dude she
used to mess with back in the day and wanted to let me know.

"At first—I ain't even going to lie—I was heated, like really mad." He
let out a chuckle as he reflected on his mood. "I had to just be myself for
a little bit, but then I had to check myself, because it was not like I owned
her or anything, and she was straight-up with me in letting me know. So
we hashed it out, but now I need to go get tested to see what is going on.
I have been feeling fine, but you know I take my health real seriously."

We drove down Manchester, east of the 110 freeway, and turned
north up Main Street headed to the Hubert Humphrey Clinic. We
joked around in the car as we were now on the "east side." Not to be
confused with East Los Angeles, the east side referred to the section
immediately east of the 110 freeway. As joked about in Marley's neighborhood and much throughout South Central Los Angeles, the east
side has connotations of being a little less refined, a little more apt to
skirt the conventions of respectable society. Marley and I joked because
there was very little difference between east of the freeway and west of
the freeway other than a mound of concrete.

Driving up Main Street, I asked Marley about using protection and
if I could be of any assistance in getting anything for him. He let out a
loud laugh and said, "Man, so this goes pretty much in two different
ways. One on hand, it is definitely on me for being so lusty!" He bel-
lowed out a deep baritone laugh. "But on the other hand, there is literally nowhere to get condoms, and I don't know what in the heck women
are supposed to get, because condoms are some of the cheapest things
that you can get."

Still reeling from his laughter, he patted down his pants and shirt to
convey that he was getting himself together to be serious. "I mean,

look," he continued. "I bet when we go up in here, there is going to be a big jar of condoms where we can take as many as we like. The problem is that they are only available at places like this, and you see how far this is from where I stay. Otherwise you have to buy them from the store. You got to drop like ten bucks for four condoms. It is almost like they want you to catch something."

Shifting his tone to become slightly more serious, Marley stared out of the window for a brief moment before he turned his attention to back inside the car and stated, "So, I know that I should be protecting myself at all times, but still, how can you blame me for everything and say it's my responsibility to use a condom and then make it so damn hard to get the things?"

We pulled into the parking lot of the clinic, which was directly adjacent to a large park. Parking the car, we walked into the medical building and, sure enough, there were condoms in a large glass jar. I laughed when I saw the jar, and Marley went to fill out the paperwork to be seen. We waited for somewhere between twenty and thirty minutes, and Marley was taken behind a door to be seen by a health professional.

He came back out fairly quickly with a handful of pamphlets. And in typical Marley fashion, he was in great spirits. We walked out of the building and he showed me all of the information that he had received. "Yeah, she pretty much lectured me on being safe and that I need to always use protection. She was not mean or anything, but just telling me stuff that I already know." He continued, "So, I need to come back in like a week, they are supposed to call me and let me know when the test is ready. You know how my phone situation is, so if it is cool, I gave them your number." I told him that it was cool as long as they didn't need any personal information. "Naw, it is just like a call to let me know to come in. They don't share anything like that over the phone. They'll mail it to your address, so I gave them the Library's address and your phone number." "Sounds good to me," I replied, and we headed back to the car.

I got a call within the week from the Los Angeles County Health Department letting me know that Marley's test results were in. I called the most recent phone number that I had for him and let him know that I had gotten the call. We made arrangements to meet up the following Tuesday and head over to the facility. The interim time period flew by pretty quickly and before I knew it, it was Tuesday. I made my way down the 110 freeway and now, knowing my way to his new residence, I was able to quickly find a parking spot in front of the house. I called Marley to let him know that I was outside, and he came out within five minutes and jumped into the car.

"Whew brother, you ready to do this?" he asked. I laughed in my response, "Yeah, I am, but the stakes for me are much lower." "You know, to be honest," he issued back, "I really ain't tripping that much over any of it. I know that I got to be careful out here, but it's not really that big of a deal." At this point, I knew Marley well enough to know between issuances of prideful bluster and his honest truth, and now was a little mixture of both. He indeed was worried, but I could very well understand that he was trying to calm himself. I also knew that when he was in moments such as these, talking brought him a sense of peace.

Following the same route that we had taken just over a week prior, we took Manchester Avenue east to avoid the traffic of the freeway. However, Marley had to go to a different facility closer to downtown Los Angeles, and thus our jaunt up Main Street was much longer than going to the clinic. He began to release the tension from his mind and remarked, "Man, you know what is crazy is what we got to go through just to even get the test results. I mean, how is it that we have to go way the hell over here to this facility that is so far away to get the results? I'm just going to put it mildly, the health care system in this city is the worst."

Much different than our previous trip, Marley was jovial, and thus his insight was more pressing in tone. "I mean, for those who can afford it, I am sure it is good, but for us, this shit is deplorable. You'd think they want us to die. And really, I don't think I am asking for that much.

You know, all I really want is to be able to reach a doctor, to be able to get good medical advice for whatever I need, and to not have to use the damn emergency room or urgent care as a default."

As he looked out of the window in a very pensive manner, Marley's fingers tapped on the seat as the words streamed out of him. "And the thing is, the damn city and county spend so much money on so much other bullshit, that the thing that should be of the utmost importance, the health care of Black people, is just cut out. That is why I say I think that they want us gone. Just look around, I mean, nobody around here has decent health care."

His finger-tapping increased and the tone in his voice matched the quick, staccato nature of his rapidly moving fingers. "The city can say 'Oh, we provide services here and here in your community, so we are doing a good job.' Man, that is bullshit," Marley fervently declared. Somehow picking up the pace, he ever so subtly exclaimed, "The health care that we have is not good, and sometimes I think that having no health care at all would be better than having this little bullshit that we have. That way we could at least call it what it is. They throw us some crumbs and act like they just gave us a ten-course meal."

The vibration of the car, the music, and the timbre in Marley's voice seemed to all be on the same frequency. As he looked out the window again, the pain and frustration were evident in his voice. "There is no way these city council representatives have the same damn health care I have," he pleaded to me. "I promise you the city council or county supervisor for this area has never stepped a foot in this damn facility for health care. They probably came up here to take a photo to promote all the 'good' they are doing," he stated, raising his hands to form air quotes around the intonation of the word *good*. He pressed on: "But believe me, after the cameras were put away, they were out of there, back to their plush lives. And then you know that the doctors aren't getting paid hardly anything. I only say that because the facilities look way too old, as if they have not been touched in decades."

The pulsing of his finger slightly decreased in speed, and the pace of his breath slowed as he added, "So my guess is that you have doctors who aren't paid hardly anything and facilities that are old, and pretty much you only go to them when something is terribly wrong. That is why I say that they want us gone."

Marley's body slightly relaxed from the tense state it had been in since entering the car. He stretched out his legs and took a deep breath. "The bottom line is that it should be so easy to go and see a doctor. There should be some type of doctor on like every block. We are living in a community where people have all types of things going wrong and it is so easy to fix." Looking straight out of the window, you could see the list forming in his mind, as he explained, "I am talking about diabetes, high blood pressure, heart issues—all of this stuff is easy to fix. And instead of giving us the most amount of resources to fix it, they leave us to figure out how to make it on our own. Like I said, they want us gone."

By this time of our ride, Marley was visibly more relaxed, but he had not lost the passion in the tone of his voice. "But trust me, I am not going anywhere. I was put here for a purpose and I have not fulfilled that purpose. They are not going to get rid of me like that. We are going to change all this, because this is not how we were made to live." I slowed the car as we were getting close to the building, but I had never been to the location and wanted to make sure that we did not pass it.

As I was looking for the address numbers on buildings, Marley stated in a fairly calm tone, "All of this stress of trying to find a job, trying to get money, trying to get some healthy food, the air is filthy as hell and the ground is contaminated too. Then we try to duck and dodge from the craziness because of the craziness that we live in. All of that contributes to our awful health situation, and then on top of all of that, we have to drive twenty to thirty minutes away to get a damn test result."

Right on cue, we pulled into the parking lot of the county health building. The look of worry was still there, but he was more relaxed. He became quiet, took a deep breath, and we walked through the doors.

Marley checked himself in at the front desk, grabbed a number and, as we waited, began maybe eating more vegetarian-type foods, but lamented that he liked meat too much. Before he could explain more, a nurse called his number. He looked at me with a hopeful expression, took a deep breath, and walked through the doors.

Socialist Visions

Ownership—that was the topic of the week. Not that I had selected the topic, but rather, it was on everybody's tongue. It was an impromptu meeting in what had been referred to as the garden just adjacent to the Library: a group of young men, all of whom took the craft of cooking food and harvesting crops very seriously.

Marley initiated the conversation as he manned the massive grill that had been wheeled over from Harvard Park to the garden. The smoke billowed out from the roasting charcoal that sat right beneath the metal grates of the rectangular grill. It was a beautiful day, with the brightness of the sun offset by the passing of the occasional cloud, which momentarily muted the intensity of the heat emanating from the sky. The heat from the grill, however, increased, and it was time to let the charcoal rest for just a moment. Marley closed the grill, and a chorus grew as they all spoke about the need to own everything from houses to businesses in the neighborhood.

The general ethos was that ownership would provide autonomy and autonomy would provide the basis to engage with the state. Ranging from the ability to grow their own food to being able to house everyone in the community, the focus was on providing resources for everyone. It was of note that no one spoke of getting rich or buying the trappings of ostentatious wealth. The entire discussion revolved around developing a plan to support the entire community and breaking away from the clutches of the city and state.

The weeks prior and following were devoted to mapping out the political gene-
alogy of communal organizing pertaining to structures of need—such as housing,
food, and material resources. Discussion was never in short supply, and the imagi-
nation of what was possible overflowed.

•   •   •

BLACK PANTHER PARTY PLATFORM POINT #4

We Want Decent Housing Fit For The Shelter Of Human Beings.

We believe that if the White Landlords will not give decent housing to
our Black community, then the housing and the land should be made into
cooperatives so that our community, with government aid, can build and
make decent housing for its people.

BLACK PANTHER PARTY PLATFORM POINT #2

We Want Full Employment For Our People.

We believe that the federal government is responsible and obligated to
give every man employment or a guaranteed income. We believe that if
the White American businessmen will not give full employment, then the
means of production should be taken from the businessmen and placed in
the community so that the people of the community can organize and
employ all of its people and give a high standard of living.

My focus on the BPP in the opening salvo of this chapter has much to
do with how the organization still resonated amongst Black young people in Los Angeles. In particular, among organizations such as BRIM,
the BPP has a salient political genealogy. This genealogy is largely
informed by the work of Alprentice "Bunchy" Carter. Bunchy was a
charismatic and vital member of the LA chapter and recruited many
members from the Slausons, of which he was a member. While the
foundational organizations such as the Slausons, the Gladiators, the
Businessmen, and Dodge City are no longer active in the city, their history remains intact and is passed down from generation to generation.
In this manner, we can understand organizations such as BRIM as
direct political descendants born from a very particular history of
political, communal, and social organizing.

Perhaps the common archival source of information for this history is the Black Panther Party's ten-point platform. From that platform, I would like to focus on two of those points during this chapter as a means to provide the context of Los Angeles during the late 1960s and early 1970s. My aim is to demonstrate how the BPP's social vision for the future had a great impact upon the socialist fringe of the Democratic Party and how that vision was picked upon by conservative ideologues in an attempt to counter and violently smash socialist possibilities in the United States.

THE FEAR OF THE FRINGE

The conventional rendering of Jimmy Carter's presidential administration is that while he was very astute in the world of international politics, he did not have a good pulse on the domestic front. I have heard this logic spewed numerous times, from high school textbooks to family conversations. Yet while that conventional wisdom has consistently spread from one generation to the next, in rhetorical posturing about the failures of the Democratic Party during the 1980s, the historical record uncovers a much different narrative.

Much of the problem with Carter's domestic policy stems not from its failure, but to the contrary, from the potential of what ardent capitalists understood as an existential threat to their very existence. In 1978, Carter had a meeting with Thomas Hayden in the latter's official capacity as the founder of the Campaign for Economic Democracy (CED). Hayden expressed his frustration with the state of affairs within the formal political sector. Of their conversation, Hayden recounted:

> Jimmy Carter's first question to me was whether I was "satisfied" at seeing so many once controversial ideas finally being carried out as national policy. The radicalism of the 60's, he seemed to imply, was becoming the common sense of the 70's. His question reminded me of something which Norman Thomas once said when asked if his ideas had been carried out by

the New Deal. "Yes," the old social crusader answered, "they were carried out—but in a coffin." So I'm not satisfied, I told the President. The federal budget, I said, expands the Pentagon's war chest while doing nothing new for our ailing cities; increases a dangerous commitment to nuclear power plants over solar energy; seems to blandly accept massive unemployment, particularly among youth, combined with permanent inflation in the cost of the basic necessities of life. The greatest issue, I continued, is a lack of power to do anything about these crises. Then followed this exchange. "Even you, the elected President of the United States, really have less power than the heads of the giant multinational corporations whom we do not elect and rarely see." "I believe that's true," he told me. "I've learned that these past twelve months." (Poole 1980, 4–5)

As evident some forty years later, the promise of Thomas Hayden's quasi-socialist vision for the future never materialized. However, what is important to note is that the political establishment took note of Carter's meeting with Hayden as a potential threat. The Heritage Foundation, the preeminent think tank of ardent capitalist values, sent out several reports concerning the threat that Hayden posed to the established capital class. In a multipart report that focused on Hayden and the Campaign for Economic Democracy, The Heritage Foundation's report stated, "One of the preeminent radical leaders of the 1960's … and several of the CED's principal activists are also veterans of the Hayden [Senate] campaign and of Students for a Democratic Society, a militantly leftist organization in which Hayden played a pivotal role both as founder and as principal author of its basic manifesto, the 'Port Huron Statement'" (Poole 1980, i).

While The Heritage Foundation's focus was upon Hayden as a charismatic force and the CED as his base of operations, they understood Hayden as giving voice to key ideological tenets that were antithetical to a free-market style of political and economic governance. Two of these big tenets were housing rights and a government apparatus that would gradually remove the economic, political, and social power of private businesses. One of the primary campaigns of the CED was a platform that placed rent control and tenants at the forefront of its agenda. From The Heritage Foundation report:

> An account published in the January 26, 1980, edition of the *Washington Star* indicated that CED's political activism is taking on a distinctly national emphasis in at least one area of concern to the Campaign over the years: so-called tenants' rights. Headlined "Tenant Associations Trying to Form a National Lobby," this article mentioned a meeting in Newark, New Jersey, "last month" attended by representatives "of 50 local tenant organizations" interested in "formation of a national tenants' rights coalition" with one of the actions agreed upon at the meeting being "a national convention next summer, possibly in Los Angeles." (Poole 1980, 21)

The report went on to describe the infrastructure of the tenants' rights organization and the ability of smaller grassroots movements to gain traction within several states. With the victories mounting, these local organizations sought to link up under a broader umbrella with a goal of forming a national union that would be able to draft federal legislation and put forth candidates who would enact measures favorable to mass tenant movements.

There was particular attention paid to CHAIN, the California Housing Action and Information Network, as a model that could have dire consequences upon free enterprise and capitalist endeavors. According to the report,

> CHAIN ... the California Housing Action and Information Network, a new statewide coalition to fight for housing rights for tenants as well as homeowners, recently kicked off with a well-attended, all-day conference in Los Angeles. CHAIN held 2 regional organizing meetings in San Diego and San Francisco in mid-March, and is now working against efforts to outlaw local rent control ordinances, and for bills to force landlords to pay interest to tenants of more low-cost housing. (Poole 1980, 15)

While the CED's stance upon housing was a point of particular angst for The Heritage Foundation, another major issue pertaining to the CED's stance was perhaps even more troublesome—solar energy.

GOING SOLAR = GOING SOCIALIST

When Jimmy Carter won the presidential election of 1976, there was a real possibility that energy sources other than fossil fuels were going to be placed at the forefront of the US national energy agenda. Carter's installation of solar panels on the grounds of the White House was a signal that he was serious about government investment into alternative energy formations. The federal government had infused money into research programs that investigated wind, solar, and other nonfossil energy sources. Yet, it was also Carter's investment in renewable energy that in part paved the way for his defeat to Ronald Reagan in the 1980 election. Using the White House's solar panels as a red herring during the campaign, Reagan successfully attacked solar panels as a foil to the logics of capitalism. True to his word, and as an effective publicity stunt, Reagan had Carter's solar panels removed from the White House. This in effect declared his allegiance to both the fossil fuel industry and the free market.

Shifting the administration's priorities to the fossil fuel industry, namely oil and coal, Reagan's tenure as president was a dramatic shift in energy policy. Heavily funded by the oil and coal industries, Reagan's administration issued serious changes to energy regulation standards and reforms that Carter had implemented. Through systematic deregulation of energy, the proverbial floodgates were opened to profit schemes regardless of the environmental consequence and impact. Utilizing free-market thinking as cover, Reagan handed the keys of the administration's energy program to the fossil fuel industry and simultaneously killed off federal funding for renewable energy:

> Reagan's political philosophy viewed the free market as the best arbiter of what was good for the country. Corporate self-interest, he felt, would steer the country in the right direction. To liberate corporate enterprise, Reagan

undertook a wholesale abolition of government regulations that oversaw corporate action in the public interest. Out went stringent fuel-efficiency standards and conservation incentives.... Tax and other incentives to promote alternative energy were rolled back or eliminated. Between 1981 and 1987, federal funding for alternative energy projects, such as solar, wind, and geothermal, was cut by 80 percent. In this same period, the DOE conservation budget was cut 70 percent; in 1988, it was slashed by a further 50 percent, essentially killing government research in this field. (Goldstein 2009, 72)

Reagan's free-market ideology has to be placed in the context of an attempt to thwart the socialism and socialism-based practices that had gained public momentum during the 1960s and '70s. While bits and pieces of socialist-based philosophies had seeped into parts of the New Deal, the Carter administration represented a serious turn in the eyes of ardent capitalists. Carter himself was not a stalwart socialist; rather, many of the left-based forces that came out to vote to propel Carter to the White House saw his administration as the beginning of the push toward a more radically democratic society.

For entities such as the CED, solar energy represented much more than a switch to a renewable source of energy. It represented the opportunity to push private capital out of influence and positions of power within processes of US statecraft. The shift to renewable energy for the CED also represented the opportunity to establish new formations as to the dissemination and implementation of energy sources. Rather than an industry governed by private capital, the vision for solar energy was a state-run project that controlled all means of facilitation. By 1977 CED had already gained traction within California and CED representatives had been in conversations with the governor and established a solar energy council that was actively seeking to establish a state-run solar operation that would create four hundred thousand jobs and become the model for future forms of economic development.

In this manner, the shift to renewable energy was as much a shift for the environment as it was a shift in economic and ideological philosophy. The Heritage Foundation was adamant that such thinking was a threat to US national interests. While there is a much-needed conversation about what forces actually propelled Reagan into office and created a mythical narrative of Carter's domestic policy, what is of greater importance is how Hayden and the CED came to their positions and how The Heritage Foundation was in fear of the logics of radical Black organizing coming to fruition on a national stage.

In describing Hayden's transgressions against the interests of US nation-building, The Heritage Foundation report goes into some detail about his then relationship with Jane Fonda. The basis of vitriol directed at Fonda was her connection to, support of, and learning from anti–Vietnam War organizations and radical-based communal groups. Of note, the report pointed out Fonda's connections to the Black Panther Party: "Fonda's support for such groups as the violence-oriented Black Panther Party is a well-known matter of public record, as is her equally vehement support for the cause of Hanoi during the war in Vietnam" (Poole 1980, 11). While there is a great amount of debate that can be had about the seriousness or level of investment that Fonda had to the long-term success of the BPP, what is of note is the fear that the BPP stoked among defenders of the status quo of US governance.

HOUSING IN LOS ANGELES, 1965–1992

The connection between Jane Fonda and the BPP gave pause to The Heritage Foundation due to matters of ideology. The support for the BPP was understood as an attack upon the very tenets of capitalism. The framing of housing and employment within the BPP platform as a basic human right targeted the power and influence of the private capitalists in matters of policy, legislation, and ideological praxis. For the private capitalist class, in particular land speculators, real estate developers, and finance capitalists, such overtures to socialist-leaning pursuits had to be dampened. What emboldened the spirit of the BPP to take such a brazen stance against capitalism were events that unfolded in cities across the United States during the 1960s. Focusing on Los Angeles, the 1965 Watts Rebellion was a high-water mark that was the direct result of mass organizing on the part of Black communities throughout the city. The effect of several years of animus directed at Black Angelenos at the hands of city planners, officials, real estate developers, and sworn officers had worn thin and Black Angelenos took to the streets and set the city ablaze.

What is evident from the historical archive of Los Angeles during the 1950s and '60s is that Black Angelenos were consistently positioned to receive the worst housing conditions, the lowest forms of education, and the least amount of health care and forced to survive within the most precarious of employment situations. Thus, while police abuse of Black people was rampant within the city, police abuse has to be understood as the proverbial heavy hand of the city to enforce Black Angelenos' place within the social, political, and economic hierarchy of city governance.

When the rebellion occurred in 1965, the attempts of the state and federal government to dampen Black critique of the long-standing violence in the city were quickly countered by the weight of ash that rained down upon the city. The bottom line was that the rebellion exposed to a global audience the systematic effect of racial capitalism upon a population that had a different vision of the world than the one that was being imposed on it. The McCone Commission Report, which was the official State of California report of '65, attempted to sugarcoat several of the key issues brought forth by the rebellion. As an example, reporting about the housing conditions in South Central Los Angeles, the report states:

> Compared with the conditions under which Negroes live in most other large cities of United States, Los Angeles conditions are superior. This has been confirmed by witnesses before this commission who noted, for example, that the majority of dwelling units in Watts are single-family structures and that the streets and lawns are well kept for a poverty area. (McCone Commission 1965, 26A)

Yet, the report could not simply sweep away a massive rebellion with dismissive rhetoric and patronizing language. Further along, when the report goes into the testimony of Black Angelenos, the structural scale of housing violence becomes evident:

> Nevertheless, we have received extensive testimony expressing residents' dissatisfaction with the area's physical facilities. Of particular concern to us is the fact that a serious deterioration of the area is in progress. Houses are old and require constant maintenance if they are to remain habitable. Over two thirds of them are owned by absentee landlords. In numerous instances neither landlords nor tenants appear willing to join in a cooperative effort to halt the deterioration. Many landlords are faced with problems of a high turnover and tenants do not consider themselves responsible for assisting to maintain the property. Tenants resent the high proportion of their income which they must devote to rent for shelter which in many instances is more deteriorated than housing in the total county.
>
> Compounding the problem is the fact that both private financial institutions and the Federal Housing Authority consider the residential multiple unit in the curfew area an unattractive market because of difficult collection problems, high maintenance costs, and a generally depreciating area resulting from the age of surrounding structures .... At the same time, the development of public housing has been limited by the failure of voters to improve governmental development of low-cost housing, as required by the California Constitution. (McCone Commission 1965, 27A)

While the city made promises to address the concerns of the rebellion, many of the core structural issues such as housing were not addressed. A mere fifteen years later, in 1980, the same year that Reagan defeated Carter, the housing crisis in Los Angeles reached a peak level. Sparked by severe land speculation, housing inflation, and stagnant wages, the vast majority of renters in the city (84 percent) were not able to purchase a home. This is of note as with land speculation came increased rents, and without rent control, many people were finding themselves without homes (Boyarsky 1980). In a federal audit administered by the Department of Housing and Urban Development (HUD), investigators found that while the city had allocated over $150 million of HUD funds during a five-year time period, it had stockpiled in excess of $50 million that was to have been spent on the development of affordable housing (Boyarsky 1980). In a contentious battle with HUD, then mayor Tom Bradley attempted to deflect attention from the failed building of affordable housing by stating that the problems had been "blown out of proportion by the news media." However, such claims were determined to be unfounded, and as journalists went through their archives they found that, to the contrary, the media had been generally supportive of his plans (Marten 1980). Further, Bradley used the media to gain attention and praise for garnering the HUD resources, but failed to deliver on his promises. Two years after he hosted a press conference in 1978, where he promised to build twelve thousand new affordable units in the city, it was discovered that the city had not built a single unit (Marten 1980). The Bradley administration came under even more scrutiny when the Coalition for Economic Survival held a news conference in 1980 and stated that the federal audit demonstrated that money that was earmarked for affordable housing had been spent on the construction of hotels and retail stores (Los Angeles Herald Examiner Staff, 1980).

In the wake of misappropriation and nonuse of funds, a coalition of nine organizations formed to thwart the city's actions (Weinstein 1979). The Los Angeles Group for Community Development Reform filed a petition with HUD to prevent a $53 million block grant from being excised by the city. The petition stated four key points as to the city's malfeasance with respect to the construction of housing:

(1) The city has not involved neighborhood residents in overall planning of housing and economic development programs, thereby creating inappropriate and unworkable projects.

(2) The City has not committed itself to an aggressive housing production program, which is the most obvious solution to Los Angeles' housing crisis.

(3) The city has overlooked the most severe housing needs, giving preference to moderate- and middle-income needs, rather than low-income needs.

(4) The city has not developed a workable strategy to stabilize neighborhoods, slowing the transition of mixed neighborhoods to higher-income ones which present residents will be unable to afford. (Weinstein 1979)

The coalition also pointed out that 45 percent of the budget for the funds was going to be allocated to specific target areas located between Chinatown and the University of Southern California, which was already deemed an area of developmental focus in preparation for the 1984 Olympic Games (Weinstein 1979).

By 1983, a year before the Olympic Games, and with mounting pressure placed in light of the HUD fiasco, the housing and overall economic situation in Los Angeles was a disaster. A survey of one of the poorest areas in the city near Downtown LA found that 70 percent of the population had less than $300 a month and many were dealing with a variety of health crises. Further, with the rash of government cutbacks implemented at the federal and state level, there was virtually no safety net offered. Seventy-six percent of the population stated that they received no public assistance and that, while they looked for work, a third of the population related their economic situation to a lack of steady income (Ropers 1983).

At the close of the decade, the economic vulnerability of the city's Black population was palpable, and, while the popular news media focused on drugs and gangs to highlight the city's issues, the very basics of housing and employment went by the wayside. These issues lay at the core of Los Angeles's foundation being ready to explode, which it did in 1992 when, similar to 1965, the city opened up in flames. Unable to contain the furor of the dispossessed, Los Angeles was engulfed and the ills and horrors of the city were placed on center stage for the world to see.

ALBUM 5

Liberatory Vibes

Freedom Ain't Free

Marley's father had been incarcerated for a long stretch of time. He had several friends who were either facing or enduring lengthy sentences or dealing with the treacherous road of the probation system. Aside from those close to him, Marley had an intimate familiarity with the carceral state as he had been arrested several times and had to serve time in both juvenile hall and the juvenile camps. Whenever he discussed his time inside camp, there was a new energy to the conversation. In the midst of the sheer madness of incarceration, Marley saw possibility and beauty. Rather than interrupt his thoughts with my voice or scene placement, the remaining pages are dedicated to Marley's experience and insight as told in his own words. My goal is to allow the depth of his story and the horrific absurdity of incarceration to bear its strange fruit through his narrative and unwavering commitment to the possibility of a better tomorrow.

THE LONG JOURNEY

It is the craziest thing that I have ever seen, like something out of a movie. They put us on this bus and we have these cuffs on and we are sitting there just waiting to be taken to who knows where. You really don't think about it too much, you kind of are just glad to get out of the place that you are in, because it is really wild in the halls, and human beings should not be forced to live in such situations. Anyway, we are waiting there to be taken up into the larger facility and then put on the bus. So you get on the bus and then you start moving. The whole time you are looking out the window because you have been stuck inside this huge holding cell and now you get just a small glimpse of freedom, or what feels like freedom.

You have no idea where you are going. Have you ever felt like you were going somewhere, but you had no control over it? Your body was just moving in a direction and you were along for the ride? Well, that is how I felt on that bus. We were on the freeway for a long time, but it was weird because it did not seem like a long time. No one really said anything at all, you kind of just sat there in silence and looked out the window.

I think it was the newness of everything. What I mean by newness is the fact that so many of us were from all over LA. You had folks in there who did not know each other, but we still knew each other. We saw ourselves in each other. We didn't have any stable housing, our school situation was just miserable, and we for sure did not trust anything that resembled authority. We all had the same experience: no matter how many times you moved or switched schools, the neighborhood was always the same. It is just like the whole damn city said "fuck you." There are plenty of neighborhoods like that all over and you can always tell when someone has lived there. They carry it in their eyes, it is on their face. The way that they sit, how they talk in a crowd. So, here we are all together, all at the same time seeing a different side of life that we had never experienced before.

Let me be clear, I am not talking about big houses and crazy cars. All of that stuff, that is like whatever. I have had a whole bunch of money, I have been up in clubs in Hollywood and experienced all that. I am not talking about that. I am talking about being far away from the superficial madness. We were on the freeway and I never forget it, because we are riding and there came a point where the houses, strip malls, and all of that just stopped. There was nothing but open space. Like space to move and be about. And like I said, all of us were from the same type of environment where you never see space like that at all. So that was the newness, the being able to just feel a freedom of movement and space.

Then there was the nature. It was like you could see your life getting better. The bus pulled off the exit and then started going up this mountain. As we went up the mountain, there were trees everywhere. Pine trees, just as far as the eye can see, pine trees. It is one of the most beautiful things that I have ever seen. So here we are just moving up, and while I had seen nature—I had been to the beach and on hiking trails—here we were, like removed from everything and a long way from home. Then the bus turns right and you look over and you can see just how far up we are. What really let me know how high we were was the smog. Now, that was the craziest thing I have ever seen. As we were making our way up you could see the layers of smog sitting right beneath us, and as the bus pulled up higher and higher, there were more and more layers of smog. It was just crazy to see.

Then we got to a certain point, and then you realized that we had reached the highest level of smog and we were in the clean air. The smog just sat over the city. It is crazy to think that is how we live, that we are trapped under a layer of dirty, filthy air. It looked like someone put a lid on top of a jar and we were now looking at the jar from the outside. Don't get me wrong, I knew about smog, but to really see that we are living in such a filthy environment was shocking to see.

ARRIVAL

So then we get way up there and it was like another world. The bus stops and they tell us to get off the bus in our handcuffs. Now this may sound wild, but the very first thing that I noticed once we got off the bus was the air. It just smelled so fresh. You could smell every single tree. I think they were pine trees, because everything to me smelled like pine. I had never smelled nature so fresh. The air was light, I felt as if I was moving on a cloud. I knew that air got thin the higher up you went, but for the first time I could actually feel it. It just felt so good to take a deep breath in and have clean air going down into my lungs. Then that got me thinking again about the smog that we just went through and how bad the air that we have to breathe every day really is. That got me thinking about where I live. You know we are pretty close to the ocean, so every now and then we should be able to smell the salt from the wind that blows in during the evening. But I can't remember a time in my life where I have smelled the ocean besides when I have been at the beach. But here up in the mountains, I could smell everything. It was as if we were finally free from all of that trash that we had been forced to live with for all that time. So here we are just out in the nature, in all this air, but we got these chains on and these folks looking over our every move. I looked around and felt like, damn, ain't this a fucked-up situation! The guards then put us in two-by-two lines and began to sort us out, and eventually we get to our rooms where we were going to be staying while we served our time. So I am in there with this other dude and I am just looking out at this little sliver of a window and you can see all of this beauty on the other side and I was just like, damn, this is truly fucked up.

TRAINING VS. LEARNING

I remember going to sleep, and the reason why I remember going to sleep is that I will never forget what woke me up. It was this noise that sounded like someone was tapping a hammer, but they are tapping a football field away. I was thinking, what in the hell is that sound so early in the morning? We had to get up early anyway because they did not allow us to sleep too late. We were up like by 6:00 A.M. every morning. When we get outside, I am super curious as to what in the hell that sound is. Then I see it. It is a damn woodpecker. I was blown away. I have seen these birds on the internet and read about them, but now to actually see one and I was just in amazement. Like, is this really real? I swear, I just stood there in amazement. This little bird is pecking away at the tree, and when we were outside, it echoed throughout the whole forest. It was crazy.

Once again, man, it was just freedom. Freedom to be able to hear, to think, to just be able to soak in all of this. They had us doing all of this work outside in the woods and forest. And the crazy part is that I loved every minute of it. While we were out there, the lesson that we were supposed to be getting was the value of hard work and the need to have strict discipline and all of that bullshit, but you know what? We already had all of that! What I learned more than anything was about all of this shit that they keep from us. All of the air that we could not breathe, all of the freedom that we did not have, all of the ways that we were being trapped. Then they want to act like all of this is because of a lack of discipline and not having a work ethic. So yeah, I did learn a lot while I was at camp—just probably not what they wanted me to learn! They went on and on about how we all made mistakes and we need to learn from our mistakes and what we had to do to become better people and how I was hurting my family and neighborhood. All I could think about was that I wasn't the one who forced our whole damn neighborhood to live in these conditions of not having clean soil, fresh air, or just freedom to move around.

Being in camp opened my eyes to so much about myself. Now, I'm not saying that I needed to be in camp to learn this. Let's get that straight. I get tired of that bullshit-ass idea. You hear that all the time, "If I didn't go to prison, then I would have wound up dead." Like really, come on. That is the lamest thing I have ever heard. How about if you would have had a million dollars, or if you would have been born in Beverly Hills? Like you were predestined to go to prison or something. Come on, you have got to be kidding me. That shit ain't real. Going to prison did not save your ass.

What saved your ass was being able to have the space and freedom to think, which ironically happens when you are locked up. And that is exactly what you don't have when you are trying to think how to survive. You are trying to figure out how to get that next meal or where you are going to be living, you don't have time to think. When you are hungry, broke, and are in bad physical shape, that is going to mess with your mind. You ain't thinking straight. You're on edge and you just might snap at the smallest thing that ain't got nothing to do with nothing. Trust me, that has happened to me more than once. All that does is makes a bad situation worse. So you can miss me with that whole madness that you as an individual made a bad decision. Shit, then what in the hell do you call the decision to put me and all of my family and friends in the situation that we are in? Who decided to pull all the jobs out of South Central? Who decided to close all the hospitals and health care facilities? Who decided to set it up so that the police hunt us down? Who did all of that? Why aren't they in prison? I'll tell you why, because prison was never made for them. Prison was never made for those who make the system function as it should. Prison was designed for the folks who call out the system or make it look like exactly what it is—a damn joke.

When I was in camp, I was able to think about all of this. It opened my eyes—all of a sudden I was locked up right next to a dude who on the street might be my enemy. Now, all of a sudden, we are talking, and you know what? We have way more in common than we are different. We grew up in the same neighborhoods, we did the same things. So, I met dudes from rival hoods, and back home, it would have been a problem on sight. But locked up here, it was way different.

Now, I will say this. The camp situation is different than being locked up in County or being sent away on a bid doing real time. In County, the politics from within the jail really controls what happens between people. But in camp, the politics are way different, because of the age of who is in here and who runs the show. So, in camp, you can really sit down with a dude from a rival hood and begin to chop it up and be cool. I ain't saying y'all are going to be best friends or nothing like that. But there is much less in the way of rivalry and about who is claiming certain sets. As a result, we had the time to just be and freedom to think.

Now, just to be clear, I ain't saying that folks should be locked up so they can think straight. What I am saying, though, is that all of this shit is ironic. Our neighborhoods and communities have been structured in such a fucked-up way that being locked up gave us more time to actually think and plan than being in the supposed comfort of our home. Now don't get me wrong, that does not mean that it was all gravy up in camp. Like I said, you had to follow a strict discipline structure and life was extremely tough in many ways, because you are far away from your family, friends, and all those things that made you who you are. But now that I am locked up and my enemy is locked up right next to me, now we have to work together, eat together, and live together. Now that we get to start talking, I see that we ain't enemies at all and in another life, we probably would be cool as hell. But, now I have the time to think about all of this, because many of my basic needs are being met. They are being met in a fucked-up way, but they are being met. Now just imagine if we lived in a situation where instead of having just our basic needs met, we actually thrived. Like everything was good, we had more than enough. We could actually roam around and when we did meet, it wasn't under hostile terms, but we were actually cool with seeing one another.

Remember what I said earlier about being on the bus and being able to see a dude for who they were? This is what I am trying to say, but in a more concrete way. We were all the same. We all came from the same damn place, and that place led us to this crazy-ass beautiful place up in the mountains where we had to walk around in chains. Like, how much more crazy does it have to be? Just think about that. That is some shit that you would expect to see in a science fiction movie or book or something, but we were living it.

PEOPLE GET READY

So there we were, and then I begin to learn not only about myself and the ways that these others dudes were, but I begin to get confirmation on what I suspected. Even if their schools were on the other side of LA or if they lived somewhere else, we all had the same experience with school. We all had the same experience in trying to deal with housing, we all had the same experience in trying to get food, in trying to see that our younger brothers and sisters, nieces, and nephews all had a better way than what we had.

When I was back home, many of the big homies would try to encourage me to be on a righteous path and use my intellect for helping the hood. My mind state at the time was, we can try with all of our might to be on the righteous path and be the best individuals that we can be, but none of that can really counter so much of what we cannot control on the day-to-day. But then when I was up at camp, I was like, oh, shit, we really *can* control this. We really *can* start making this different, it just is not based on us being better individuals or anything having to do with our morals or ethics. Well, it is about morality, because you know I am real big on having moral principles, but not the type of moral principles that only work when I am subservient to you in some kind of way. That shit is not going to work. I am talking about having real integrity when dealing with me on a human level. That is the type of moral compass I am talking about. Anyway, I am there at camp and it hit me what we could really do if we really came together and made shit different.

We do a helluva job of organizing ourselves. I began thinking, what if we got all these hoods all over LA, where we are all going through the same shit—getting the same shitty-ass education, shitty-ass health care, shitty-ass jobs, shitty-ass housing, and get shitty answers to our very real questions? What if we all got together? Then it would be a whole different game. That is, in large part, why so many of us are locked up. I mean, we were the damn problem and they had to keep us locked away. They had to keep us from each other. Like I told you about the times that I would be walking with the homies and one of my best friends who was from El Salvador, and the police would always roll up on us and tell us that since it was three of us we had to disperse because we were considered a gang.

So anyway, when I get to the camps, I realize that if we all link up and get together then we can actually make some shit happen. Like the same shit that we as Black people have been going through in this country, in this city. This same shit is about to happen to all these folks coming here from Mexico, El Salvador, all over Central America. They have already perfected the shit on us! They have already locked us up, took our little bit of property, and threw us into the cages, camps, and halls. That shit is a done deal. In their minds, they already have a plan of action of how to move forward in order to make sure that things remain the same.

So, rather than beefing with each other and having the ability to turn on each other, we should link up and make our hoods even stronger. And I am not talking about some Kum-ba-ya type of stuff, I mean some real neighborhood-type stuff that will make all of this shit way different. Let's learn from one another. It's like, oh, so you know how to do this, let me teach you how to do *this*. And I ain't even trying to make money off you, I am trying to figure out how to live in a way that is going to make everyone's life better.

We all were working together out there, and were learning skills that were actually useful out there for that context. We were out in nature and we were doing things that were very appropriate for being out in the forest and the woods. I learned that nature is key to the whole process. Back home we may not be able to grow those huge pine trees that were up there in the forest, but we could grow all kinds of fruits and vegetables. We live in the perfect environment to do all of that. You know what we don't need anymore, is any damn smog! Man, you see all of that pollution from the sky, it looks crazy. Now I know the easy thing to say would be to get rid of cars from off the street, that is the cause of the smog. But for me, that is the easy way out. What about all these damn refineries that we have all over the place. You drive over by the 405 over there in Long Beach and Carson and it looks like they built the damn city around a huge oil refinery. The environment can't take any of this.

A HOUSE IS NOT A HOME

But the environment is more than just the air and the ground. It is the people that make you whole. And this is what I missed more than anything else while I was locked up. That is one of the truly fucked-up things about being incarcerated in any form. Just think about what that means, to rip you from everything that you hold dear. They just take that from you. That is a cold situation. I don't know the logic behind that other than just being down-right evil. I mean, if you really had my best interest in mind, how in the hell do you think taking me away from the people who I love the most is going to solve those problems? Then think about it from the other side. Very often you are taking away people who really help out in their community and neighborhoods. In addition to putting food on the table or helping pay some of the bills, you are taking away people who have been instrumental in creating a new kind of life for the neighborhood. It is just a foul system.

When I was away from my family, all I could think about was how they were doing. My granny was sick and I did not know what was going on with her. I had been trying to watch over my brother and I did not know what was going on with him. Then you are in there and your mind starts overthinking. You can start to think, like, oh man, this is all my fault. Like if my granny dies while I am locked up, then it is my fault that it happened. Or if something happens to my brother, then that is my fault. Now take all of those little thoughts and multiply them times a hundred or a thousand, and that is what you have going on while you are locked up. Then, say something does happen, now you've got to deal with all that guilt and grief. There are no psychologists around, and if they are around, then you don't trust them because you have no idea where that information is going back to. So you just hold all of that in. Walking around with all of this just raw emotional feeling, and you can't do anything with it because you are locked up and the guards are just looking for a reason to get some work in. So you just hold all of this in, and then you get sent back home and you have to deal with all of that. How fucked up is that?

We are talking about kids here. You know, we are still trying to work shit out and figure out how the world operates, and you are playing with our minds at such a young age and there is no one there to support us. And they know that all of this is bad for your mind and overall health. They have had prisons around for long enough to know that what is happening is not healthy. It is like some crazy long-term experiment or something. I swear we were the mice in those experiments where they take the mice and separate them from their family just to see what happens. With all of their psychologists and supposed experts who know so much about prisons and what prisons do to us, they really are just experimenting, because all of us who have been locked up, we already know what in the hell it does.

Then when you get back home, everything is all messed up, because now you have to deal with all of the shit that you have been going through while you were away in addition to all of the just regular shit that you got to deal with on the day-to-day. This is then what creates a hostile situation. It creates people being on edge and who are ready to snap at any minute. Folks are not in their right state of mind, because they have been pushed to the brink. Then when something does go down—as can be expected—guess what, you get sent right back to the place that just made a bad situation worse. This truly makes no sense at all.

And I haven't talked about the stress that it puts on your family. Just being locked up that far away and what that means for them. I mean, you really can't even put a number on it. Think about this—there are no phone calls, no visitations, no real contact. Can you imagine the type of stress that puts on grandmothers, aunts, uncles, moms, dads, and children? You know I told you about my granny being sick, and you know she wants nothing more than to see her grandchildren doing well and living life to the fullest, and how do you think she is doing when you begin to pull away family like that? Like, why would you put kids—and I am talking about kids—that far away from their family and loved ones?

But you know, this is the United States of America. This is the country that perfected the separation of families. They literally ripped families apart and sold them across the whole damn country. So, it can't be a surprise that a country that would be that vicious and cruel would accept tearing families apart. We live in a country where that has been made normal. There really is no other way around it. This society is profoundly corrupt, and its corruption can be seen most clearly when looking at how it treats Black children.

And I am really talking about children, because you know, being locked up, you can really forget that we are talking about young kids here. That is the thing about jail, prison, all of that. Once you accept that you are really going to put somebody in that type of situation, you know, lock them up, you accept the fact that you do not view them as a human being. You don't care that they have a family, you don't care that they may have children of their own. You don't care because you don't see them as even worthy of breathing the same air as you or walking the same streets as you or damn sure having the same job, same house, or same type of lifestyle. You don't care and that is where we are. Then you go and put Black children in that situation, and that really shows what type of place that we live in.

You know, I thought about that a lot when I was locked up. I really thought about my family and the homies and what it means to continuously lock up people day after day, week after week, year after year, decade after decade. You know it ain't nothing for them to just throw crazy time at us. Three hundred years there, two hundred years there. It is like a sport or something to them. How can you really look at someone and just treat their life as if it is a game? It is something that I have never been able to fully understand. Just what kind of person does that make you, that you can treat someone else's life with so little value?

THE RETURN

These thoughts constantly went through my mind while I was locked up, and then one day, it was time to go back. It was like going back down into a deep hole in the bottom of the ocean. I did not know where I was going back to. Which is crazy, because I knew exactly where I was going back to in terms of the street, neighborhood, and everything. We took that same path back down the mountain that I told you about before, but now instead of seeing everything in grey, it was like everything was in bright color. I have never gone through any type of religious experience, but from what I understand, it is that moment of clarity, when you really see the world for what it is. It was like that. I had already felt like I knew a lot about where I came from and what my family, the homies, and the hood meant to me, but having that time to think just made me slightly more focused, you know. But also, I was mad, like really, really mad. With all of the time to think and reflect on life, it just got me thinking so much differently about my life, my family, and how all of that was just treated in such a matter-of-fact type of way. It was during that trip back home that I started to really think about how my time locked up was so much like my pop's when he was locked up. He was in prison for a good solid chunk of my life, and I think about what they did to me, to take someone like that from my life.

When I was younger, I found all of these old tapes that my dad sent my mom when he was locked up. There was a whole shoebox of tapes that she had kept that he sent her. So I started listening to them and I was just blown away. He was rapping on the tapes and was really flowing, and then I knew right then and there where I got my love for music and rapping. Our flow sounds just the same, and it is wild that the two of us can have the same love for music. You know, it made me so mad also, because I began thinking about all of the things that we shared in common, but I just never got to experience. Now, I am not saying that my life would have been different or that things would have gone better for me because of my dad in the picture. That is not it at all. I hear that type of stuff all the time and just laugh. I laugh because it is not just the fact of having a man around, and that bullshit about all boys need a man around to teach them to become a man is some garbage. What I am talking about is just having a parent around, somebody who could possibly understand me in the way that a parent could, that was taken away from me.

Like, what would it have been like to for him to have seen his son have the same love for music as himself? So at this point now, you are talking about jacking up two lives. You are talking about messing up his life, because who knows what it would have done for him as an adult? I mean, just seeing something that you helped create and now is a mirror of yourself. Like a walking mirror of yourself. All of your good qualities, all of your bad ones, all of the things that you love are right in front of you. How would that affect you as a person? I would like to think that it would have a profound effect upon him, and not saying that it would have improved his life or made him a better person, but that it would have given him experiences that otherwise he never would have had.

And that opportunity was all taken away when he was locked up, and for what? If you really care about people and you really think that people need to learn and grow, why would you send them somewhere where they are going to be stunted in life? I mean, that is what being locked up seemed like to me. Sure, I had time to think, because I had more time, but I also realized very quickly that I am not actually experiencing the things that I will need to actually function in the world. So, if I have a child when I am locked up, and then when I get out that child is sixteen or seventeen years old, what in the hell am I supposed to do? You just locked me up, and now how am I supposed to relate to this person? I don't have the skills to do so. I have the words, sure, because I have been thinking all that time, but I don't have the experience and skills to actually actively contribute to their lives.

Let alone the fact that I don't have a job or anything that I can contribute resource-wise to their lives. So that is going to just add more drama to the situation, because now there is going to be problems between me and the child's mother. Then add to that the child who is wondering, where in the heck did you go, why did you leave? All of these things happen now, and for what? What was the point of doing all of that?

Then on the other end of the equation, you have the child. So in my situation, having my dad around would not have meant that I would have been a better man or anything like that, or even know the difference between right and wrong and all of that stuff. My mom, granny, aunts, and cousins, I learned how to become a human being from having these people around. I had love in my family, so it is nothing like that. It just blew my mind when I heard him on those tapes, because all I could think of is what it would have been like to have someone around who could have taught me everything that he knew. And shit, maybe I would not have been the best student or would have fought back, but all I can think about is the fact that there is so much that we had in common and yet we hardly spent any time together, and how much different my life could have been from that perspective. All of that was taken away because of the way that we just rip people away from their families.

This is all going through my mind as we make our way back home. I can see things that I have not seen in a long time. Everything is coming into color. The streets look the same, I know where I am and what I am up against. But at that moment, I also knew what I had to do and how much of a challenge it would be, but the moment was ripe for me. I knew what I could do in the hood. I knew that I could get everyone on the same page. For some reason, I can't put my finger on it, but I have always been able to get people together and ready to move into action. But more importantly, I have always had passion. Whatever it was that I was doing, I knew that I had to do it to the highest level. That is how I saw my situation going back home. I had so much love for the hood, but I wanted to see my homies thrive and I knew that we had to get right because we had a large task ahead of us. This whole prison shit, this whole not having a home, not having any food or being able to go to the doctor—all of this shit was over. It was time to get things moving in the right direction. When I stepped off that bus, I knew things would never be the same.

The Price of Freedom

Virtually everyone from the neighborhood who walked through the doors of SCL had either served time or had an immediate family member or close friend who served time in the myriad of carceral networks throughout the city, county, and state. The carceral state in this manner was the most pressing and readily identifiable marker of any vestige of state life within the community. More so than any other state structure, carcerality permeated throughout the lives of so many Black Angelenos. It also was all-encompassing in its approach, encroaching upon the lives of the young, the elderly, men, women, it truly knew no bounds.

The question/framing/context that Marley and his comrades wrestled with was how and why carcerality had such an outsized impact upon Black life in the neighborhood. Being voracious learners, they demanded that more study was needed to understand the processes that facilitated the growth of the carceral state.

•   •   •

Perhaps the most infamous case of government subterfuge and malfeasance in the city of Los Angeles involved Geronimo Ji Jaga (formerly Elmer Gerard Pratt). Ji Jaga was a member of the LA chapter of the Black Panther Party (BPP) and trained as a soldier in the United States armed forces. Ji Jaga did two tours of duty in Vietnam and put his skill set to use when he came back to the United States and rose through the ranks to become minister of defense of the LA BPP. He would later state that he was instructed by a group of elders, a loose conglomerate better known as the Deacons of Defense, to enlist in the military to get the training and bring it back to fight against agents of white supremacy. A very effective strategist, Ji Jaga was instrumental in keeping several members of the Panthers alive when the Los Angeles Police Department (LAPD) raided their headquarters on December 8, 1969. Given a tip that the LAPD was going to attack the building with the intent on killing as many Panthers as possible, the Panthers barricaded themselves in military fashion and not one member of the group was killed.

In large part due to his effectiveness as a strategist and organizer, Ji Jaga was targeted by both the city of Los Angeles and the national government as a person to monitor and later to "neutralize." In a very deliberate miscarriage of justice, he was arrested and charged with the attempted murder and murder of Keith and Caroline Olsen. The trial had garnered significant news attention and was dubbed the Santa Monica Tennis Court Murder. Ji Jaga was convicted of the murder of Caroline Olsen from evidence that largely hinged on the testimony of an LAPD informant, Julius Butler. Butler, who was a member of the BPP, would later be identified as an informant working in tandem with both the LAPD and the FBI in an effort to thwart the efforts of the BPP.

Butler wrote in a letter that found its way to the LAPD and the FBI that Ji Jaga bragged about killing Caroline Olsen. Butler's letter was countered by Ji Jaga's defense where he stated that he was in Oakland, California, at a BPP meeting with members of the Oakland chapter. Ji Jaga was convicted of the murder in 1972, sentenced to life in prison, and immediately began the long fight for release from prison. He was finally released in 1997, thanks in large part to FBI counterintelligence documents that revealed that Ji Jaga was indeed in Oakland. The gross irony is that this became substantiated as state fact, as the FBI was keeping strict surveillance on Ji Jaga and was fully aware that he was in Oakland on the date and time of the murder.

Ji Jaga's countless appeals revealed the depths to which the city and national governments went in order to suppress the work of the Panthers in Los Angeles. The plot by the FBI to counter the work of the BPP was laid bare in its explicit attempts to destroy the organization. In a January 28, 1970, internal FBI memo to the FBI director that was made public during one of Ji Jaga's appeals, the correspondence stated:

> Bureau approval is requested in the creation of an anonymous paper underground to attack, expose, and ridicule the image of the BPP in the community and to foment mistrust and suspicion amongst the current and past membership, through participation and dissemination of information embarrassing to the BPP.... Operation Number One is designed to challenge the legitimacy of the authority exercised by ELMER GERARD PRATT, BPP Deputy Minister of Defense for Southern California, and JOHN WILLIAM WASHINGTON, an active member of the BPP in Los Angeles. (McCloskey 1980)

This was followed up six months later by a memo within the LA FBI office that stated, "Constant consideration is given to the possibility of the utilization of counter-intelligence measures with efforts being directed toward neutralizing PRATT as an effective BPP functionary" (McCloskey 1980).

While the case against Ji Jaga is a spectacular example of the lengths to which the LAPD and the FBI would go to eliminate the BPP, it was by no means an isolated affair. However, the case against Ji Jaga did tip off LA-based activist organizations that the level of surveillance, spying, and subterfuge was more intense than previously imagined. In the wake of rooting out the infiltration scheme that was at the heart of Ji Jaga's conviction, it was revealed that the LAPD had a secret intelligence division—Public Disorder Intelligence Division (PDID)—that had been infiltrating and spying on organizations for over five decades.

The unit that became PDID was founded in the 1920s and was heavily focused on the activities of the Communist Party in the City of Los Angeles. By the late 1960s, the unit had expanded its capacity and had detailed records on countless organizations and people including the

Industrial Workers of the World (IWW, or Wobblies), labor organizers, interned Japanese and Japanese Americans whose land and homes were taken from them in the 1940s, anti–Vietnam War demonstrators, and general "subversives." The unit became much more refined and was organized into a formal part of the bureaucratic structure of the LAPD at the close of the 1960s. In 1970 it was reconstituted under the Division of Special Services and given the designation Public Disorder Intelligence Division. Even by the LAPD's own admission, the focus of the PDID until the mid-1970s was "intelligence gathering ... directed towards organizations or individuals with 'subversive' ideologies" (Los Angeles Board of Police Commissioners 1975).

It was during this critical period that Ji Jaga's appeals were revealing the extent to which the LAPD had been involved in the attempted destruction of the LA chapter of the BPP. Having the acute sense that something much larger was afoot, activist organizations and legal advocates wanted to understand the depths of the LAPD's infiltration. The initial push was a twofold campaign. On the first front, the American Civil Liberties Union (ACLU) launched a lawsuit against the LAPD in an effort to release access of the PDID files and their contents to the public or at the very least to the people and organizations who were the target of the LAPD's infiltration schemes. The second campaign was spearheaded by a group of organizations in which Dr. Mae Churchill, director of the Urban Policy Research Institute, played a major role. The primary objective of the group was to build up a wide base of support in the effort to abolish the PDID. Corresponding with a wide array of city, county, state, and national officials, this collective doggedly pressured officials to shut down the intelligence-gathering arm of the LAPD.

Rather than comply with the wishes of the lawsuit and in an effort to stave off closure, in 1975 the LAPD took the very drastic step of destroying over two million files before the public could view the records. Further, the agency refused to grant access to the remaining files on the grounds of "public safety." However, the ACLU had serious doubts that the LAPD had decided to destroy the files without any contingency plans. In response to the LAPD's action, Ramona Ripston of the ACLU stated, "We wonder about the purported, and I say purported, recent destruction of almost 2 million old index cards after a period of 50 years. One wonders why. We have recently gone through a period where those in high places, oblivious to the right of the governed, have publicly stated they would have been wiser to destroy incriminating evidence. A good way to insulate yourself from civil damage actions is to have destroyed the evidence" (Townsend 1975).

While the lawsuit and subsequent action by the LAPD did not result in the viewing of the documents, as part of a negotiated settlement, the LAPD was forced to provide an audit of the organizations that the PDID had infiltrated and surveilled over the fifty-year time period. The list revealed that the PDID had kept detailed information on more than 170 organizations that included the Black Panther Party, the Black Liberation Army, the Nation of Islam, US Organization, Black student unions from several California State and University of California schools, the Southern Christian Leadership Conference, the Community Freedom School, the Black Guerrilla Family, and the Congress of African People. The fallout from the named organizations was tremendous, as the LAPD became increasingly defensive about the PDID and its intent. In reaction to the fallout from the news coverage and organizing against the PDID, the LAPD attempted to draw a proverbial line in the sand to separate the bad intentions of the previous regime to surveil "subversive" organizations from a new iteration of the PDID that sought to maintain public safety.

In order to achieve this goal, the LAPD agreed to develop a new set of guidelines for the PDID as a means to rebrand the unit. In 1976, the LAPD set forth new guidelines to legislate the parameters of the PDID. One of the major shifts was to move from surveilling "subversive" people and organizations to those that were "threatening" to "public order." With the new guidelines set in place, the LAPD attempted to squelch the concerns of the pending lawsuit and wrestle public opinion back onto their side. Yet, the LAPD would not get off so easily, as organizations such as the Urban Policy Research Institute placed forth a detailed analysis that spoke to the major problems of the new guidelines. Writing directly to the Board of Police Commissioners, Dr. Churchill shared a general consensus among communal organizations that the new PDID guidelines strengthened the unit rather than limited its power.

In her correspondence to the Board, Churchill stated:

Careful reading of the proposed standards and procedures for the public disorder intelligence division reveals the following:

1) Evasion of the fundamental constitutional question, namely, the right of police to collect, analyze, record, store and disseminate information on individuals and/or organizations charged with no crime but perceived by police as "threatening" to "public order," as defined by police.

2) No amount of legalese language can conceal the basic fact that the police commission, presumably representing citizens of Los Angeles and presumably responsible for the lawful operation of the Police Department, is proposing to legitimize, by administrative fiat, a largely covert operation seriously threatening to individual privacy, chilling to the rights of assembly, freedom of speech and other cherished American values.

3) Not only are the police authorized to initiate and maintain files on thousands of individuals and organizations; they are completely anonymous in their operation, accountable only internally within a sealed system. (Churchill 1976, 1–2)

At the close of her letter, she reframed the function of the PDID as an apparatus of ideological contestation. Rather than having the "public's" interests in mind, there was a concerted effort by organizers to clearly articulate that the PDID was an agent of political and social repression. In the last paragraph of her letter she argued:

In conclusion: since the operation of a political intelligence division within the Los Angeles Police Department is of dubious constitutionality as well as dubious effectiveness, I urge that the board of police commissioners abolish the division and require the police department to protect the public order by constitutional means. (Churchill 1976, 4)

Churchill's reframing of the "public intelligence division" to the "political intelligence division" signifies the magnitude of the role and function of the police within the social and political landscape of Los Angeles. The organizations that were being targeted were putting forth policy, plans, and practices that radically altered the political, economic, racial, and gendered geographies of a harsh racial capitalist nightmare. The established hierarchies that subjected countless Angelenos to far too little food, minimal health care, a sordid education system, and decrepit, if any, housing demanded unquestioned adherence to a multiracial fantasy that was void of a material reality. The on-the-ground struggle revealed that in order to dampen the social visions of those who knew better, the LAPD was utilized as the "heavy hand" in order to ensure that the callous devices of gross exploitation remained intact.

Rather than hyperbolic rhetoric used to rile up crowds, the descriptors exercised by organizers such as Churchill were rooted in the fact that, although the PDID claimed that it limited its techniques to "threatening" organizations, the LAPD was being far from truthful. Not only did the new guidelines provide the PDID with far more leeway to infiltrate a wide swath of organizations, it was not transparent in its audit procedures and continued to infiltrate organizations that directly challenged the power of Los Angeles's governing elite. Speaking to the problematics of the new guidelines, Churchill was a part of a committee that sought to expose the true intentions of the newly established guidelines. In direct response to the guidelines, the committee issued a report that detailed key problems with the new branding of the PDID. The report was broken down into sections that provided a step-by-step analysis of the new guidelines and procedures set forth in the PDID's purported new turn to the public good. One of the key issues raised in the report was the questioning of key terms:

On Basic Definitions

1. Who is to define what acts are ideologically motivated?
2. Who is to define what acts may result in a disruption of the public order?
3. Are gatherings of more than one person in front of a building which may result in the blocking of citizens' access to that place an act of public disorder? Is a picket line?
4. Is mere participation in a demonstration which ended up being declared an "illegal gathering" enough of a basis for inclusion?
5. Is advocating or planning such a demonstration sufficient for an organization or individual to be included?
6. And if the police, themselves, are the ones to declare an act or demonstration an illegal gathering, can they be expected to be the sole definers of what is, for the purpose of the files, to be considered advocacy or participation in an act of public disruption?
7. Is this not a merging of the legislative and administrative functions? (Citizens Committee of Inquiry 1975, 1)

In addition, through alluding to cases such as Geronimo Ji Jaga's, they pointed out the glaring pitfalls located in the newly constructed methods, which appeared to be pathways to justify techniques of entrapment:

Sources of Information

Clearly the events of the last years have shown us that intelligence reports are, at times, generated by agents, informers, and agent provocateurs, not on the basis of what they have seen or heard, but rather in order to meet the expectations of their superiors or to maintain employment. In other instances, we have learned that it is the informer or agent themselves that have created the advocacy or the plan. Nothing in this section corrects or inhibits the use of erroneous data, unreliable and self-seeking informants or the all-too-pervasive agent provocateur.

1. Where is the prohibition of illegal methods of surveillance?
2. Where are the controls on agents, informers or agent provocateurs?
3. Where is the prohibition of entrapment, the encouragement of illegal acts, etc.?

4. What shall be the cause that generates an investigation?
5. Who shall be held responsible for the initiation of an investigation which results in inclusion of a group or individual in the files?
6. Who is to attest to the validity of information? (Citizens Committee of Inquiry 1975, 3)

The concerns of the committee turned out to be prophetic when, in 1979, the American Friends Service Committee published a nationwide study of the relationship between dissension and government in the United States titled *Police Threat to Political Liberty.* Among the key cases highlighted in the report were the sordid details of the LAPD's attempt to suppress the organizing efforts of the Coalition Against Police Abuse (CAPA):

In March 1978 one of the organizations in the Citizens' Commission found that it had been infiltrated by an LAPD undercover officer. This organization, the Coalition Against Police Abuse (CAPA), had obtained a partial list of LAPD officers, and the name of CAPA's secretary, Georgia Odom, was on the list. CAPA and the Citizens' Commission decided to investigate the matter further, and after obtaining Odom's voter registration affidavit and other public documents, concluded that she was, in fact, a police officer. Odom had belonged to CAPA for over two years. She had worked quietly in the background and had slowly risen to a position of trust and leadership. As secretary of the organization she had access to membership lists and was responsible for the minutes of the meetings. Odom also involved herself in numerous demonstrations against officer-involved shootings. In 1977, she attended several demonstrations organized by the friends of Ron Burkholder, a group which was seeking an investigation into a fatal shooting of a Los Angeles man by an LAPD officer. Odom attempted to disrupt the protests by chanting anti-police slogans. This created dissension among members of the group, most of whom preferred silent vigils to rancorous demonstrations....

The citizens commission and CAPA began quietly to circulate a list among progressive and liberal groups in Los Angeles. Two more names surfaced. Eddie Solomon, another member of CAPA, an office manager for the National Alliance Against Racism and Political Repression, was one of the suspected other officers. Solomon had been active in progressive groups, including the Young Workers Liberation League, for almost 3 years. He was a quiet, diligent man who tended to steer clear of internal political disputes. An investigation revealed that Solomon, too, was a police officer.

Cheryl Bell, a young woman active in the anti-nuclear movement, was the third suspect. Another quiet, "background" person, Bell had participated in the alliance for survival for a little more than a year. She was also active in the committee on nuclear information at California State University in Los Angeles, where she was ostensibly attending classes as a full-time student. Bell's identity was not confirmed until the following August.

Odom, Solomon and Bell all subsequently dropped out of sight when the covers were blown. Odom is now working in the South Central division as a "community relations officer." Solomon is working in uniform in the Hollywood division. Bell's status is not known. (American Friends Service Committee 1979, 41–42)

Informed by the vast spy operation launched against CAPA, organizations across Los Angeles banded together to counter the actions of the LAPD. They launched a forty-plus-member collective—the Citizens Commission on Police Repression. Included were CAPA, the Urban Policy Research Institute, the Black Panther Party, La Raza Unida, the Feminist Women's Health Center, Union of Lesbian and Gay Men, and Radical Women. The organization set in motion several lawsuits, procedural changes, political education campaigns, and strategic tactics to limit the power of the LAPD. One of the immediate effects that the Citizens Commission had was to illuminate the insidious tactics that were utilized by the LAPD in order to gain information on organizations. Ranging in actions from sexual impropriety and manipulation to tampering with court files, the LAPD's desire to root out radical politics knew no bounds (Johnston 1982).

The influence of the Citizens Commission expanded as institutions across the region found that they were the subject of the LAPD's nefarious plan. In 1982, the Student Senate at the California State University, Northridge (CSUN), which represented the CSUN student body, approved a measure to file a lawsuit against the LAPD. The basis of the suit was the discovery that during a seven-year period, undercover LAPD agents had infiltrated student organizations and monitored the teaching of university professors on the college campus. With an explicit focus on Black and Mexican American student organizations, courses, and professors, the agents reported their findings back to the PDID (Nordwind 1982; Campaign for Political Rights 1982). The filing of the CSUN lawsuit came on the heels of a lawsuit filed by a group of Black ministers who had been organizing against the infamous LAPD murder of Eula Love. It came to the ministers' attention that the cochairman of a protest march was an undercover police officer who operated as an agent provocateur and attempted to incite violence in what was originally planned to be a peaceful march (Sappell 1982).

In addition to the filing of lawsuits, there was a demand put forward for the establishment of a citizens' review board that would have extensive power to curtail the reach of the LAPD. As stated in the mission of the proposed review board:

> Any effective Review Board must contain the following:
>
> 1. The Board must be formed and controlled by that section of the community that has been most abused by the police, mainly poor and minority people.
> 2. Its make-up must consist of people democratically chosen from the community and subject to total recall by the community.
> 3. Our Review Board must include an independent special prosecutor to replace the District Attorney's office which has not, to date, indicted any LA officers for murderous shootings or chokeholds.
> 4. Our Review Board must include special investigators to replace the LAPD's Internal Affairs Division. We fail to see how police can objectively investigate police crimes; in fact, many times in the past, it has been shown that they are illegally covering up police crimes.
> 5. Our Review Board should include a section that will investigate the many illegal acts of spying and harassment by the LAPD and PDID (Public Disorder and Intelligence Division).

6. Our Review Board should have access to records and vital information of incidents in which police officers are involved. (Interim Steering Committee of the Coalition for a Civilian Review Board 1979)

In the midst of the struggle over the future of the PDID, the LAPD doubled down on the need for the PDID and adopted the language of terrorism as a means to justify not only its existence but expansion. In a 1980 press conference regarding the 1984 Summer Olympics (which were to be held in Los Angeles), LAPD chief Daryl Gates pleaded his case that the PDID division needed to be bolstered in order to prevent international terrorism from spilling over into Los Angeles during the Olympic Games. Given that the PDID's budget had been cut in light of the lawsuits and reports of spying, Gates made a bold move to use the 1984 Olympics as a springboard to increase funding and resources for the PDID (Johnston 1980). Yet, despite Gates's attempts to revive the PDID, the coalition against the secret division proved to be too much for Gates to endure. However, rather than fold in defeat, the LAPD changed tactics and in many respects emerged a more powerful force.

Realizing that the fight for the PDID was facing a monumental challenge, the LAPD was able to reorient the division within the rhetoric of the time period. Rather than focus on issues of "subservience," "disorder," and "ideology," the new unit had a new prime directive: terrorism. Informed by national discussions pertaining to the Cold War, but more importantly by the increased connection that linked Black organizations such as the Crips and Bloods to a terroristic framework, the LAPD jumped headfirst into the racket of "defense against terrorism." The PDID unit was effectively dropped from the department and replaced by the Anti-Terror Division (ATD). While the LAPD was castigated as the lone wolf in the case of PDID, the ATD found much support from county and city legislators who champion the cause of taking down Black organizations in the name of fighting domestic terror. The zenith of this alliance was codified into law with the passage of the Street Terrorism Enforcement and Prevention (STEP) Act in California in 1988. The LAPD no longer had to act in a clandestine manner to achieve its goals as the STEP Act effectively rendered Black organizations such as the Crips and Bloods as residents of a police state.

The guidelines of the STEP Act provided the means for the state attorney and district attorneys' offices across the state to develop procedures to limit the freedoms of Black people. One of the results of these procedures was gang injunctions. In Los Angeles County, the test-case model, established in Norwalk, California, was successfully utilized throughout the region. Following the test run in Norwalk, the City of Pasadena worked in conjunction with the District Attorney's Office to effectively quarantine the mobility and action of the Pasadena Denver Lanes, a Blood set based in Pasadena, California. One of the first steps of the injunction was to issue a temporary restraining order on the group and anybody associated with the organization. The list of who was affiliated was left to the discretion of the police, who were granted autonomy to place all known members and affiliates within an ever-growing gang database. As issued by the restraining order, anybody associated with the Denver Lanes was prohibited from the following within the one-mile radius that was considered to be the hub of the Denver Lanes community:

a) Selling, possessing, or using any controlled substances or related paraphernalia, including rolling papers and straight shooters, without a prescription;

b) Remaining in the presence of anyone selling, possessing, or using controlled substance-related paraphernalia without prescription;

c) Possessing or using any pager, beeper, cellular phone, or walkie-talkie in any public space;

d) Approaching or signaling to any vehicle on any street, alleyway, or other area of public passage, thus causing the vehicle to stop, unless legitimate emergency situations are required;

e) Throwing a rock, bottle, brick, or any other item at a vehicle, animal or person;

f) Blocking the free passage of any person or vehicle on any street, walkway, sidewalk, driveway, alleyway, or other area of public passage;

g) Riding a bicycle in any public space;

h) Being present or causing others to be present, on the private property of others, except (1) with the prior written consent of the person in lawful possession of the property, or (2) in the presence and with the voluntary consent of the person in lawful possession of the property;

i) Being present on the premises of an uninhabited or abandoned apartment or building;

j) Being present on the roof of any building, or climbing over any fence or wall, unless a legitimate emergency situation so requires;

k) Acting as a lookout, whistling, yelling "Five-O" or "One Time," or otherwise signaling with a flashlight or other means to warn another person of approaching law-enforcement officer, or soliciting, encouraging or employing another to do so;

l) If under the age of 18, being in a public space between the hours of 10 P.M. on any day, and sunrise of the immediately following day, unless (1) accompanied by a parent or legal guardian, or by spouse 18 years of age or older, or (2) performing an errand directed by a parent or legal guardian, or by a spouse 18 years of age or older, or (3) returning directly home from a public meeting, or a place of public entertainment, such as movie, play, sporting event, dance or school activity, or (4) actively engaged in some business, trade, profession, or occupation with requires such presence;

m) If 18 years of age or older, being in a public space between midnight on any day and sunrise of the immediately following day, unless (1) going to/from a legitimate meeting or entertainment activity, or (2) actively engaged in some business, trade, profession or occupation which requires such presence;

n) Making, causing, or encouraging others to violate noise restrictions as defined in P.M.C. 9.36.020 et. seq., including playing loud music; participating in loud parties; and engaging in exhibitions of speed in vehicles with the attendant noise, roaring engines, and screeching tires;

o) Fighting in public or any space open to public view or hearing;

p) Harassing, intimidating, threatening to peace or safety of any person, including by the use of vulgar or abusive language, whether in retribution for any past complaint or to prevent a future complaint about Defendant's gang activities, including complaints to law enforcing officers;

q) Gambling, including playing of cards, dice, or dominoes for money, in public or any place open to public view. (*City of Pasadena v. Denver Lanes* 1995)

The end result proved to be that the injunctions were much less about targeting terroristic plots than about stamping out dissent and agents of rebellion. This distinction, of course, was not lost upon the CAPA, which fought against both the establishment of the ATD and the gang injunction procedure.

The absurdity of the fight against the PDID in the 1970s was that by the 1990s, the spy tactics were not as pressing, given that the burgeoning carceral state effectively made the suppression of Black people a part of the state bureaucratic process. The result was the rapid increase of Black youth into the expanding juvenile carceral system that sent Black youth from areas such as South Central Los Angeles to far-flung regions of the county. Once the order was granted, which was a matter of procedure, and the injunction was formerly placed upon the organization, matters of due process and civility were off the table as fines and prison sentence guidelines were drastically increased. Youth were tried as adults and sentences, which had previously been contested as too long by CAPA, were now doubled and in some cases tripled. The effect was that rather than spy upon Black organizations, the LAPD, now in lockstep with city and state officials, could "legally" suppress Black freedom.

It is only after decades of fighting from organizations such as CAPA that the absurdity of incarceration has been made apparent on a local and national level. However, while many claim victory, it is ever-important to heed the lessons of the fight over the PDID and be prepared for the next reactive move against Black freedom.

Closing Note

Freedom on the Mind

VERSE ONE

OCTAVIA BUTLER: "What I wanted to write was a novel of someone who was coming up with solutions of the sort. My main character's solution ... grows from another religion that she comes up with. Religion is everywhere."

MARLEY: "I am here for a reason. My purpose has yet to be fulfilled. There are too many times when I should have been killed or died. You can call it God, Allah, whatever you want, but there is a higher power that has made sure that I stayed alive. My community needs me. My story is not done."

Visions, or religion, provide a guide, a path to a life that extends beyond the here and now. For Black people, visions have been at the center of "breaking on through to the other side." Contrary to popular depictions via cinematic and written mediascapes, Black people do not think of themselves as downtrodden or relish their own trauma. Rather, they have relied upon visions of other worlds, other places, other times, and conjured realties to craft a more humane existence.

Marley's life is indicative of not only the beautiful struggle that is Black existence, but more important, the power of belief in a vision that extends beyond the individual experience. Marley wanted freedom and liberation for his entire community. The conventional reaction is to laud Marley if only he had ascended into the classical narrative of the individual hero who positioned his community as something that he had to overcome. Marley was and still is not interested in personal accolades or achievements. He had several opportunities to turn his life into a trope and become a poster child for foundation-based campaigns and state projects that laud the success of wayward souls and their return to the proverbial fold of the respectable citizen. No doubt, this would have secured him a modicum of financial security and enabled him to bridge that story into future endeavors that very easily could have turned into greater personal success. But as Marley has told me several times, he is interested in only one thing: Black freedom. In this way, Marley is a portal into understanding the impulse, driven by visions, of Black people living in Black communities around the world. Freedom is on the mind. A freedom that is not dictated by an edict of exploitation, manipulation, and conquest. It is a freedom that allows for the multiplicity of life to exist at the same time.

> REFRAIN (MARLEY): We need strategies for living . . . We are working to get free and that means making a better world right now, not just for when we are gone.

In the midst of not knowing where you are going to sleep, when or where your next meal is going to come from, the next occasion to bathe or just exhale without worry in the midst of constant stress is a vision, a path forward, that not only does away with the horrors of this world but is focused on the possibilities that have existed in past lives and future undertakings. Such visions have been the imperative of Black liberation struggles. In the face of Marley's direct inquiries and demands upon his schools, housing officials, and employment officers, the response has been consistent: do the impossible. You want a housing voucher? Find your way to an office building twenty miles away between the hours of 8:00 A.M. and 10:00 A.M. and make sure you have proof that you do not have housing and do not have any income. You want more health services in your neighborhood? Well, we would love to help, but there is not any money or space for such facilities. Yet there is money to build new police substations and leave lots vacant until they become profitable enough to develop. The absurdity never fell flat upon Marley. "If they want me to make manna fall from the sky, I'm going to do it on my own terms." And thus, from a very young age, visions take shape and form into a collective apparition of known worlds and profound possibilities.

VERSE TWO

The interplay between the A side and the B side represents a way of looking backward to move forward. The political education courses, workshops, and symposiums that were and continued to be held at SCL are a critical component to the communal organizing logic against the multifaceted nature of the carceral state within Southern California. The archives housed at SCL were eagerly embraced by Marley and his peers as a way to understand how to live. Learning about tactics, strategies, successes, and failures was critical in order to develop a politics of liberation that was a part and parcel of Black radical genealogies that demanded rigorous analysis. While such a methodology might seem commonplace, it must be stated that the social milieu within which the story was told continues to be dominated by narratives of Black suffering and trauma. Yet, the archives from the Coalition Against Police Abuse, the Urban Policy Research Institute, and the Los Angeles chapter of the Black Panther Party reveal that the positioning of Black people as bedazzled, trauma-ridden spectacles has been an age-old tactic that seeks to diminish Black radical thinking, planning, and action.

The result was a symbiosis of thought. Black people in South Central Los Angeles did not claim suffering as a politics; rather, it was a readily available frame provided by a variety of state actors including foundations, schools, and health care professionals. The archives reified the genealogical presence of these inclinations and situated the experiential within a broader context of historical reality.

> REFRAIN (MARLEY): We need strategies for living ... We are working to
> get free and that means making a better world right now, not just for
> when we are gone.

The energy and spirit of Marley and his comrades was a constant drive, an unrelenting set of demands that did not acquiesce to the trappings or heavy hand of the broad range of liberal and draconian state tactics. Similarly, the politics of the Southern California Library inform the need to reframe the terms of analysis and thus debate. In the middle of the A side and B side is the archive of the experiences, cultural mores, and traditions of Black life that expose the fallacy of carceral-generated myths centered in Black suffering, misery, and pain. The complexity of Black life is revealed in the fact that the state cannot squelch Black love: a love that supported each other when there was no place to sleep, when disengagement was the only solution, when the state failed to keep its promise, or when freedom was taken, no matter the reason. It is a requited love that is constantly paid forward, yet it is not always easy to process as the frame demands Black repentance for unabashedly loving each other. Thus, the connective tissue that binds the archival material to the present is an ethos of love and unabashed embrace of Black people.

VERSE THREE

There were many funerals, visits to the hospital, late-night phone calls, and tense moments of high anxiety. There were also birthday parties, cookouts, easy conversations, and times of extreme jubilation. In the midst of the proverbial ups and downs, the joy and pain, there was the consistent knowing that the vision was not fulfilled. Marley is still organizing, planning, studying methods to achieve freedom for his community. The Southern California Library is still standing as a critical community hub of intellectual, emotional, social, and cultural support. It is by no stretch of the imagination idyllic.

In many respects things have gotten worse since Marley and I first met over ten years ago. The community, designated as the Vermont Corridor by the City of Los Angeles, has suffered from carceral-based policies and legislation that have literally swept people from off the street. What once was a vibrant space, with a constant flow of people on street corners and walking, is very often eerily quiet and sometimes desolate. The streets are lined with cars as exploitative development schemes in Los Angeles have left far too many people without shelter, and vehicles have turned into homes. Many of those who organized with Marley are no longer in the neighborhood. Many have moved to neighboring states such as Nevada and Arizona in the hopes of living a life that is more humane. Many have been placed in the clutches of the carceral state. Many are on the brink.

> REFRAIN (MARLEY): We need strategies for living ... We are working to get free and that means making a better world right now, not just for when we are gone.

Yet, many still reside in the community and continue to live, to fight and struggle alongside each other. Similar to the political framing that emanates from the lives of Marley and his peers and from the ethos of the archives that are housed at the Southern California Library, there are no endings, there are only social visions that serve as guides, providing a metaphysical roadmap to another world. Passed down as communal knowledge, they exist in a subtle glance, head nod, and in moments of deep, rigorous study. Legible only to the believers, the struggle continues, and its beauty is profound.

GROUNDING MATERIALS

The writing of Joy and Pain *is indebted to the thinking, research, genius, and creativity of so many writers, artists, scholars, and teachers. The following provocation is an opening to the myriad of works that have been instrumental in the development of this book. Rather than a foreclosed experience, it represents merely the beginning of the process that documents the joy and pain of Black life. The stated categories below are merely for organizational purposes, but many of the texts can easily float betwixt and between each subheading. I offer this list as a starting point, and it is my hope that we can add to it in a collective fashion to document the multiplicity of Black liberatory theories, methods, and practices.*

THEORIES OF BLACKNESS

Alexander, M. Jacqui. 2005. *Pedagogies of Crossing: Meditations on Feminism, Sexual Politics, Memory, and the Sacred.* Durham, NC: Duke University Press.

Allen, Robert L. 1969. *Black Awakening in Capitalist America: An Analytic History.* Garden City, NY: Doubleday.

Borges, Sónia Vaz. 2019. *Militant Education, Liberation Struggle, Consciousness: The PAIGC Education in Guinea Bissau 1963–1978.* Berlin: Peter Lang.

Browne, Simone. 2015. *Dark Matters: On the Surveillance of Blackness.* Durham, NC: Duke University Press.

Du Bois, W.E. Burghardt. (1935) 1998. *Black Reconstruction in America, 1860–1880.* Edited by David Levering Lewis. New York: Free Press.

Fanon, Frantz. 2008. *Black Skin, White Masks.* Translated by Richard Philcox, foreword by Kwame Anthony Appiah. New York: Grove Press.

Harney, Stefano, and Fred Moten. 2013. *The Undercommons: Fugitive Planning and Black Study.* Wivenhoe, UK: Minor Compositions.

Kelley, Robin D. G. 1996. *Race Rebels: Culture, Politics, and the Black Working Class.* New York: Free Press.

McKittrick, Katherine. 2006. *Demonic Grounds: Black Women and the Cartographies of Struggle.* Minneapolis: University of Minnesota Press.

Robinson, Cedric J. 2007. *Forgeries of Memory and Meaning: Blacks and the Regimes of Race in American Theater and Film before World War II.* Chapel Hill: University of North Carolina Press.

———. 2021. *Black Marxism: The Making of the Black Radical Tradition.* Revised and updated 3rd ed. Chapel Hill: University of North Carolina Press.

Rodriguez, Dylan. 2020. *White Reconstruction: Domestic Warfare and the Logics of Genocide.* New York: Fordham University Press.

Sharpe, Christina. 2016. *In the Wake: On Blackness and Being.* Durham, NC: Duke University Press.

Snorton, C. Riley. 2017. *Black on Both Sides: A Racial History of Trans Identity.* Minneapolis: University of Minnesota Press.

Spillers, Hortense J. 1987. "Mama's Baby, Papa's Maybe: An American Grammar Book." *Diacritics* 17 (2): 65–81. https://doi.org/10.2307/464747.

Willoughby-Herard, Tiffany. 2015. *Waste of a White Skin: The Carnegie Corporation and the Racial Logic of White Vulnerability.* Oakland: University of California Press.

Wilson, Bobby M. 2019. *America's Johannesburg: Industrialization and Racial Transformation in Birmingham.* Reprint ed. Athens: University of Georgia Press.

Woods, Clyde Adrian. 2010. *In the Wake of Hurricane Katrina: New Paradigms and Social Visions.* Baltimore: Johns Hopkins University Press.

———. 2017. *Development Arrested: The Blues and Plantation Power in the Mississippi Delta.* 2nd ed. London: Verso.

Woodson, Carter Godwin. (1919) 2017. *The Education of the Negro Prior to 1861: A History of the Education of the Colored People of the United States from the Beginning of Slavery to the Civil War.* Midland Park, NJ: Pinnacle Press.

Wynter, Sylvia. 2003. "Unsettling the Coloniality of Being/Power/Truth/Freedom: Towards the Human, After Man, Its Overrepresentation—An Argument." *CR: The New Centennial Review* 3 (3): 257–337.

ETHNOGRAPHY

Alves, Jaime Amparo. 2018. *The Anti-Black City: Police Terror and Black Urban Life in Brazil*. Minneapolis: University Of Minnesota Press.

Ambikaipaker, Mohan. 2018. *Political Blackness in Multiracial Britain*. Philadelphia: University of Pennsylvania Press.

Camp, Jordan T. 2016. *Incarcerating the Crisis: Freedom Struggles and the Rise of the Neoliberal State*. Oakland: University of California Press.

Costa Vargas, João Helion. 2006. *Catching Hell in the City of Angels: Life and Meanings of Blackness in South Central Los Angeles. Foreword by Robin D. G. Kelley*. Minneapolis: University of Minnesota Press.

——. 2008. *Never Meant to Survive: Genocide and Utopias in Black Diaspora Communities*. Lanham, MD: Rowman and Littlefield.

Drake, St. Clair, and Horace R. Cayton. 2015. *Black Metropolis: A Study of Negro Life in a Northern City*. Foreword by Mary Pattillo. Enlarged ed. Chicago: University of Chicago Press.

Gordon, Edmund Tayloe. 1998. *Disparate Diasporas: Identity and Politics in an African Nicaraguan Community*. Austin: University of Texas Press and Institute of Latin American Studies.

Gregory, Steven. 2011. *Black Corona: Race and the Politics of Place in an Urban Community*. Princeton, NJ: Princeton University Press.

Grigsby, Julie Renee. 2014. "Grim Sleeper: Gender, Violence, and Reproductive Justice in Los Angeles." PhD diss., University of Texas at Austin. *https://doi.org/10.15781/T27H3D55Z*.

Jackson, John L., Jr. 2001. *Harlemworld: Doing Race and Class in Contemporary Black America*. Chicago: University of Chicago Press.

Lara, Ana-Maurine. 2021. *Queer Freedom / Black Sovereignty*. Albany: State University of New York Press.

Perry, Keisha-Khan Y. 2013. *Black Women against the Land Grab: The Fight for Racial Justice in Brazil*. Minneapolis: University of Minnesota Press.

Reese, Ashanté M. 2019. *Black Food Geographies: Race, Self-Reliance, and Food Access in Washington, D.C.* Chapel Hill: University of North Carolina Press.

Rosa, Jonathan. 2019. *Looking like a Language, Sounding like a Race: Raciolinguistic Ideologies and the Learning of Latinidad*. New York: Oxford University Press.

Shange, Savannah. 2019. *Progressive Dystopia: Abolition, Antiblackness, and Schooling in San Francisco*. Durham, NC: Duke University Press Books.

Skipper, Jodi. 2022. *Behind the Big House: Reconciling Slavery, Race, and Heritage in the U.S. South*. Iowa City: University Of Iowa Press.

Vaught, Sabina E. 2017. *Compulsory: Education and the Dispossession of Youth in a Prison School.* Minneapolis: University of Minnesota Press.

Williams, Bianca C. 2018. *The Pursuit of Happiness: Black Women, Diasporic Dreams, and the Politics of Emotional Transnationalism.* Durham, NC: Duke University Press.

Williams, Erica Lorraine. 2013. *Sex Tourism in Bahia: Ambiguous Entanglements.* Urbana: University of Illinois Press, National Women's Studies Association.

Wun, Connie. 2016. "Against Captivity: Black Girls and School Discipline Policies in the Afterlife of Slavery." *Educational Policy* 30 (1): 171–96.

LOS ANGELES

Banks, Ingrid, Gaye Johnson, George Lipsitz, Ula Y. Taylor, Daniel Widener, Clyde Adrian Woods, and Santa Barbara Center for Black Studies Research University of California. 2012. *Black California Dreamin': The Crises of California's African-American Communities* Santa Barbara: UCSB, Center for Black Studies Research.

Campbell, Marne L. 2016. *Making Black Los Angeles: Class, Gender, and Community, 1850–1917.* Chapel Hill: University of North Carolina Press.

Davis, Mike. 2006. *City of Quartz: Excavating the Future in Los Angeles.* New ed. London: Verso.

Felker-Kantor, Max. 2018. *Policing Los Angeles: Race, Resistance, and the Rise of the LAPD.* Chapel Hill: University of North Carolina Press.

Horne, Gerald. 1997. *Fire This Time: The Watts Uprising and the 1960s.* New York: Da Capo Press.

Johnson, Gaye Theresa. 2013. *Spaces of Conflict, Sounds of Solidarity: Music, Race, and Spatial Entitlement in Los Angeles.* Berkeley: University of California Press.

Kennedy, Scott Hamilton, Danny Glover, Daryl Hannah, and Antonio Villaraigosa. 2014. *The Garden.* Documentary. Black Valley Films.

Lipsitz, George. 2011. *How Racism Takes Place.* Philadelphia: Temple University Press.

Masilela, Ntongela. 1993. "The Los Angeles School of Black Filmmakers." In *Black American Cinema*, edited by Manthia Diawara, 107–17. New York: Routledge.

Osuna, Steven. 2019. "The Psycho Realm Blues: The Violence of Policing, Disordering Practices, and Rap Criticism in Los Angeles." *Chiricú* 4 (1): 76–100. *https://doi.org/10.2979/chiricu.4.1.06.*

Sloan, Cle, and Antoine Fuqua. 2006. *Bastards of the Party*. Film. Fuqua Films, HBO Documentary Films.

Tapscott, Horace. 2001. *Songs of the Unsung: The Musical and Social Journey of Horace Tapscott*. Durham, NC: Duke University Press.

Widener, Daniel. 2010. *Black Arts West: Culture and Struggle in Postwar Los Angeles*. Durham, NC: Duke University Press.

AGAINST CARCERALITY

Abu-Jamal, Mumia. 1995. *Live from Death Row*. Introduction by John Edgar Wideman. Reading, MA: Addison-Wesley.

Burton, Orisanmi. 2018. "Organized Disorder: The New York City Jail Rebellion of 1970." *The Black Scholar* 48 (4): 28–42. *https://doi.org/10.1080/00064246.2018.1514925.*

———. 2021. "Captivity, Kinship, and Black Masculine Care Work under Domestic Warfare." *American Anthropologist* 123 (3): 621–32. *https://doi.org/10.1111/aman.13619.*

Gilmore, Ruth Wilson. 2007. *Golden Gulag: Prisons, Surplus, Crisis, and Opposition in Globalizing California*. Berkeley: University of California Press.

———. 2022. *Change Everything: Racial Capitalism and the Case for Abolition*. Edited by Naomi Murakawa. Chicago: Haymarket Books.

INCITE! 2006. *Color of Violence: The Incite! Anthology*. Edited by Incite! Women of Color Against Violence. Cambridge, MA: South End Press.

———. 2007. *The Revolution Will Not Be Funded: Beyond the Non-Profit Industrial Complex*. Edited by Incite! Women of Color Against Violence. Cambridge, MA: South End Press.

Jackson, George, Jean Genet, and Jonathan Jackson Jr. 1994. *Soledad Brother: The Prison Letters of George Jackson*. New ed. Chicago: Lawrence Hill Books.

James, Joy, ed. 2005. *The New Abolitionists: (Neo) Slave Narratives and Contemporary Prison Writings*. Albany: State University of New York Press.

Kaba, Mariame, and Naomi Murakawa. 2021. *We Do This 'Til We Free Us: Abolitionist Organizing and Transforming Justice*. Edited by Tamara K. Nopper. Chicago: Haymarket Books.

Meiners, Erica R. 2007. *Right to Be Hostile: Schools, Prisons, and the Making of Public Enemies*. New York: Routledge.

———. 2016. *For the Children? Protecting Innocence in a Carceral State*. Minneapolis: University of Minnesota Press.

Olsen, Jack. 2001. *Last Man Standing: The Tragedy and Triumph of Geronimo Pratt.* Reprint ed. New York: Anchor.

Richie, Beth E. 1996. *Compelled to Crime.* New York: Routledge.

———. 2012. *Arrested Justice: Black Women, Violence, and America's Prison Nation.* New York: NYU Press.

Robinson, William I., and Cesar Rodriguez. 2020. "Militarised Accumulation." *Journal of Australian Political Economy,* no. 86: 256–79.

Rodríguez. Dylan. 2006. *Forced Passages: Imprisoned Racial Intellectuals and the U.S. Prison Regime.* Minneapolis: University of Minnesota Press.

Shakur, Assata. 2001. *Assata An Autobiography.* Chicago: Lawrence Hill Books.

ART AND FICTIVE THINKING

Butler, Octavia E. 1993. *Parable of the Sower.* New York: Four Walls Eight Windows.

———. 2000. *Parable of the Talents.* New York: Warner Books.

DuVernay, Ava. 2008. *This Is the Life.* Documentary. The DuVernay Agency.

Hathaway, Lalah. 2008. *Self Portrait.* Beverly Hills: Stax Records.

The Internet. 2018. *Hive Mind.* Audio CD. New York: Columbia Records Group.

Jones, Kellie, ed. 2011. *Now Dig This! Art and Black Los Angeles, 1960–1980.* Los Angeles: Hammer Museum.

King. 2016. *We Are King.* Audio CD. Los Angeles: King Creative.

Lamar, Kendrick. 2013. *Good Kid, M.A.A.D. City.* Short film. Santa Monica, CA: Top Dawg Entertainment.

Mingus, Charles. 1980. *Mingus ah um.* Audio CD. New York: Columbia.

Mosley, Walter. 2002. *A Red Death: An Easy Rawlins Novel.* New York: Washington Square Press.

———. 2008. *Little Scarlet.* Reprint ed. New York: Grand Central Publishing.

Pac Div. 2009. *Church League Champions.* Los Angeles: Artist Release.

Pharcyde. 1995. *Labcabincalifornia.* LP recording. Los Angeles: Delicious Vinyl.

Rushen, Patrice. 1982. *Straight from the Heart.* Audio CD. Los Angeles: Elektra Records.

Schoolboy Q. 2016. *Blank Face.* Explicit version. LP recording. Santa Monica, CA: Interscope.

Staples, Vince. 2015. *Summertime '06.* Explicit version. Audio CD. New York: Def Jam.

Tapscott, Horace, Pan Afrikan Peoples Arkestra, and Great Voice of UGMAA. 2010. *Little Afrika.* Audio CD. Los Angeles: Interplay Records.

Thundercat. 2017. *Drunk.* Audio CD. Los Angeles: Brainfeeder.

Washington, Kamasi. 2015. *The Epic.* Audio CD. Los Angeles: Brainfeeder.

THE ARCHIVE AND ITS DISCONTENTS

Fuentes, Marisa J. 2016. *Dispossessed Lives: Enslaved Women, Violence, and the Archive.* Philadelphia: University of Pennsylvania Press.

Gordon, Avery F. 2017. *The Hawthorn Archive: Letters from the Utopian Margins.* New York: Fordham University Press.

Haley, Sarah. 2019. *No Mercy Here: Gender, Punishment, and the Making of Jim Crow Modernity.* Chapel Hill: University of North Carolina Press.

Hartman, Saidiya. 2020. *Wayward Lives, Beautiful Experiments: Intimate Histories of Riotous Black Girls, Troublesome Women, and Queer Radicals.* Reprint ed. New York: W. W. Norton and Company.

Hicks, Cheryl D. 2010. *Talk with You Like a Woman: African American Women, Justice, and Reform in New York, 1890–1935.* Chapel Hill: University of North Carolina Press.

LeFlouria, Talitha L. 2016. *Chained in Silence: Black Women and Convict Labor in the New South.* Reprint ed. Chapel Hill: University of North Carolina Press.

Thomas, Deborah A. 2019. *Political Life in the Wake of the Plantation: Sovereignty, Witnessing, Repair.* Durham, NC: Duke University Press.

Trouillot, Michel-Rolph. 2015. *Silencing the Past: Power and the Production of History.* Boston: Beacon Press.

WORKS CITED

American Friends Service Committee. 1979. *The Police Threat to Political Liberty.* Philadelphia: American Friends Service Committee.

Biondi, Martha. 2014. *The Black Revolution on Campus.* Berkeley: University of California Press.

Black Panther Party. 1972. "Sister Bobbie Watson Won't Play the City's Games." *Black Panther Intercommunal News Service,* February 12, 1972.

Black Panther Party: Southern California Chapter. 1969. "Watts Summer Festival: 1969." *The Black Panther Community Newsletter,* August 11, 1969.

Black Panther Party: Southern California Chapter. n.d., a. "Black Panther Party Free Breakfast Fundraiser Letter." Southern California Library: Los Angeles Black Panther Party Collection, box 1, folder 3.

Black Panther Party: Southern California Chapter. n.d., b. "Through It All, the Black Panther Party Has Survived." Southern California Library: Los Angeles Black Panther Party Collection, box 1, folder 3.

Boyarsky, Bill. 1980. "While City Government Fiddles, Los Angeles' Housing Crisis Burns: Inaction Fuels Los Angeles' Housing Crisis." *Los Angeles Times,* February 3, 1980.

Butler, Octavia E. 1993. *Parable of the Sower.* New York: Four Walls Eight Windows.

———. 1998. *Parable of the Talents.* New York: Seven Stories Press.

Campaign for Political Rights. 1982. "LAPD Infiltrated California Campus." *Organizing Notes,* October 1982. Southern California Library: Coalition Against Police Abuse Collection, box 4, folder 13.

Churchill, Mae. 1976. "Standards and Procedures of the Public Disorder Intelligence Division, Los Angeles Police Department," November 20, 1976. Northridge, CA: Urban Policy Research Institute.

Citizens' Committee of Inquiry. 1975. "Statement of The Citizens' Committee of Inquiry into Los Angeles Law Enforcement Intelligence Practices Concerning the Proposed Standards and Procedures for the Public Disorder and Intelligence Division of the Los Angeles Police Department." Review of Police Intelligence Activities. Northridge, CA: Urban Policy Research Institute.

City of Pasadena v Pasadena Denver Lanes. 1995. Los Angeles Superior Court: Superior Court of the State of California for the County of Los Angeles.

Costa Vargas, João H. 2004. "The Los Angeles Times' Coverage of the 1992 Rebellion: Still Burning Matters of Race and Justice." *Ethnicities* 4 (June): 209–36.

———. 2006. *Catching Hell in the City of Angels.* Minneapolis: University of Minnesota Press.

Davis, Mike. 2006. *City of Quartz: Excavating the Future in Los Angeles.* Revised ed. New York: Verso.

Fogelson, Robert M. 1967. "White on Black: A Critique of the McCone Commission Report on the Los Angeles Riots." *Political Science Quarterly* 82 (3): 337–67. https://doi.org/10.2307/2146769.

Franklin, Bruce. 2000. "The American Prison in the Culture Wars." Presented at the Modern Language Association, Washington, DC. www.hbrucefranklin.com/articles/the-american-prison-in-the-culture-wars/.

Gilmore, Ruth Wilson. 2007. *Golden Gulag Prisons, Surplus, Crisis, and Opposition in Globalizing California.* Berkeley: University of California Press.

Goldstein, Natalie. *Global Warming.* New York: Facts on File, 2009.

Gordon, Avery. 2018. *The Hawthorn Archive: Letters from the Utopian Margins.* New York: Fordham University Press.

Holland, Randy. 1994. *The Fire This Time.* Documentary. Blacktop Films.

Horne, Gerald. 1997. *Fire This Time: The Watts Uprising and the 1960s.* New York: Da Capo Press.

Interim Steering Committee of the Coalition for a Civilian Review Board. 1979. "Initiative Campaign Meeting." Interim Steering Committee of the Coalition for a Civilian Review Board. Los Angeles: Coalition Against Police Abuse. Southern California Library: Coalition Against Police Abuse Collection, box 16, folder 4

Johnston, David. 1980. "Gates to Seek Bigger Anti-Terrorism Unit." *Los Angeles Times,* October 15, 1980.

———. 1982. "New Probe Ordered on Spying by LAPD." *Los Angeles Times,* December 15, 1982.

Kelley, Robin D. G. 1996. *Race Rebels: Culture, Politics, and the Black Working Class.* New York: Free Press.

———. 1998. *Yo' Mama's Disfunktional!: Fighting the Culture Wars in Urban America.* Boston: Beacon Press.

L.A. Friends of the Panthers. 1969. "SEARCH and DESTROY" (pamphlet). Los Angeles: L.A. Friends of the Panthers. Southern California Library: Los Angeles Black Panther Party Collection, box 1, folder 3.

Los Angeles Board of Police Commissioners. 1975. "Statement of the Los Angeles Board of Police Commissioners: The Public Disorder Intelligence Function of the Los Angeles Police Department." Los Angeles: Los Angeles Police Department.

Los Angeles Herald Examiner Staff. 1980. "Is L.A. Mismanaging Housing Funds?" *Los Angeles Herald Examiner,* January 25, 1980.

Mae Churchill. 1976. "Standards and Procedures of the Public Disorder Intelligence Division, Los Angeles Police Department," November 30, 1976. Northridge, CA: Urban Policy Research Institute.

Marten, Michael. 1980. "What's Wrong with L.A.'s Public Housing Programs?" *Los Angeles Herald Examiner,* February 19, 1980.

Mayor's Office of Criminal Justice Planning. 1975. "Project Heavy/Gang Consortium." City of Los Angeles.

McCloskey, Congressman Paul, Jr. 1980. Letter to Honorable Don Edwards, Chairman, Subcommittee on Civil and Constitutional Rights, Committee on Judiciary, May 9, 1980. Southern California Library: Coalition Against Police Abuse Collection, box 8.

McCone Commission. 1965. *McCone Commission Report: Complete and Unabridged Report by the Governor's Commission on the Los Angeles Riot.* Los Angeles: Kimtex Corporation.

Meiners, Erica R. 2007. *Right to Be Hostile: Schools, Prisons, and the Making of Public Enemies.* New York: Routledge. https://doi.org/10.4324/9780203936450.

Nordwind, Richard. 1982. "Northridge Students to Sue LAPD Over Campus Spies." *Los Angeles Herald Examiner,* June 10, 1982.

Office of Urban Affairs. 1966. *Implementation of Ad Hoc Directives on Equal Educational Opportunity.* Los Angeles: Office of the Superintendent.

Oliver, Melvin L., James H. Johnson Jr., and Walter C. Farrell. 1993. "Anatomy of a Rebellion: A Political-Economic Analysis." In *Reading Rodney King / Reading Urban Uprising*, edited by Robert Gooding-Williams, 117–41. New York: Routledge.

Ortiz, Paul. 2000. "The Anatomy of a Rebellion." *Against the Current* 84 (January/February). https://againstthecurrent.org/atc084/p1696/.

Patterson, William L., ed. 1951. *We Charge Genocide: The Historic Petition to the United Nations for Relief from a Crime of the United States Government against the Negro People*. 2nd ed. New York: Civil Rights Congress.

Poole, Wiliam. 1980. "Campaign for Economic Democracy: Part 1, The New Left in Politics." 13. Institutional Analysis. Washington, DC: Heritage Foundation.

Redmond, Shana L. 2013. *Anthem: Social Movements and the Sound of Solidarity in the African Diaspora*. New York: NYU Press.

Robinson, Cedric J. 1993. "Race, Capitalism, and Antidemocracy." In *Reading Rodney King / Reading Urban Uprising*, edited by Robert Gooding-Williams, 73–81. New York: Routledge.

Ropers, Richard. 1983. "Basic Shelter Research Project of Los Angeles." Research study. Los Angeles: Coalition Against Police Abuse.

Sappell, Joel. 1982. "Officer Helped to Organize Eulia Love March, Suit Says." *Los Angeles Times*, February 9, 1982.

Schnyder, Damien. 2012. "Criminals, Planters, and Corporate Capitalists: The Case of Public Education in Los Angeles." *Black California Dreamin'* 1, no. 1: 107–26.

Sloan, Cle. 2006. *Bastards of the Party*. Film. Produced by Antoine Fuqua. www.imdb.com/title/tt0455913/.

Sojoyner, Damien M. 2013. "Black Radicals Make for Bad Citizens: Undoing the Myth of the School to Prison Pipeline." *Berkeley Review of Education* 4 (2). https://doi.org/10.5070/B84110021.

———. 2014. "Chapter Three: Changing the Lens: Moving Away from the School to Prison Pipeline." *Counterpoints* 453: 54–66.

———. 2016. *First Strike: Educational Enclosures in Black Los Angeles*. Minneapolis: University of Minnesota Press.

Thomas, Deborah. 2019. *Political Life in the Wake of the Plantation: Sovereignty, Witnessing, Repair*. Durham, NC: Duke University Press.

Townsend, Dorothy. 1975. "Critics Assail Destruction of Intelligence Files." *Los Angeles Times*, April 27, 1975.

Weinstein, Henry. 1979. "L.A. Housing Funds Opposed: Coalition Asks HUD to Withhold $53 Million." *Los Angeles Times*, June 4, 1979.

Willmarth, Susan, Ellen Miller-Mack, and Lois Ahrens. 2005. *Prisoners of a Hard Life: Women and Their Children*. Northampton, MA: The Real Cost of Prisons Project.

Woods, Clyde. 2017. *Development Arrested: The Blues and Plantation Power in the Mississippi Delta*. 2nd ed. London: Verso.

ILLUSTRATION CREDITS

Frontispiece.   Illustrated map by Michelle Ott *ii*

Album 1.   110 and 105 Freeway Intersection. Credit: Damien M.
                Sojoyner *16*

Album 2.   Watts Towers. Credit: Juli R. Grigsby *58*

Album 3.   SCL Mural of Michael Zinzun and Annette McKinley. Credit:
                Damien M. Sojoyner *96*

Album 4.   Venice Beach. Credit: Juli R. Grigsby *130*

Album 5.   Black Panther Party Mural on Slauson Avenue. Credit: Juli R.
                Grigsby *172*

INDEX

accountability: community engagement and, 44; environment creation and, 3; expectations based in, 4

album template: as archetype, 6; institutional sites and, 7; A side/B side analogy, 6, 11

American Civil Liberties Union (ACLU), 192

American Friends Service Committee, 197

Anti-Terror Division (ATD), 200, 203

archive(s): as generative theory, 10–11; as historical, 10; interplay with power, 11; models of, 11–12; organizers use of, 11; as prophetic, 10; theorization and framing of Black Life through, 12; UPRI archives, 10–11; visionary aspects of, 11

A side/B side analogy, 6, 11

basic necessities: Black precarity and, 119–20; Free Breakfast Programs, 120–23, 125; of housing, 145–48; Marley on, 73; Moynihan Report on, 122; struggle for, 5

Bell, Cheryl, 198

Black communities: impact of carceral state expansion on, 3; leaders and, 14; "making it out" mentality, 36; multifaceted nature of, 23; patrolling of, 80; relationship with carceral state, 2. *See also* Black Los Angeles

Black cultural production: articulation of, 6; castigation of, 14

Black education: operational dysfunctionality of, 83. *See also* education

Black freedom, embodiment of spirit of, 4

Black Guerrilla Family, 193

Black intellectual thought, complexity of, 6

Black knowledge formation, castigation of, 14

Black Liberation Army, 193

Black life: complexity of, 207; historical knowledge production of, 6; multifaced nature of, 5; precarity in, 9; social visions of, 9; strategies against forces encroaching on, 10

Black lived experience: Black music and, 6; Marley's, 7; nonprofit/state-partnered campaigns and, 13

Black Lives Matter (BLM), 12–13
Black Los Angeles: intellectual infrastructure of, 3; Los Angeles Rebellion and, 3; SCL documents lived experience of, 3. See also Black communities; Los Angeles
Black masculinity: issues around, 21, 23; recycling center and, 32–33; targeting of, 26
Black music: Black lived experience and, 6;
Black nationalism, 82
Blackness: dislike for in LA, 29; education to contain, 93–95; exploration of life of, 5; expressions of, 5; limited framework of, 5; progressive mobilizations and, 24–25
Black Panther Party (BPP): Fonda and, 167; logics of racial capitalism and, 121; members of, 189–90; neutralization of, 120–21; platform points, 161–62
Black Panther Party (BPP), Los Angeles chapter: about, 119–21; archives of, 3, 20, 206; battle for the community, 124–25; campaign to neutralize, 126–29; against capitalism, 167–68; Citizens Commission on Police Repression and, 198; Free Breakfast Programs, 120–23, 125; gun ownership, 120; Liberation Schools, 120; members of, 87; neutralization, 120, 126–29; PDID's information on, 193; police violence against, 128; Watts Rebellion of 1965 and, 127–28. See also Ji Jaga, Geronimo
Black precarity as overwhelming, 9. See also precarity
Black Revolutionary Independent Mafia (BRIM), 29–32, 74, 75, 140, 161
Black senior citizens, 123
Black struggle: collective aspect of, 12; visionary aspects of, 10
Black student unions, 193

Black vulnerability, 4. See also vulnerability
Black women: as caretakers and nurturers, 26; Moynihan Report on, 122; precarity and, 27; as vulnerable populations, 25–26
Black world-making, 10
Black youth: communal organizations and, 83; engagement with, 45–46; physical containment of, 85; precarity and, 27; SCL summer course for, 35–46; targeting of, 55; treatment of, 26–27. See also Marley (and his peers)
Bradley, Tom, 51–53, 170
Bradley administration, 53, 55, 170
BRIM (Black Revolutionary Independent Mafia), 29–32, 74, 75, 140, 161
Brown, Pat, 79
businesses, in Black neighborhoods, 32–33
Butler, Julius, 190
Butler, Octavia, 8, 9, 10, 204

California Housing Action and Information Network (CHAIN), 164
California State University, Northridge (CSUN), 198–99
Campaign for Economic Democracy (CED), 162–64, 162–65, 166–67
campaigns' unfinished work of, 12–14
Campbell Village housing project, 125
CAPA archives: about, 10–11. See also archive(s); Coalition Against Police Abuse (CAPA)
capitalism, 121, 126, 165
carcerality: logics of, 9, 10; mechanization of carceral-based relationships, 10; multifaceted nature of regime of, 8–9; reconceptualization of, 2; state governance structures and, 7; understanding of, 2

carceral state: archives' use to inform on power of, 11; basic necessities and policies of; buildup of, 71; development of, 1; docility as prescribed by, 5; education and, 1; expansion of, 8; fight against, 1, 7; framing of, 1; freedom from, 9; housing and, 1; impact of expansion on Black communities, 3; liberation efforts against, 2; political economy and, 1; precarity of Black life and, 9; relational aspect of, 7, 10; relational organizational structure of, 7, 10; SCL as part of regional communal struggle against, 3; servility as prescribed by, 5; state structures that animate, 2; structural conditions of, 42–43; struggle against, 2; theorization and framing of, 12; violence's multifaceted nature in, 2

Carter, Bunchy, 126–27, 161

Carter, Jimmy, 162–63, 165

Carter administration, 162–63, 165, 167

CED (Campaign for Economic Democracy), 162–65, 166–67

CHAIN (California Housing Action and Information Network), 164

Chavez, Raquel, 4, 119

Churchill, Mae, 192, 194–97

Citizens Commission on Police Repression: about, 198; Black Panther Party (BPP) and, 198; CAPA and, 198; Feminist Women's Health Center and, 198; LAPD and, 198; La Raza Unida and, 198; Radical Women and, 198; Union of Lesbian and Gay Men and, 198; Urban Policy Research Institute (UPRI) and, 198

city politics, SCL knowledge of, 25

Civil Rights Congress (CRC), 8

climate change: Carter administration, 165–66; Marley on, 148; Reagan administration, 165–66

Coalition Against Police Abuse (CAPA): about, 9–10; archives of, 20; Citizens Commission on Police Repression and, 198; spy operation against, 197–98, 203

Coalition for Economic Survival, 170–71

collective process formation, 13–14

Combahee River Collective Statement (CRCS), 21–22, 23

communal resources as limited for Black women, 26

community: BPP's battle for, 124–25; community engagement event, 113–18; community garden plans, 33–34; community policing, 31; community scholars, 11; government programs for, 128–29; knowledge sharing in, 11; SCL as hub of, 3

Community Freedom School, 193

community organizations: knowledge passed on from, 11; SCL and, 3; Watts Rebellion of 1965 and, 83. *See also* Black Revolutionary Independent Mafia (BRIM); *specific organizations*

condoms, 154–55

Congress of African People, 193

consistency, appreciation of, 40

conspiracy theories, 64, 66

courts, relationship with carceral state, 2

CRCS (Combahee River Collective Statement), 21–22, 23

creativity, Black music and, 6

criminal justice system: Black lives and, 14; costs of involvement with, 63; housing assistance and, 63

Crips and Bloods, 54, 55, 200, 201

critical node locations, 2

CSUN (California State University, Northridge), 198–99

curriculum, engagement with, 44

Deacons of Defense, 190

Democratic Party, 162, 166

demographics, Black women as hidden, 26

Department of Housing and Urban Development (HUD), 169–70

detention centers, relationship with carceral state, 2

docility as prescribed by carceral state, 5

Dodge City (communal organization), 83, 161

dream(s): freedom to have, 9; of new ways of being, 11. *See also* vision

dress: as form of protection, 42–43; logics of, 102; Marley's style of, 138; shoes, 138–32

dropouts, problem of, 83–84

dystopic futures, 9

economic oppression: Civil Rights Congress petition and, 8; ideology and, 126–29

education: about, 60–67; Alain Leroy Locke High School, 60; Black precarity and, 9; to contain Blackness, 93–95; containment of Black radical action and, 84, 85; disdain for Blackness in, 29; Liberation Schools, 120–21; logics of carcerality in, 9; of older generations, 78–79; policies related to, 80; punitive formations of public, 13; at SCL, 44–45; as a tool, 87–90. *See also* schools

educational oppression, Civil Rights Congress petition and, 8

employment: BPP's battle for, 161; policies related to, 79, 80

ethnography: as generative theory, 10–11; interplay with historical archives, 12; of A sides, 7, 10

exploitation, logics of, 12, 126

FBI investigation, 191

Federal Housing Authority, 169

Feminist Women's Health Center, Citizens Commission on Police Repression and, 198

Fonda, Jane, 167

food insecurity: as commonplace, 5; community engagement and, 110–11; connections to, 73; Marley on, 145, 147–48

Free Breakfast Programs, 120–23, 125

Freed, Emil, 3

freedom: arrival at prison, 176–77; from carceral state, 9; difficulties in obtaining, 9; to dream, 9; family separations and, 183–85; to live in laughter and joy, 9; price of, 189–203; returning home, 186–88; SCL as space for, 3; training vs. learning, 177–80; transport to prison, 174–76; from violence, 9; ways of attaining, 9; working together for, 180–82

Friends of the Panthers pamphlet, 121–22

gang problems: about, 47–49; gang injunctions, 63; gang resource specialists, 53; Gang Task Force, 52; Gang Truce of 1992, 55, 56; "gang violence," 54, 55; LA Bridges program, 56; Los Angeles Rebellion of 1992, 55–56; Project HEAVY, 52–55, 56; Watts Rebellion of 1965, 50–51; Welfare Planning Council and, 49–50, 51, 53, 57

Gates, Daryl, 200

gender issues: disagreements over, 36–43; gendering norms, 41–43

genealogical tradition of study, 11

generative theory, 10–11

genocidal violence, 8

Gladiators (communal organization), 83, 161

Gordon, Avery, 11–12

grant project development: framing
documents, 21–24; initial meeting
for, 18–21

Harlins, Latasha, 139–40
Harvard Park, 33–34
The Hawthorn Archive (Gordon), 11–12
Hayden, Thomas, 162–63, 167
health care: Black precarity and, 9;
disdain for Blackness in, 29; Marley
on, 146–47; as state apparatus of
carceral state violence, 13; staying
healthy without, 148–59; void of, 13
Heritage Foundation, 163–64, 167
honesty: appreciation of, 40;
expectations based in, 3, 4; radical
honesty, 4; SCL project and, 26.
hope and vulnerability, 104–5
Horne, Gerald, 82
houseless persons: Black women as, 26;
Marley (and his peers) and, 27–28,
133–38, 143–44; SCL and, 25
housing: about, 132–33; basic necessities,
145–48; Black precarity and, 9;
Black women and, 37–38; BPP's
battle for, 161; criminal records and,
63; efforts to secure, 5; federal
funding, 169–71; lack of, 13; lack of
affordable, 27; Marley (and his
peers) plans for, 35–36; Marley as
houseless, 27–28, 133–38, 143–44;
policies related to, 79, 80; project
housing, 62; public housing, 9; as
socialist vision, 167–71; as state
apparatus of carceral state violence,
13; staying healthy with no health
care, 148–59
housing assistance and criminal
records, 63
Huggins, John, 126–27
hunger. *See* food insecurity

Ice Cube, 69
idealism, visions labeled as, 9

illegible existences: Black lives cast as,
14; listening to, 9
*Implementation of Ad Hoc Directives on
Equal Educational Opportunity* (Office
of Urban Affairs) report, 11, 83–84
institutionalization. *See* punitive
institutionalization
insurgency acts against carcerality, 11.
See also Los Angeles Rebellion of
1992; Watts Rebellion of 1965
intellectual infrastructure of
neighborhoods, 3
International Oil Workers Union, 3
interpersonal dynamics of
neighborhoods, 27
intersectionality, 23
invisibility, silencing and, 41–42

Ji Jaga, Geronimo, 126, 189–92, 196
jobs and work link to poverty, 83
joy: Black music and, 6; freedom to live
in, 9, 207
juvenile detention and Black
precarity, 9

King, Rodney, 55
knowledge: accumulation of at SCLA,
19; knowledge traditions, 78;
knowledge transference, 19; passing
on of, 11; production of, 45;

LA Bridges program, 56
land: food insecurity and, 73–74;
homeless people and, 72–73;
landfills in Black LA, 65
La Raza Unida, Citizens Commission
on Police Repression and, 198
Latino communities, 81
Lauren Oya Olamina (fictional
character), 9. *See also Parable* series
(Butler)
leaders, Black communities and, 14. *See
also* Marley (and his peers)
Liberation Schools, 120–21

logics: of capitalism, 121, 126, 165; of
carcerality, 9, 10; dress, 102; of
exploitation, 12, 126; of radical Black
organizing, 167
Los Angeles: activist and organizing
history of, 19; life in, 1. *See also* Black
Los Angeles
Los Angeles Group for Community
Development Reform, 170
Los Angeles Police Department
(LAPD): audit of PDID information,
193; in Black high schools, 82; CAPA
and, 197–98, 203; Citizens Commission on Police Repression and, 198;
communal organizations and, 83;
CSUN lawsuit against, 198–99;
information collected on organizations by, 198; Los Angeles Rebellion
of 1992, 55; Mexican-American
community and, 81–82; patrolling of
Black communities by, 80; raid on
BPP headquarters, 121–22; Review
Board, 199–200; special gang teams
of, 55. *See also* policing apparatus of
carceral state
Los Angeles Rebellion of 1992: gang
problems and, 55–56; LAPD and, 55,
85–87; photograph of SCL after, 25
love: Black music and, 6; capacity to, 5;
community engagement and, 44; of
neighborhoods, 36
Love, Eula, 199

Marley (and his peers): about, 28; on
Black freedom, 204–5; on Black
organizations in LA, 29; on buildup
of carceral state, 71; capacity to love
in, 5; on climate change, 148;
community engagement event,
113–18; community garden plans,
33–34, 35–36; daily lived reality of, 14;
on dental health, 150–52; disengagement from formal school, 78;
event politics and, 111–13; family
separations, 183–86; first meeting

with, 3, 4; food insecurity, 145,
147–48; food insecurity and, 110–11;
on health care, 13, 146–47; on health
issues, 153–59; as houseless, 133–38,
143–44; incarceration experiences,
174–82, 186–88; introduction of, 27;
on land and homeless people, 72–73;
leadership style of, 4, 112–13, 116;
multifaced nature of life of, 5–6; on
music, 67–72; on neighborhood,
29–31; neighborhood plans, 32–33, 35;
phones, 133–35; on police violence, 13;
on policing of community, 31;
precarity and, 27–28; as representation of Black men, 4–6; SCL and,
2–6, 28; SCL summer course, 35;
SCL summer program and, 98–109;
shoe shopping with, 138–43; on siting
of public schools, 61–64; skepticism
of, 14; on teachers, 64–67;
theorization and framing of Black
Life through, 12; UC Santa Barbara
talk, 66–67, 74–77; use of archives, 11
mass mobilizations, radical politics
and, 3–4
McCone Commission, 79–80, 84,
168–69
mentor role, 14, 20–21, 23
Mexican-American community, 80–82
micro/macro engagements against
Black people, 1–2
movements, unfinished work of, 12–14
Moynihan Report, 122
multiplatform social media
engagement, ethnography informed
by, 7
music: Black lived experience and, 6;
as common thread, 7–8; Marley on,
67–72
mutual respect, expectations based in,
3, 4, 14

narrative/vision schematic, 9–10, 12
National Alliance Against Racism and
Political Repression, 197

Nation of Islam, 193
neighborhoods: collective aspect of, 36;
    documents on removal of Black
    people from, 10; foundational
    political impetus governing Black
    life in, 10; importance of, 29–31;
    intellectual infrastructure of, 3;
    internal/external politics of conflict
    in, 31–32; interpersonal dynamics of,
    27; mechanization of, 25; policing
    of, 31–32; political infrastructure of,
    27; political knowledge of, 13–14;
    SCL's relationship with, 3; unity
    in, 36
neutralization of Black Panther Party,
    120, 126–29
Newton, Huey, 121, 123
nonprofit sector: Black precarity and,
    9; campaigns in LA Black
    communities, 12–13; struggle
    against, 113–18; effects on
    community, 110–13; SCL summer
    program and, 98–109; Project
    HEAVY and, 54

Obama administration, 21
Odom, Georgia, 197
Office of Urban Affairs, 83–84
Olympic Games, 171
Omowale, Yusef, 3, 11, 13–14, 19–25, 28,
    38–43, 45, 99–102, 106–11, 114, 115, 119,
    135, 137, 142, 144
organizational strategies: archive use
    for, 11; critical node locations and, 2;
    SCL as host of sessions for, 3; *We
    Charge Genocide* petition and, 8
Ortiz, Paul, 79n

Parable of the Sower (Butler), 9
Parable of the Talents (Butler), 9
Parable series (Butler), 8, 9–10
parental negligence, removal of
    children under guise of, 5
Parker, William, 81
Pasadena Denver Lanes, 201–3

Patterson, William L., 8, 23
PDID (Public Disorder Intelligence
    Division): LAPD's audit of
    information of, 193; new guidelines
    for, 194; replaced by ATD, 200, 203;
    spy operation by, 191–93
Police Threat to Political Liberty study, 197
policies: policy investment, 26; public
    pitch and implementation of, 27
policing apparatus of carceral state:
    BRIM as buffer to, 32; community
    policing, 31–32; forces behind, 10;
    increase in police presence, 55;
    police officers relationship with
    carceral state, 2; police violence, 32,
    82; restructuring of, 55–56; schools
    and, 62–64. *See also* Los Angeles
    Police Department (LAPD)
political education courses: archives
    utilized through, 11; young people
    in, 78
political infrastructure of
    neighborhoods, 27
political knowledge documentation, 11,
    13
Political Life in the Wake of the Plantation
    (Thomas), 11–12
political oppression, Civil Rights
    Congress petition and, 8
poverty, jobs and work link to, 83
power interplay with archives, 11
Pratt, Elmer Gerard. *See* Ji Jaga,
    Geronimo
precarity: in Black life, 9; Black women
    and, 26, 27; Black youth and, 27;
    Marley (and his peers) and, 27–28
prison system: connections to, 73;
    relationship with carceral state, 2;
    "Why We Thugs" (Ice Cube)
    on, 69
Prison Town, 35
progressive mobilizations, Blackness
    and, 24–25
Project HEAVY, 52–55, 56
Project Long Table, 54

public discourse, focus and energy of, 26
Public Disorder Intelligence Division (PDID). *See* PDID (Public Disorder Intelligence Division)
public infrastructures: abandonment of, 29; administration of, 29
punitive institutionalization, 26

race, reconfiguring race to maintain power, 90–92
racial capitalism: BBP understanding of logics of, 121; Watts Rebellion of 1965 and, 168–69
racial exploitation, traditions of, 8
radical-based organizations, strategies against, 10
radical Black organizing logics, 167
radical freedom, 9
radical love, SCL project and, 26
radical politics: education and, 84; LAPD's against, 198; mass mobilizations, 3–4
Radical Women, Citizens Commission on Police Repression and, 198
Reagan, Ronald, 82, 165
Reagan administration, 165
Real Cost Prisons Project, 35
real estate developers, relationship with carceral state, 2
record collection structure, about, 6–10
recorded conversations, ethnography informed by, 7
Redmond, Shana, 6
reform works, nonprofit/state-based, 14
relational structure of carceral state, 7, 10; abusive educational relationships, 78; Marley as attuned to, 28; relationships with carceral state, 14
respect: community engagement and, 44; expectations based in, 3, 4, 14; respectable politics, 20–21
Ripston, Ramona, 193

schools: connections to, 73; curriculum, 44; disengagement from formal school, 78, 83; LAPD in, 82; older generations' schooling experience, 78; police occupations of, 82; policing and, 62; as state apparatus of carceral state violence, 13; surveillance in, 44; teachers, 64–67; withdrawal from school system, 44. *See also* education
Section 8 housing, increase in, 27
senior citizens and Free Food Program, 123
sentencing issues, 70–71
servility, 5
sexuality issues, disagreements over, 36–43
silencing, invisibility and, 41–42
Slausons (communal organization), 83, 161
Slauson Swapmeet, 139–42
Social Adjustment Centers, 85
socialist visions: about, 160–61; Black Panther platform points, 161–62; Carter administration, 162–63, 165, 167; housing in Los Angeles, 1965–1992, 167–71; Reagan administration, 165
social justice, 129
social movements against carcerality, 11
social oppression, Civil Rights Congress petition and, 8
social services, 9
social spending, 26
social workers, 2
Solomon, Eddie, 197–98
South Central Los Angeles (SCLA): Black organizations in, 56; CAPA and, 197–98, 203; dropout rates in, 93; east side/west side division, 154; effects of juvenile carceral system on Black youth of, 203; health care system in, 156–59; health clinics in, 153–55, 155; as home, 18–19; housing

in, 112, 148–49, 168–69; on open
space in, 73; raids targeting Black
youth in, 55; SCL's importance to
Black people of, 6; siting of public
schools in, 62–63, 64; Slauson
Swapmeet, 139–40; suffering of
Black people in, 206–7;
unemployment in, 89, 179
Southern California Library (SCL):
about, 18–19; as archive of radical-
left organizations, 2–3; author and, 1,
2; education at, 44–45; founding of,
3; importance to Black people in
SCLA of, 6; initial meeting at, 18–21;
location of, 3; Marley and, 2–6;
neighborhood relationship with,
24–25; photograph after LA
Rebellion of 1992, 25; political
education courses, 119; in regional
communal struggle against carceral
state, 3; as space for activist
organizations, 19; as space for
community building, 27, 43–46; as
space for freedom, 3; summer
program for Black youth, 35–46,
98–109; symbiotic bond with, 4;
theorization and framing of Black
Life through, 12; war on gangs
and, 47
Southern Christian Leadership
Conference, 193
state violence: carceral state expansion
as, 8; removal of children as form
of, 5
Street Terrorism Enforcement and
Prevention (STEP) Act of 1988,
200–201
Student Senate at California State
University, Northridge (CSUN)
lawsuit against LAPD, 198–99
surveillance: Project HEAVY and, 55;
in schools, 44

teachers, 64–67, 78
Thomas, Deborah, 11–12

Thomas, Norman, 162–63
transparency, appreciation of, 40

Union of Lesbian and Gay Men,
Citizens Commission on Police
Repression and, 198
University of California, Los Angeles,
126
University of California, Santa
Barbara, Marley talk at, 66–67,
74–77
UPRI (Urban Policy Research
Institute) archives, 10–11
Urban Policy Research Institute
(UPRI), 10; archives of, 11; Citizen
Commission on Police Repression,
192; Citizens Commission on Police
Repression and, 198
US Commission on Civil Rights, 81
US Organization, 193

violence: Black lives cast as, 14; against
Black women, 38–40; against BPP,
122; freedom from, 9; "gang
violence," 54, 55; genocidal
violence, 8; multifaceted nature of
within carceral state, 2, 11, 13; police
brutality, 32, 82; structural violence
of whiteness, 80; traditions of, 8. *See
also* state violence
vision: belief in, 204–6; of Black love,
206–7; labeled as idealism, 9; as not
fulfilled, 207–8; social vision of
Black life, 9, 14. *See also* socialist
visions
vulnerability: hope and, 104–5; pride
and, 38–41

war on gangs, SCL and, 47
Watson, Bobbie, 125
Watts Rebellion of 1965: Black
disengagement after, 93–95, 127–28;
events of, 79–82; gang problems
and, 50–51; housing and, 168–69;
Los Angeles Rebellion of 1992 and,

Watts Rebellion *(continued)*
85–87; public education after, 82–85;
racial capitalism and, 168–69;
reconfiguring race to maintain
power after, 90–92; social
infrastructure attacks after, 87–90
We Charge Genocide petition, 8, 23
Welfare Planning Council, 49–50, 51,
53, 57
Welsing, Michele, 3, 11, 19–22, 23–28,
43–45, 99–102, 107–11, 115, 119
white backlash, 82, 84, 85

whiteness, structural violence of, 80
"Why We Thugs" (Ice Cube), 69
*Without Fear … Claiming Safe
Communities without Sacrificing
Ourselves* (SCL), 1, 2
Woods, Clyde, 6
workshops: archives utilized through,
11; SCL as host of, 3

young people: Black women and, 26;
disconnect from schools, 78; as
vulnerable populations, 25–26

Founded in 1893,
UNIVERSITY OF CALIFORNIA PRESS
publishes bold, progressive books and journals
on topics in the arts, humanities, social sciences,
and natural sciences—with a focus on social
justice issues—that inspire thought and action
among readers worldwide.

The UC PRESS FOUNDATION
raises funds to uphold the press's vital role
as an independent, nonprofit publisher, and
receives philanthropic support from a wide
range of individuals and institutions—and from
committed readers like you. To learn more, visit
ucpress.edu/supportus.